The Rediscovery of Common Sense Philosophy

The Rediscovery of Common Sense Philosophy

Stephen Boulter

First published 2007 by
PALGRAVE MACMILLAN
Houndmills, Basingstoke, Hampshire RG21 6XS and
175 Fifth Avenue, New York, N.Y. 10010
Companies and representatives throughout the world

PALGRAVE MACMILLAN is the global academic imprint of the Palgrave Macmillan division of St. Martin's Press, LLC and of Palgrave Macmillan Ltd. Macmillan® is a registered trademark in the United States, United Kingdom and other countries. Palgrave is a registered trademark in the European Union and other countries.

ISBN-13: 978–0–2300–0246–3 hardback
ISBN-10: 0–2300–0246–3 hardback

This book is printed on paper suitable for recycling and made from fully managed and sustained forest sources. Logging, pulping and manufacturing processes are expected to conform to the environmental regulations of the country of origin.

A catalogue record for this book is available from the British Library.

A catalog record for this book is available from the Library of Congress.

10   9   8   7   6   5   4   3   2   1
16   15   14   13   12   11   10   09   08   07

Printed and bound in Great Britain by
Antony Rowe Ltd, Chippenham and Eastbourne

For Eileen, Joan and Elizabeth

Contents

Acknowledgements

I have profited enormously from the advice and critical comments of many people in the course of preparing this book. Special thanks are due to Alexander Broadie, William Bechtel, Mark Cain, Jim Edwards, Mary Haight, John Haldane, Michael Lessnoff, Christopher Martin, Fred Miller, Constantine Sandis, Kim Sterelny, Neil Spurway, Steve Stewart-Williams and Kenneth Westphal. I would also like to thank my family. Without their support, this book would not have seen the light of day.

Introduction: Two Tribes

Open any history of Western philosophy and you are likely to find at least a brief mention of Thales of Miletus (640–545/8 BCE). The mention, however brief, is obligatory because Thales is generally honoured as the first recognised philosopher in the Western tradition, the first thinker, that is, who quite consciously set aside myth and religion in order to provide a rational account of the world and man's place within it. As anyone with a passing acquaintance with Presocratic thought will tell you, Thales is usually remembered for breaking new ground in cosmology with his striking conjecture that the ultimate constituent of the universe is water. He is also credited with several important geometrical discoveries. He was the first to demonstrate that a circle is bisected by its diameter, that in every isosceles triangle the angles at the base are equal, that when two straight lines intersect the angles at the vertex are equal and that a pair of triangles with one equal side and two equal angles are equal. Historians of Presocratic thought aside, it is safe to say that the earliest of the so-called "Seven Sages" of early Greek thought is remembered for little else. But it is not for these reasons that Thales is recalled here. Our interest in Thales lies rather in a curious but revealing anecdote mentioned almost in passing in a Platonic dialogue, an anecdote in which our hero is humiliated by a common barmaid.

While expounding upon the nature of the archetypical philosopher in his *Theaetetus*, Plato says that the true philosopher has no interest in practical politics, and looks disdainfully upon courts of law, social cliques, dinner parties, "merrymaking with flute girls", and all other activities associated with ordinary everyday life. The philosopher, says Plato, always seeks "the true nature of everything as a whole, never sinking to what lies close at hand" (*Theaetetus*, 173d–e). When asked what he means by this, Plato offers our anecdote by way of illustration:

> The same thing as the story about the Thracian maidservant who exercised her wit at the expense of Thales, when he was looking up to study the stars and tumbled down a well. She scoffed at him for being so eager to know what was happening in the sky that he could

not see what lay at his feet. Anyone who gives his life to philosophy is open to such mockery.

(*Theaetetus*, 174b)

This story of the first absent-minded professor is probably apocryphal. And it is likely that Plato recounts it here at Thales' expense at least in part because he liked to poke fun at Presocratic philosophers generally.[1] But there can be no doubt that this anecdote is meant to illustrate Plato's considered views on the nature of philosophy and philosophers. It also neatly captures the tone and tenor of the uneasy relationship that obtains between philosophers and the common run of mankind, an uneasiness stretching back from the very beginnings of the discipline to the present day. Between those two utterly distinct tribes of humanity, says Plato, there can be only mutual contempt. For if Thales could not see what lay at his feet, it was precisely because he maintained, like all true philosophers in Plato's view, that the grubby, everyday world of the vulgar, untutored barmaid is not worthy of serious study. The world of the true philosopher, says Plato, is on an entirely different plane, far beyond the reaches of even the most sharp-witted waitress. Moreover, it is only to be expected that barmaids and their ilk will fail to appreciate the nobility of the philosopher's aspirations. Indeed, it would be perverse to expect swine to appreciate pearls. After all, the common run of man is lost in a world of insubstantial shadows, while the philosopher alone sees the world as it truly is. Our anecdote, then, is Plato's stark warning to all philosophers that mockery and scorn will inevitably follow those who refuse to "sink" to the level of the everyday, and that this has always been so.[2]

Plato is certainly not the only philosopher to have explicitly voiced opinions of this kind. For Parmenides, there could be "no true reliance" on "the opinions of [ordinary] mortals" (Kirk, Raven and Schofield, p. 243). Heraclitus and Democritus both claimed that the untutored mass of mankind knows nothing of significance, and as Seneca pointed out, they disagreed only on whether this ignorance ought to provoke laughter or tears.[3] And this attitude is by no means confined to the ancient world. Charron, an influential contemporary of Descartes, took matters to new heights when he spoke openly of the "contagion" of the crowd and common people. "Above all", he says, the philosopher must "avoid the bog". And philosophers must rid themselves of all popular opinions, he says, for they are "base, weak, undigested, impertinent...false, foolish, flighty, and uncertain – the guide of fools and the common people".[4] Descartes himself expressed similarly unflattering opinions of the mass of mankind. In his Preface to the *Meditations on First Philosophy*, Descartes writes that his plan is to lay the foundations of first philosophy, but

> I do this without expecting any praise for it from the vulgar, and without hoping that my book will be read by many. On the contrary, I would not recommend it to any except to those who would want to meditate seriously along with me, and who are capable of freeing the mind from attachments to the senses and clearing it entirely of all sorts of prejudices; and I know only too well that there are very few people of this sort.
>
> (1986, p. 11)

Descartes' disdain for the common run of mankind is perhaps only matched in the modern period by Kant's memorable rebuke of the members of the so-called "Scottish School of Common Sense". These philosophers were foolish enough to betray their tribe and to speak up in defence of the views of the common man because they could not bring themselves to accept the counter-intuitive conclusions of their more illustrious countryman, David Hume. Of this treacherous crew Kant wrote acidly as follows:

> [T]he opponents of the great thinker [Hume] should have penetrated very deeply into the nature of reason, so far as it is concerned with pure thinking, – a task which did not suit them. They found a more convenient method of being defiant without any insight, viz., the appeal to *common sense*.... To appeal to common sense, when insight and science fail, and no sooner – this is one of the subtle discoveries of modern times, by means of which the most superficial ranter can safely enter the lists with the most thorough thinker, and hold his own.
>
> (1902, p. 6)

No doubt Bertrand Russell, a great admirer of Hume and another philosophical luminary, would have agreed with Kant's sentiments; but he did not waste much ink on the members of the Scottish School of Common Sense. It was enough for him to remark that common sense is little more than "stone age metaphysics".

No doubt it is the very idea that the true philosopher ought to expect to be mocked by the non-philosopher, and to regard such mockery as something of a badge of honour, which is at least partially responsible for the fact that philosophers have always found it easy to lend a ready ear to counter-intuitive theories. But whatever the reason for this predilection, there is no doubt that the history of philosophy is littered with truly bizarre claims. Consider this quick, but by no means exhaustive, review of some of the most famous philosophical theories from the Ancient Greeks to the present day:

- Parmenides, perhaps the first great philosopher to depart radically from common sense, denied the existence of change and motion in the natural world, and so concluded that the world available through sense experience was an illusion;
- By contrast, Heraclitus insisted that all is in flux, and was understood to have denied the existence of any permanence in the natural world from one moment to the next;
- Plato, at one stage at least, refused to regard the world known via the senses as truly real, positing instead a realm of eternal Forms of which objects in this empirical world are mere copies;
- Chrysippus and other Stoics did away with the distinction between beliefs and emotions, claiming that the "passions" – fear, anger, pity, grief, erotic love and the like – are simply false beliefs, and, like all false beliefs, need to be entirely extirpated;
- Averroes and Siger of Brabant, among others, claimed that human beings share a single mind, or more precisely, a single intellect, a view known as monopsychism;
- Descartes argued that one has no warrant to claim to know anything unless one can demonstrate that there is no possibility that one is being deceived by a malign demon, and that to be in such a position one has to know both that God exists as well as a number of his chief characteristics;
- Malbranche denied that minds and bodies causally interact, and that the appearance to the contrary is the work of God's intervening in the natural order;
- Spinoza insisted that, despite appearances, there is only one substance, God or Nature, and that apparently discrete objects are merely modes of the one true substance;
- Berkeley famously denied the existence of a material world, insisting that everything that exists is mental in nature;
- Leibniz, at one point at least, maintained that the real world consists of monads which exist neither in space nor in time, and that there are no causal relationships of any kind between these entities;

- Hume denied that it is fully rational to rely on inductive arguments, and claimed that the relation of causation is no more than that of the constant conjunction of cause and effect, any necessity thought to obtain between cause and effect being nothing more than a projection of the human mind;
- Kant claimed that the empirically available world is in part a construction of our own minds, and that any mind-independent reality is beyond our ken;
- Fichte, following Kant's lead, came to the conclusion that a free and self-producing subject is the source not only of knowledge but of the objects known, so that knowledge of the natural world is really only a form of self-knowledge;
- McTaggart continued a long tradition of denying the reality of time;
- Frege insisted that whole sentences, like names and predicates, have references, and that the referent of all true sentences is "the True", while the referent of all false sentences is "the False";
- Quine has many takers for his thesis that there are no facts about what a speaker means by his or her utterance of a sentence, a view echoed by Kripke, who claimed it was implied by his own reading of Wittgenstein; Quine also claimed that ordinary objects like tables and chairs, trees and suns are theoretical entities on a par with atoms and subatomic particles, gravitational fields and Homeric gods;
- Dummett, updating Ayer's famous verification theory of meaning, denied that a statement is true or false if there is no way in principle of determining its truth value, leading him to deny the reality of the past;
- Feyerabend, Rorty, the Churchlands and other eliminativists in the philosophy of mind appear to deny the reality of garden-variety mental states such as beliefs, desires, hopes and fears.

And this weary list could be extended almost indefinitely if one wished to include the claims of the so-called post-modern, post-structural, post-feminist, post-colonial, deconstructionist and post-deconstructionist philosophers.

When faced with this eye-watering litany of philosophical extravagance it is difficult not to sympathise with Moore when he asked, "What could these philosophers possibly *mean* by these claims?" One is also reminded of Descartes' rueful observation that there seems to be nothing so outrageous that some philosopher will not maintain it. But while this list of philosophical paradoxes certainly indicates that on the whole philosophers in the orthodox canon of the Western tradition have had scant regard for the views of the common man, this attitude has not been universal. There have always been philosophers who have instinctively felt that the pre-theoretical views of the common man had at least some claim upon them. But relatively few have thought that a deep respect for such views was an essential prerequisite for success in one's philosophical endeavours. Few, for example, would go as far as Thomas Reid, the founder of the Scottish School of Common Sense Philosophy, who wrote,

> In this unequal contest betwixt Common Sense and Philosophy, the latter will always come off both with dishonour and loss; nor can she ever thrive till this rivalship is dropt, these encroachments given up, and a cordial friendship restored; for, in reality, Common Sense holds nothing of Philosophy, nor needs her aid. But, on the other hand, Philosophy...has no other root than the principles of Common Sense; it grows out of them, and draws its nourishment from them. Severed from this root, its honours wither, its sap is dried up, it dies and rots.
>
> (*An Inquiry*, Chapter 1, Section iv)

The names now most commonly associated with this common sense tradition are Thomas Reid and G.E. Moore; but the tradition has an ancient pedigree, stretching back to Plato's greatest critic, Aristotle.

What would philosophy look like if it struck up a "cordial friendship" with common sense? And why should the philosopher go about his or her business in this fashion? This book is an exploration of these and related questions, and contains an extended exposition, defence and illustration of a metaphilosophy of common sense broadly in the spirit of Aristotle, Thomas Reid and G. E. Moore. But by relying heavily on evolutionary biology and psychology, I hope to provide a thoroughly modern doctrine.

The basic structure of the book is as follows: In Chapter 1, after a preliminary discussion of the nature of the philosophical enterprise and what it can legitimately be taken to be in a modern context, I set out the characteristic claims and distinctive project of the common sense philosopher, and draw up a provisional list of common sense beliefs that I argue philosophers would do well to respect. In Chapter 2, I offer a defence of the key claim of the common sense philosopher, namely that common sense beliefs ought to be treated as default positions. Here I rely on a revised version of an argument based on current work in evolutionary biology and cognitive psychology, the key claim being that beliefs are adaptations. In Chapter 3 I tackle a difficult question head-on: Why it is that philosophers so frequently end up denying what we all know to be true? In this Chapter I review suggestions offered by others on this score, and offer the tentative beginnings of a taxonomy of philosophical error. In Chapter 4 I go on to offer a new suggestion based on a largely forgotten episode deep in our medieval past. An important thesis of this book is that philosophers from the early modern period to the present day have often erred for the most unlikely of reasons: Unwittingly, they have been conducting their philosophical business according to rules and expectations appropriate, not to philosophers, but to medieval theologians.

The last half of the book is then devoted to dealing with particular contemporary challenges to common sense beliefs on a range of topics from metaphysics to ethics. These chapters are set-piece defences of certain target theses, but there are important connections between them, and they point towards a philosophical account of the world that takes common sense as its point of departure. A common theme running through these efforts is the attempt to capitalise where possible on the work of Aristotle, as well as developments in evolutionary biology and cognitive psychology. I begin with a response to McDowell's neo-Kantian constructivism and defend the view that the external world is independent of our representations of it and that this world is perceived via non-projective perception. Moving from the nature of perception to the philosophy of language, Chapter 6 is devoted to Dummett's semantic anti-realist challenge to metaphysical realism. Here I argue that the Dummettian reductio provides no good reason to give up the principle of bivalence. In Chapter 7 I turn to the philosophy of mind and focus on the work of the Churchlands, particularly their eliminativist approach to beliefs and desires and the other elements of folk psychology. In Chapter 8 I respond to the arguments of Peter van Inwagen and Galen Strawson, and provide an analysis and defence of the claim that human beings are, at least on occasion, responsible for their actions in a way that renders them fit subjects of reactive attitudes. Finally, I examine the so-called "moral problem", recently brought back into focus by Michael Smith, which purports to threaten moral realism and moral cognitivism.

Some of the material in this book has appeared previously as stand-alone journal articles. Chapter 2 is an expanded version of "The 'Evolutionary Argument' and the Metaphilosophy of Commonsense", *Biology and Philosophy*. Chapter 5 draws on "Metaphysical realism as a pre-condition of visual perception", *Biology and Philosophy*,

19: 243–261, 2004, while Chapter 6 draws on "Whose Challenge? Which Semantics?", *Synthese*, **126**: 325–337, 2001. Material from these three articles appears with kind permission of Springer Science and Business Media. Chapter 4 draws on material which first appeared in "Hume on Induction: A Genuine Problem or Theology's Trojan Horse?", *Philosophy*, **77**, pp. 67–86, 2002, and again appears with kind permission of the editor.

1
The Metaphilosophy of Common Sense

> In the absence of critical reflection on the nature of the philo-
> sophical enterprise, one is at best but a potential philosopher.
> Wilfred Sellars[1]

Introduction

The primary purpose of this chapter is to set out as clearly as possible
a general account of the metaphilosophy of common sense. To be sure,
the account provided here does *not* appear in all details in the work
of any single thinker in the common sense tradition. It does, however,
incorporate the central pronouncements of the likes of Aristotle, Reid,
Moore and other central figures of the tradition, and it is certainly
consistent with the general tenor of their thought on these matters.
Nonetheless it has been necessary first to gather and then to meld these
pronouncements into a coherent whole in order to arrive at a complete
metaphilosophy. Following the lead of Sellars, the account begins with a
general statement on the nature of the "philosophical enterprise" from
the common sense point of view. I then go on to consider the methodological approaches it sanctions as well as what one might call "the
common sense project" as a whole. To add some flesh to these otherwise
abstract bones, I end with a provisional list of putative common sense
beliefs in order to provide the reader with some concrete examples.

On the need for a general account of the "philosophical enterprise"

Arguably the most distinguishing, and certainly the most eye-catching,
feature of the metaphilosophy of common sense is its iconoclastic

nature. Common sense philosophers are not impressed by philosophical paradoxes, however venerable their origin. And common sense philosophers are not always very polite when it comes to expressing their dismay at the extravagances of their philosophical brethren. One is likely to be struck, for example, by Reid's rather intemperate remarks in *An Inquiry* where he sets out, in particularly uncompromising tones, the tenor, if not the nuanced details, of this tradition. "I despise Philosophy", he writes, "and renounce its guidance – let my soul dwell with Common Sense" (Chapter 1, Section 3). And it is difficult not to be taken aback by Moore's confident, defiant and shaming claim that he knows certain common sense beliefs to be true, and that they are known with certainty to be true even by those philosophers who deny them (1963, p. 41).[2] But for all their initial iconoclastic appeal, it is only when seen against a wider picture of the philosophical enterprise in general, a picture in which the metaphilosophy of common sense is embedded, that these claims can be properly appreciated and common misconceptions avoided. It is necessary then to begin an account of the metaphilosophy of common sense with a higher level description of the nature of philosophy itself.

There is a further reason for beginning this chapter, and indeed this work, with a discussion of the nature of philosophy in general. It is worth acknowledging at the outset that the account of the philosophical enterprise to be offered below has more than a purely expository role to play in this chapter. The reason for this is that the defence of common sense is made that much easier if something like this account of philosophy is considered plausible and attractive. Indeed part of the defence of common sense to be offered in what follows is that its characteristic approach to philosophical problems is the most reasonable approach to take given the nature of philosophy in general. To be sure, the common sense tradition does not stand or fall with the acceptability or otherwise of this account in all its details. And, as noted at the outset, it is fair to say that neither Reid nor Moore, the two most prominent figures in the common sense tradition, ever wedded themselves explicitly to any fully fleshed-out account of the discipline in general.[3] Nonetheless, if the picture of philosophy offered here is plausible, then the virtues of the common sense approach will be all the more apparent. But given that this account of philosophy is more than an expository aid, it is important that great care is taken, and be seen to be taken, to ensure that the account is plausible and robust.

Now one could be forgiven for suspecting that linking one's metaphilosophy in this fashion to a particular account of the nature of philosophy itself is something of an own goal, for the nature of the philosophical enterprise is a notoriously vexed question on which there is currently little substantial agreement. In a recent survey article on the direction of the discipline at the turn of the century, a prominent and well-placed member of the profession rightly characterised twentieth-century philosophy as ending in "diversity and fragmentation". After listing the philosophers thought to have been the most influential in the last 20 years – Dummett, Kripke, Rawls, Armstrong, Derrida, Levinas and Habermas – it is noted that "... without exception, everyone had a different philosophical agenda and a different pursuit".[4] It is hard to disagree with this observation, at least at first blush. But care should be taken not to make too much of this potentially embarrassing situation. For if the common sense philosopher is wedded to an account of the discipline in general, so too is every other philosopher. For if, following Sellars, one assumes that engaging in philosophical activity at a reasonably sophisticated level presupposes *some* conception or other of the nature of philosophy itself (however incomplete and undeveloped it may be); and if an aspiring philosopher wishes to flatter himself or herself with the belief that he or she is at least a "potential" philosopher; then whatever his or her philosophical stripe, he or she will have to be able to offer something sensible about the nature of philosophy and the philosophical enterprise. It simply will not do, when pressed on this matter, to frown significantly and say, "Well, the nature of philosophy is itself a philosophical question, for 'philosophy' is an 'essentially contested concept'", and then hope no one will be so impolite as to press us further. Nor will it do to suggest that philosophy is just whatever academic philosophers happen to get up to in their working hours. Despite the fact that philosophers are now accustomed to the idea that one ought not to look for the essences of things, it is difficult to accept that there is nothing that our various and disparate activities have in common that makes them distinctly philosophical. In the absence of very strong evidence to the contrary, it is safer to assume that there is at least a family resemblance to be uncovered here, and perhaps even a focal sense of the term "philosophy" on which various analogical senses are dependent. If there is no such focal sense or family resemblance, then the term "philosophy" is a mere *flatus vocis*.

The upshot is that at some point *all* philosophers must address the discipline's embarrassing question, and so the common sense philosopher is in no worse position on this score than any other. But our collective embarrassment may be alleviated somewhat if we pause for a moment to consider carefully what constraints should be placed on any such account. Surely one cannot say just anything one likes about the nature of philosophy. For all that "philosophy" is a contested concept, it is not an entirely subjective matter. Presumably some accounts are better than others, and the criteria by which such judgements are made ought to be identified and brought out explicitly. I begin then by taking what amounts to yet another step back from my primary task by sketching in a cursory fashion some purely formal criteria I think any plausible account of the nature of philosophy ought to satisfy. Having thus retreated the better to advance, I proceed to the account itself. That account in place, we can then safely move on to the primary business of this chapter, namely, the exposition of the metaphilosophy of common sense.

Some formal constraints on accounts of philosophy

Let us proceed without further ado to the first constraint.

Any plausible account of the nature of Western philosophy ought to be able to accommodate a good number, if not most, of the central metaphilosophical insights of its greatest figures. The intuition here is that a plausible account of philosophy will not force one to maintain that many, and certainly not most, of the discipline's greatest lights were ignorant of the nature of their own enterprise. After all, it is from precisely these figures that subsequent generations have learned their trade. Of course this is *not* to say that the philosophical greats cannot be corrected on these matters, merely that our default position ought to be that the great practitioners were not hopelessly confused about the nature of their discipline.

This charitable but not unreasonable constraint raises two tricky questions: Who is counted among the greats of Western philosophy? and, How many metaphilosophical insights constitutes "a good number"? Neither question can be given a precise answer, but plausible, if rough and impressionistic responses are available. Taking the second question first, clearly it is unlikely that a single coherent account of the nature of philosophy can accommodate all metaphilosophical views; but if we agree to wave difficulties concerning how one individuates metaphilosophical insights, our general rule of thumb should be that of two otherwise equally matched accounts the one which is able to save more of the central metaphilosophical insights is to be preferred to one that does not.

As to the first question, there will always be some debate about which philosophers ought to be included on the list of outstanding figures. But I think the matter is made less contentious if it is agreed that one ought *not* to include any philosopher whose work has not stood the test of time, or, perhaps more importantly, has yet to stand the test of time. This effectively removes from our considerations contemporary figures and those from the recent past, say the last 50 years, that is, precisely those about whom there is likely to be little widespread agreement.

Against those who would maintain that this constraint is excessively conservative and will only lead to accounts of what philosophy has been like in the past and not what it is like at the moment, I would suggest that this alleged vice is really a virtue. First of all, there is nothing in this stipulation which prevents the discipline from changing and developing over time. Nonetheless the range of activities into which philosophy, or any other discipline for that matter, can plausibly be thought to mutate is limited by the discipline's past. If it changes too much, it is reasonable to say that a new discipline has arrived on the scene.[5] The second reason for not fearing the conservative tendency of this time constrain is that philosophers are notoriously poor judges of the lasting impact or import of the work of their contemporaries. This point can be graphically illustrated by looking at edited collections of philosophical works published a considerable time ago. Consider, for example, a now infrequently consulted work published originally in 1908 entitled *Modern Classical Philosophers: Selections Illustrating Modern Philosophy from Bruno to Bergson*. This edited collection was compiled by Prof. Rand of Harvard University, and published by Houghton Mifflin Company. This work reveals what an informed professional considered to be the list of philosophical greats of the modern period. Rand's list is as follows: Bruno (1548–1600), Bacon (1561–1626), Hobbes (1588–1679), Descartes (1596–1650), Spinoza (1632–1677), Leibniz (1646–1716), Locke (1632–1704), Berkeley (1685–1753), Hume (1711–1776), Condillac (1715–1870), Kant (1724–1804), Fichte (1762–1814), Schelling (1775–1854), Hegel (1770–1831) Schopenhauer (1788–1860), Compte (1798–1857), Mill (1806–1873), Spencer (1820–1903), Herman Lotze (1817–1881), Charles Renouvier (1815–1903), Bradley (1846–1924), Josiah Royce (1855–1916), James (1842–1910) and Bergson (1859–1941). What the list reveals is that agreement on who counts as a significant figure is easier to secure the more historically distant the figure under consideration happens to be. I would suggest that between Bruno and Kant there is substantial agreement between ourselves and Rand (the status of the other German Idealists is less certain); but between Compte and Bergson there are figures many professional philosophers working today will have never heard of, let alone read. Apart from Mill, who among them would be included as a matter of routine in an undergraduate programme of study? And where, one wants to ask, are the likes of Frege, Brentano, Nietzsche or Moore?

Any plausible account of the nature of philosophy ought also to square with the actual practice of its greatest figures. The intuition here is that philosophy ought not to be characterised in such a way as to force one to maintain that the great practitioners of the discipline were not actually engaged in philosophy at all. At issue here is the observation that theory and practice can at times come apart, even among the greats. The point of this constraint is simply that we ought to pay attention to what the great philosophers actually do, as well as to their explicitly expressed metaphilosophical statements. A corollary to this is that a plausible account of the nature of the discipline ought to be able to point to historical examples drawn from a variety of thinkers of different complexions as illustrations of certain key points contained in the account.

Thirdly, a plausible account of the nature of philosophy ought not to depart too widely from the expectations of the educated non-philosopher. If the account provided bears no relation whatsoever to what those working in other disciplines associate with the term "philosophy", then a question mark ought to be placed next to that account. This is not to say that the philosophical layperson ought to be able to understand the work of professional philosophers without a great deal of effort and help (if at all), anymore than the layperson understands advanced theories in physics, mathematics or engineering. But the layperson can usually recognise a biological theory or mathematical theorem as belonging to biology or mathematics, even if they do not understand the theory or the theorem. In an ideal world, the same would hold for philosophy. I say "ideal" because I fear that the nature of philosophy is something of a mystery to many academics working in other disciplines. But what is worse is the very real possibility that, on the contrary, many have quite definite views about what philosophy is, a view derived from a limited exposure to only a few selected figures rather than engagement with the discipline as a whole. Consequently, this constraint cannot be given priority over the first two.

The last, but by no means least of the formal constraints I wish to insist upon is the following: It seems plausible, as well as highly desirable, that accounts of philosophy should identify a distinctive role for the discipline within the general intellectual economy. The intuition here is that one can begin to formulate a clearer idea of the distinct nature of philosophy by placing the discipline in the wider university context and identifying the role it plays in the interactions of the various disciplines. There must be such a distinctive and legitimate contribution philosophy makes in this context if it is to avoid redundancy or the fate of all hermetically sealed endeavours, namely, a lingering death due to its irrelevance to the wider context. I am assuming therefore that any account of philosophy will have missed something essential if the account portrays philosophy as redundant (because replaceable at least in principle by another discipline or disciplines), or trivial (because it is a mere intellectual amusement for a group of specialists). No doubt philosophy is not as important as some have made out; it is no longer "The Queen of the Sciences"; it certainly does not solve the problems of the world, nor is it likely to provide effective treatment for existential anxieties born of the human condition. In fact good philosophy is often rather dry, difficult and obscure. But our default position ought to be that, when properly conducted, philosophy is not trivial (despite the fact that the relevance of the work of some philosophers may not be immediately obvious) or replaceable even in principle by some other discipline.

I have suggested, then, that an account of the nature of the philosophical enterprise is plausible if (a) it is largely consistent with the metaphilosophical insights of the discipline's greatest practitioners; (b) it is consistent with the actual practice of the discipline's greatest practitioners; (c) it is not wildly at odds with the expectations of educated non-philosophers and (d) it identifies a distinct role for the discipline within the general intellectual economy. It is with these constraints in mind that the substantive account of the nature of philosophy presented below is to be considered. My hope is that by respecting these constraints the account will gain some measure of objective validity, and so will serve both as a backdrop against which to better appreciate the metaphilosophy and overall project of the common sense philosopher, but also as a point of departure in their subsequent defence. It is also hoped that the account presents philosophy in an attractive light, with its own distinctive and legitimate purpose in the twenty-first century.

Philosophy and co-ordination problems

As stated above, the account of the general nature and aim of philosophy to be offered here draws heavily on the work of previous philosophers, although it does not match in all details any account given by a common sense philosopher, or any other philosopher for that matter. And, as I will show, something close to this picture of philosophy is consistent with the efforts of its greatest practitioners, and so deserves to be taken seriously as a picture of philosophy in general. But a word of qualification. Philosophy is a slippery discipline. It is therefore unlikely that any account, however satisfactory from a formal point of view, will succeed in capturing all aspects of our elusive quarry.

The account of philosophy provided here is based primarily on Aristotle's remarks in the *Topics, Posterior Analytics, Nicomachean* and *Eudaimon Ethics*, and *Metaphysics*. But it also builds explicitly on the views of modern philosophers, such as Gilbert Ryle and Wilfred Sellars. That this account shares features with those offered by thinkers of a variety of different stripes and historical periods suggests that the account offered here has some staying power. But however that may be, the general strategy has been to seek to accommodate a wide range and variety of metaphilosophical insights by recognising that there are different stages of the philosophical enterprise, with different metaphilosophical views accurately describing these different stages. And while it is no part of my claim that all philosophers consciously progress through all the stages I set out – they most certainly do not – I would claim that they provide a rational reconstruction of the processes undergone by the philosophical community as a whole in its treatment of a problem, while the careers of individual philosophers may be entirely devoted to only certain phases of the process.

In accordance with my fourth criterion, namely, that any account of philosophy ought to be able to identify the, or at least a, distinctive role for philosophy in the general intellectual economy, I begin with the general aim of philosophical activity in its broadest sense. Trying always to avoid the twin dangers of pomposity on the one hand and undue understatement on the other, it is not implausible to suggest that the end of the discipline throughout most of its history has been to provide a description and explanatory account of the nature of the Universe and the place of human beings within it. It is this aspect of philosophy which forever ties it to the so-called "Big Questions" – much to the embarrassment of most professional philosophers and the delight of undergraduates. What distinguishes philosophy from religion and myth, which share similar aims, is (i) philosophy's commitment to employing reason, evidence and argument alone in the pursuit of this goal, (ii) the level of abstraction attained in the descriptions and explanatory accounts and (iii) its desire for comprehensiveness. Of course professional philosophers rarely, if ever, have this grandiose end in mind on a Monday morning on the way to work; but the core sub-disciplines of philosophy, when taken together, do go some way to completing what one might call "The Big Picture". These sub-disciplines are devoted to developing descriptions and accounts of (a) the kinds of things to be met with in the Universe, and their most general features (ontology and metaphysics); (b) the most general features of the mind and its relation to the body (philosophical anthropology and philosophy of mind); (c) how human beings come to know and understand something of themselves, the natural world, and whatever else the Universe may contain (epistemology) and finally (d) how human beings ought to comport themselves, and what we ought to strive for, both privately and collectively (theories of action, theories of the good, ethics and politics). The Holy Grail of philosophy has been a set of descriptions and accounts covering areas (a)–(d) which are not just satisfactory on their own when taken in isolation, but which are consistent with each other and mutually reinforcing. Moreover, it is arguable that many of the great philosophers have hoped that accounts (a)–(c) will provide some guidance in the area of human action. It is commonly assumed, at least implicitly if not explicitly, that knowing something about the nature of the world we live in, and something of our own human nature, is bound to shed some light on what kind of life human beings should lead and what kinds of actions human beings ought to perform and which to avoid. Implicit in this picture of philosophy then is the claim that philosophy is not just a theoretical exercise, but is ultimately connected, if at times somewhat distantly and indirectly, with the practical and existential concerns of ordinary life.[6] This is one way, but only one, in which philosophy has justified its claim to being more than a trivial pursuit.[7]

I suspect that this account of the ultimate aim of philosophy will be familiar to most. I also suspect that the attempt to provide "The Big Picture" will strike many as hopelessly grandiose, laughably old-fashioned and maybe even dangerous. And of course, there is a very respectable and longstanding tradition within philosophy which maintains that such a project is an impossible undertaking. But despite the fact that many a philosopher has made it his or her business to attack something like this vision of philosophy, or at least some element of it, their work as philosophers would be unintelligible without it. And those who would reject this picture as hopeless must themselves defend a set of philosophical theses which inevitably fall into the recognised sub-disciplines of philosophy as I have just sketched it. Consequently, in addition to the foregoing, one should say that philosophy has also included an ongoing discussion as to whether this grand project is in fact achievable.

But I want to insist that the project as outlined above is, at least in one important respect, not as grandiose as one might think.[8] And the reason for this is that philosophers *qua* philosophers do *not* provide the basic materials out of which "The Big Picture" is developed. It is not the job of philosophers to spin castles of their own imaginings and then attempt to pass these off as a picture of reality. If one is to understand the distinctive nature of philosophy one must begin by recognising that a division of intellectual labour exists in the general intellectual economy between philosophy on the one hand and the sciences and truth-directed subjects of the humanities on the other. It is the role of the special sciences, for instance, to conduct investigations into that aspect of reality peculiar to them, and to discover new facts and develop theories within and about that particular realm or domain. By contrast, there is no particular aspect or element of reality that philosophers study *qua* philosophers, as there is, say, for the biologist, chemist or economist. Nonetheless, philosophy is not open to the complaint (as perhaps is theology as traditionally understood) that it is a subject without an object, because philosophy is not a first-order discipline on a par with the special sciences. Philosophy does not provide new first-order information about any aspect of reality; rather the contribution of the philosopher *qua* philosopher to the grand project is to draw on pre-existing materials derived from the special sciences, the truth-directed subjects of the humanities, as well as our store of pre-theoretical beliefs, and to *co-ordinate* this material into a coherent picture of human beings and our place in the Universe. It is this task of co-ordination, lying outside the remit of any special science, which is specifically philosophical, and the problems encountered in the pursuance of this task are specifically philosophical problems.[9]

This is not to say that philosophers have not often tried, sometimes successfully, to provide theories concerning matters which strictly speaking belonging to the special sciences. This has occurred repeatedly, particularly when the relevant science had yet to emerge. It is this historical fact which prompts some to say, erroneously, that philosophy is what one does with a problem until one can hand it over to the sciences. But on the account of philosophy offered here such efforts are not strictly philosophical, although they are often prompted by philosophical investigations, and put to philosophical use.[10] It is precisely because philosophers historically have worn many additional hats (scientist, mathematician, theologian, historian, to name just a few) that philosophical activity has often been mistaken for activities of a different sort. And this is a relatively easy mistake to make. For while we all recognise clearly enough, for example, that Aristotle is wearing his philosopher's hat in the *Metaphysics* and *Nicomachean Ethics* and his biologist's hat in *Parts of Animals,* things are not always so clear-cut.

Consider, for example, Searle's *Speech Acts*. Is this a work of philosophy or linguistics? While it was motivated by philosophical concerns, and can be put to philosophical use, I would suggest that its ultimate home is within linguistics, but is no less valuable for that. Similar considerations apply to Berkeley's *A New Theory of Vision*, and to much of the work of Descartes. But the point to emphasise here, however, is that it is precisely because philosophy is *not* a first-order discipline that it *cannot* be a proto-science, or worse, science carried out by philosophers. It is also for this reason that one cannot reasonably expect philosophy to be replaced by the sciences.

A principal thesis of this account of philosophy then is that strictly philosophical questions *begin* their careers as co-ordination problems. It is important therefore to say something further about the nature of co-ordination problems in general. A co-ordination problem initially arises when one notices a tension, real or apparent, between beliefs or lines of thought that one is otherwise inclined to accept – beliefs derived from the sciences, the truth-directed subjects of the humanities, perhaps religious doctrine and humanity's common store of pre-theoretical beliefs. But not just any tension between beliefs produces as a philosophical problem *per se*. A philosophical problem emerges when the beliefs in question originate in *different* domains, when a line of thought from one special science, for instance, appears to clash with a belief from a distinct science, or theology, or, as we shall see, common sense. The problem is that both lines of thought are attractive and well established within their respective domains, but the taking up of the one precludes, or at least appears to preclude, the taking up of the other. Such tensions are commonly felt to be of some significance because the conflicting beliefs are usually important elements of The Big Picture, it is the aim of philosophy ultimately to generate. But the crucial point for present purposes is that such problems fall to philosophy, as opposed to a special science, because such problems do not arise *within* the domain of any special science, but are due to a prima facie clash *between* first-order disciplines, or between first-order disciplines and common sense, and thus lie outside the competence of any first-order discipline.[11]

Consider Hume's problem of induction. At its simplest, this notorious problem is a co-ordination problem. The problem is to accommodate beliefs emanating from logic on the one hand with another set of pre-theoretical beliefs on the other. The problem emerges when one acknowledges (i) the pre-theoretical view that experience is generally a good guide to action, and that this is so because similar causes tend to produce similar effects, a belief which grounds our expectation that in the future events will unfold much as they have done in the past, and (ii) the logical point that a finite set of observations provides no logical guarantee of the truth of any universal generalisations, thus undercutting the belief that one can be sure that the future will resemble the past, a point which suggests to some that relying on experience as a guide to action cannot be justified according to the cannons of deductive logic. At the level of particular instances, one then gets a tension between the perceived reasonableness of beliefs held by all – for example, that the Sun will rise tomorrow, that bread will continue to nourish and not poison us – and the view, derived from logic, that such beliefs cannot be supported by valid rules of inference, and so cannot be fully rational. Both lines of thought seem to be well supported, and yet they appear to be inconsistent with each other. One is then left wondering whether it is or is not rational to expect the Sun to rise tomorrow or for bread to continue to nourish rather than poison. Aristotle had a name for questions of this sort. Aristotle stated that an *aporia* (problem or puzzle) arises "...when we reason on both sides [of a question] and it appears to us that everything can come about either way." This produces "a state of *aporia* about which of the two ways to take up" (*Topics*, VI, 145b 16–20).

Now if strictly philosophical problems or questions begin as co-ordination problems as described above, then the following can be said about philosophical activity in general at the highest level of abstraction: The task of the philosopher *qua* philosopher is to give an account of the initial set of beliefs that removes the prima facie tension, and so solves the philosophical puzzle. Removing these tensions constitutes success in philosophy. Indeed, on this view, solving problems of this sort is the *raison d'être* of the philosopher *qua* philosopher, and constitutes the philosopher's specific contribution to the general intellectual economy.[12] For by removing the puzzlement, the state of *aporia*, one finds that elements of The Big Picture that previously would not fit obligingly together are now co-ordinated and allotted their respective places. From this perspective, all conceptual analyses, second-order theory construction, argument development, analysis and critique, that is, all the working philosopher's bread and butter activities, are best understood as means to this end, and they receive the tag "philosophical" because they can be used to this end.[13]

Now if this is what a strictly philosophical problem looks like, and what success in philosophy consists in, then, at the highest level of abstraction, solutions to philosophical puzzles can take only a limited number of forms. After due consideration the philosopher must show either that

(a) the alleged tensions in the initial set of beliefs which lead to the puzzlement are merely apparent and not real (perhaps stemming from certain misunderstandings either of the facts of the case or of our own conceptual system), or,
(b) the perceived tensions in the initial set of beliefs are indeed real, and are best removed by modifying or qualifying or perhaps abandoning altogether one or more of the initial set of beliefs.

Other possibilities are open to the philosopher, but these options are signs of philosophical failure. For instance, a philosopher might effectively declare that the puzzle cannot be solved, and that theorising in this domain is futile (either in principle or at least for the present). In practice this amounts to saying that either

(c) no totally satisfying account of the initial data can be given (either in principle or at least at present) but that nonetheless none of the initial beliefs should be abandoned or,
(d) no coherent account of the data can be provided, and for this reason all of the initial beliefs fall under suspicion.

The third option is taken by philosophers who are willing to admit that there are some mysteries that simply cannot be solved, if only for the moment, and that such mysteries have to be accepted as features of the intellectual landscape. The fourth and final position is occupied by those willing to suggest that in a particular domain or domains human beings are subject to comprehensive and systematic error, not simply at the level of theory, but at the level of the initial beliefs themselves.

It is perhaps worth pausing for a moment to illustrate these patterns with a quick glance at two grand old philosophical chestnuts, the free will–determinism debate, and the mind–body problem. In both cases it is clear that the initial data from different domains pull in two seemingly incompatible directions, thereby creating an *aporia*. Concerning the freedom of the will, for instance, it is usually taken for granted that in the normal course of events we usually feel free, and we certainly talk and act as if we are responsible agents at least much of the time. This much appears to be just so much common sense. And yet this "freedom of the will", which lies at the heart of our picture of ourselves as human beings, is notoriously difficult to reconcile with the natural sciences. Are there not necessary and sufficient causes for every natural event? Does this not mean that all events, including human actions, are determined? And does this not preclude the very possibility of freedom? As to the mind–body problem, again we all accept initially that human beings and the higher animals have mental states with particular properties (consciousness and intentionality, etc.) and that these states are somehow related to physical bodies. What could be more obvious? But again upon reflection it soon emerges that these initially obvious claims are difficult to reconcile with the equally authoritative claims of the natural sciences. One begins to ask, "How is it that brute matter can have these properties of consciousness and intentionality?" and, receiving no answer, one is left with an *aporia*.

To continue illustrating these patterns, it is clear that on both of these issues one can find philosophers whose efforts fall more or less neatly into our four forms of solution. There are those who claim the noticed tensions are merely apparent and other who claim that the tensions are real and that more or less drastic revisions of the initial data are required. In the first camp, one finds the compatibilists in the free-will debate, while John Searle's biological naturalism serves as a good example of a philosopher claiming that the alleged tensions between the apparent properties of mental states and a commitment to physicalism are merely apparent. In the second camp, one can point to the determinists and libertarians in the free-will debate, while the eliminativists in the philosophy of mind provide a particularly vivid example of this turn of mind. On both topics one can also find philosophers who despair of ever reaching any coherent account of the data while refusing to give them up. This appears to have been Descartes' view on the freedom of the will,[14] and Thomas Nagel in the philosophy of mind. And while I am not aware of any major philosopher occupying the final position (d) on either of these topics,[15] Kant's treatment of the antinomies is the best historical example of a philosopher maintaining that there are domains in which human beings are systematically confused and cognitively incompetent, and that all beliefs in these domains ought to be viewed with suspicion.

These two classic philosophical problems, and the work carried out on them, nicely conform to one's expectations given the general account of the nature of philosophy being developed here. But confidence in this account of the philosophical enterprise would no doubt be increased if one could point to a number of recognised philosophers whose work appears to have taken its point of departure from an *aporia* of the sort described above. Again, as my methodology demands, I will confine my remarks here to a few seminal figures from the dim and distant past whose importance for the development of the discipline will go unchallenged by the vast majority of working philosophers.

It is clear, at least on a traditional reading, that Plato's metaphysical theories stem in no small part from his attempts to accommodate two influential lines of thought which appeared to be flatly contradictory, namely Heraclitus' famous observation that everything in the natural world is in flux, and Parmenides' equally striking but contradictory assertion that change is impossible. Heraclitus' contention appears to have been grounded on empirical observation of the natural world, while Parmenides reached his conclusions on the basis of conceptual considerations alone. The *aporia* emerges from the fact that two distinct sources of knowledge, reason and sense experience, deliver apparently contradictory results. What is more, both of these Presocratic positions presented challenges to yet a third plausible assumption, namely, that the cognitive capacities of human beings are such that we can rise above mere perception – something within the cognitive reach of animals – and achieve intellectual understanding of at least some features of the natural world. That humans enjoy a significantly richer intellectual life than even the highest of the other animals appears to have been taken for granted by most of the Greeks. But making sense of these three conflicting lines of thought was not easy, and this challenge lead Plato to posit a realm of eternal and unchanging Forms (a nod to Parmenides) in addition to a material world subject to change (a nod to Heraclitus) while insisting that humans, or at least philosophers, can have an intellectual understanding of reality, or at least part of it (a nod to common sense) via cognitive access to the eternally existing forms.

Since much of Aristotle's work takes as its point of departure many of the themes found in Plato, he naturally had to consider the *aporia* that spurred Plato into action. Aristotle's *Metaphysics* is an obvious example of a major philosophical work taking its start from a set of *aporia*, and is worth noting that by his time something like distinct domains had begun to emerge. The first chapter of the third book sets out explicitly the 15 *aporiai* Aristotle intends to tackle, and this he proceeds to do in the remainder of the work. Without getting into the details of the *Metaphysics*, it is clear that the central books (Zeta and Eta) are devoted to the development of a theory of substance which will do justice to three lines of thought which were not obviously reconcilable. The three lines were (a) his ultimate subject view of substance as developed in his logical work *The Categories*, (b) the hylemorphism so successfully employed in his *Physics* and (c) his pre-theoretical and characteristically

Greek assumption that the world is intelligible. One should also mention Aristotle's *Nicomachean Ethics,* another seminal work in the history of philosophy replete with *aporia*, perhaps the most famous of which is the perceived tension between Socrates' views on akrasia and those of the ordinary person.

If one moves forward in history to consider the Medieval Scholastics, often denigrated as mere theologians, one can see that they were in fact engaged in genuine philosophical activity. The drama of philosophy in the Middle Ages centres on the attempt to synthesise theology with philosophy. Aquinas' philosophical challenge, for example, was to accommodate the two great authorities from these distinct domains, (Augustine the theologian and Aristotle the philosopher and scientist) whose views were clearly not obviously compatible on all key points. In fact every scholastic article begins with the stating of a question to which contradictory answers had been given by recognised authorities from the domains of theology and philosophy. The business of the article is then to reach an answer to the set question. Even Descartes, the father of modern philosophy, was drawn into this medieval project of Faith seeking Understanding. Although Descartes is usually credited primarily with the development of new methods of pursuing the business of philosophy, and with achieving a radical break with the medieval past, it is important to recall the end to which Descartes' new method was to be the means. Already in his *De Mundo*, Descartes was trying to provide the conceptual infrastructure for a modern Christian philosophy, an infrastructure that would accommodate Athens and Jerusalem. And in the dedication to perhaps his most famous work, the *Meditations*, Descartes states that his intention is to show, ostensibly for the benefit of those seeking to "persuade infidels", that a commitment to rationalism in epistemology is not only consistent with, but can provide justification for, the Church's teachings on the existence of God and the immortality of the soul, and that these matters need not be accepted simply on faith alone. (It is noteworthy that this was precisely the motivation behind Aquinas's *Summa Contra Gentiles*.) For all his undoubted modernity on some matters, Descartes' ultimate philosophical aim was the reconciliation of the claims of two distinct domains, theology and philosophy.

Consider now the work of another great figure from the history of the discipline, Immanuel Kant. It is undoubtedly the case that reconciling the philosophical positions of rationalism and empiricism was a significant element of the Kantian project. But Kant is often read as having been spurred into philosophical action at a more profound level by the apparent tension between the Newtonian mechanics he so admired and his belief in the autonomy of the will, a belief no doubt encouraged by his religious convictions. The challenge of reconciling rationalism with empiricism in a manner consistent with both Newtonian mechanics and the freedom of the will is undoubtedly at the heart of Kant's most important metaphysical and epistemological work, and can easily be seen to conform in general outline to the account of philosophy I have been presenting here.

One final historical example will have to suffice.[16] F. P. Ramsey once called Russell's theory of descriptions a "paradigm of philosophy", and it is probably fair to say that most analytic philosophers have agreed with this assessment. It is interesting to note then that this paradigm fits the account of philosophy offered here particularly well. Consider Russell's problematic sentence "The King of France is bald". On the one hand Russell accepts and appreciates that every competent speaker of English understands this sentence, so there is no question as to its having a relatively clear meaning. Yet his commitment to the not obviously absurd view that the meaning of a referring expression is the object it picks out creates a ticklish problem. Since there is no King of France, the referring expression "The King of France" ought not to have any meaning, leaving it unclear how it is that we all understand the sentence "The King of France is bald". Russell's theory of descriptions tries to save both common sense and his theory of referring expressions by showing that definite descriptions are not really referring expressions at all, thereby neatly solving the *aporia*. While Ramsey was impressed by Russell's theory because it illustrates how the surface features of ordinary language can be misleading, and how philosophical analysis can allow one to get behind these surface features to the deep logical structure of a sentence, our interest here is confined to pointing out that Russell's problem has the form of an *aporia*, and that his solution takes the form of the first of the four possibilities noted above.

Hopefully these brief and incomplete historical observations concerning the work of some undoubtedly seminal figures does go some way to establishing that the account of philosophy offered here does indeed square with the actual practice of some the greatest philosophers. It is also hoped that this account is not too far removed from the expectations of the educated non-philosopher, at least at some stages, although this remains to be seen. But perhaps most importantly, it is hoped that this account does identify a role for philosophy as a discipline within the general intellectual economy, a role which gives the lie to those who would maintain that philosophy is either redundant or trivial.

Much more could, and perhaps should, be said about this account of the philosophical enterprise before moving on. I have, for example, said nothing about how one might individuate domains, relying instead on our intuitions regarding such things at least for the purposes of this chapter. But at least one further question ought to be considered. Even if one were to accept that this account of philosophy is more or less historically accurate, and more or less meets the formally criteria identified at the outset, does this give one grounds for saying that the *essence* of philosophy, our elusive prey, has been caught?

While confident that the forgoing general account of the philosophical enterprise does identify something fundamental about the discipline, I would not wish to suggest that every instance of genuine philosophical activity will fit our model exactly. What I would claim for the account however, is that it does capture the *focal* sense of the term "philosophy" inasmuch as strictly philosophical problems appear to begin life as co-ordination problems. This does not preclude the possibility that other sorts of problems and activities can rightly be termed "philosophical". But, to take page from Aristotle's copy book, in the same way that one can speak intelligibly of healthy diets, healthy life-styles and healthy urine only because these are the causes or the signs of health within an organism, so too I believe that other philosophical activities or problems are genuinely philosophical insofar as they bear a certain relation to co-ordination problems as outlined above. In particular, they are problems or activities that emerge in the course of a philosopher's coming to terms with a co-ordination problem (or a philosopher's attempt to come to terms with another philosopher's attempt to deal with a co-ordination problem). In short, I am claiming that all genuine philosophical activity, in whatever form it takes, can ultimately be traced back to a co-ordination problem, and that it is these co-ordination problems that provide the focal sense of the term "philosophy".

The metaphilosophy of common sense

Our digression on the nature of the philosophical enterprise complete, I can, at long last, turn to the primary business of this chapter, namely, providing a general characterisation and initial defence of the metaphilosophy of common sense. We can begin simply by stating that the common sense philosopher broadly accepts the account of the nature of the philosophical enterprise sketched in the previous section. What distinguishes the common sense philosopher from their philosophical brethren then is how he or she sets about this shared task. There are two chief characteristics of the common sense approach to the business of philosophising that set the common sense philosopher apart. These are (a) a decisive rejection of certain Cartesian assumptions concerning methodology and (b) the championing of the views of the philosophical laity when these come into conflict with the sophisticated theories of philosophers. An extended word on each of these points is in order.

In the *Essays on the Intellectual Powers of Man* Reid writes, "[this] may be considered as the spirit of modern philosophy, to allow of no first principles of contingent truths but this one, that the thoughts and operations of our own minds, of which we are conscious, are self-evidently real and true; but that every thing else that is contingent is to be proved by argument" (VI, vii, p. 464). The Cartesian project, namely, the attempt to derive a complete scientific and philosophical world view consistent with Catholic doctrine solely from what are taken to be the certain foundations of what is provided in consciousness, a project accepted by rationalists, empiricists and Kantians alike, is categorically rejected by Reid and all other philosophers working in the common sense tradition. Reid insists that there is much that we are right to believe, and cannot help but believe, despite the fact that such beliefs are not, and could not be, the conclusions of deductive proofs erected on the certainties available to consciousness. The beliefs which Reid is particularly concerned to safeguard are the assumptions that lie behind our ordinary everyday judgements about the world, for example, that objects which we perceive really do exist and are what we perceive them to be, and that events which we distinctly remember really did occur (*Essays on the Intellectual Powers of Man*, VI, v). These are the sorts of assumptions that the philosophical layperson takes for granted in his or her everyday dealings with the world (although he or she may never have explicitly entertained them); but they are precisely the sorts of beliefs that modern philosophers have had great difficulty justifying in the face of well-known sceptical arguments.

Now it is frequently thought that by refusing to engage with the Cartesian project, which ultimately boils down to declining the invitation to deal with the challenge of Cartesian scepticism, the common sense philosopher is simply begging all the interesting questions, or worse, displaying a crude, anti-intellectual denseness by simply refusing to acknowledge existing problems. But this is not the view common sense philosophers have of themselves, as should be plain from the account of philosophy offered above. The refusal to deal with Cartesian scepticism stems from a radically different conception of the philosophical enterprise. As set out above, it is definitely not the business of philosophers to provide the initial data on which philosophers then set to work. These are provided by the first-order disciplines such as the sciences and the truth-directed subjects of the humanities, and the common experience of mankind. Moreover, there is no need for the philosopher *qua* philosopher to worry about whether the initial data can be known "with certainty" in the fashion demanded by Cartesianism. Such a worry is inappropriate; for it is enough that the data be sufficiently reputable within their "home" domain to merit their being taken seriously by the philosopher. Indeed, if the philosopher was not already sufficiently confident about the initial data they would not give rise to *aporia* in the first place. It is only because these opinions are reputable *prior to any philosophical handling* that they cause concern when they are found to conflict.

So when Descartes writes of his desire to "reform the body of the sciences", and that to this end he had resolved to "sweep away" *all* the opinions he had hitherto embraced and to accept only those that had successfully undergone the "scrutiny of reason";[17] and when Kant wrote that "Everything ... which bears any manner of resemblance to an hypothesis is to be treated as contraband" and "not to be put up for sale even at the lowest price, but forthwith confiscated immediately upon detection",[18] the common sense philosopher has two objections. The philosopher will say first: "Look for certainty if you wish, and play cat-and-mouse games with the radical sceptic if you must; but don't pretend that this is the proper business of philosophy. On the contrary, you are neglecting the proper business of philosophy, which is to deal with co-ordination problems, and have begun to encroach on the territory of other intellectual domains and enterprises, in violation of the principle of the division of intellectual labour, and at the risk of rendering philosophy redundant." But the philosopher will also say, with unmistakable exasperation, "Besides, surely grown men have more pressing concerns to attend to than proving, for example, that I know that I'm not an insect, and the like. Taking time to prove what no one has any reason to doubt is at best a waste of time, and at worst, the high road to philosophical disaster."

Now as important as this rejection is to the metaphilosophy of common sense, it is its second chief characteristic which no doubt provides the tradition with its name. Put crudely, the common sense philosopher has more confidence in a specific sub-set of the opinions of the common man than he or she does in the sophisticated theories and arguments of learned philosophers. As a consequence, if common sense beliefs come into conflict with the theories and arguments of learned philosophers, they will always give the vulgar commoner the benefit of the doubt, and put the question mark over the philosopher.

This crude account of (b) can be expressed more precisely using aspects of the account of philosophy provided in the previous section. Using the terminology of that account, we can say that the second chief characteristic of the metaphilosophy of common sense concerns how the philosopher ought to respond to *aporia*. In particular, the common sense philosopher is distinguished from his or her philosophical brethren by his or her adoption of a twofold hierarchy of preferences. The first hierarchy assigns an order of preference to the four forms a solution to a philosophical puzzle can take. The second hierarchy concerns which kinds of data should be saved and which sacrificed when an *aporia* involves a genuine and not merely a prima facie conflict. A word on both hierarchies is required.

In the first instance it is important to recognise that all four methods of resolving a puzzle are in principle open to the common sense philosopher. That is, he or she can, after due consideration, opt for positions (a)–(d) outlined in the previous section, and he or she is not committed to the employment of any one type of solution for all philosophical problems. However, the common sense philosopher would prefer to be able to show that the perceived tensions that make up the *aporia* are merely apparent, and that all of the initial data leading to the *aporia* can be preserved if understood aright. However, in the real world this is not always possible, and there are instances where the tensions are indeed genuine and some of the initial data has to be modified, qualified or perhaps abandoned entirely. Nonetheless, revising the initial set of data is not to be undertaken lightly, and this option is to be pursued only if the tension is genuine. Put another way, one ought not to go in for revision for revision's sake, but only if revision is needed to resolve an *aporia*. Of the final two options (c) is preferable to (d) despite the fact that both are signs of philosophical failure. The reason for preferring (c) to (d) is that (d) is extremely revisionist while (c) is not.

The second hierarchy of preferences is more important than the first, and concerns precisely what kinds of initial data are to be saved and which dropped when the *aporia* is genuine and not merely apparent. Here the common sense philosopher has an order of preference that puts his or her decidedly at odds with the majority of philosophers in the Western tradition. If a puzzle is genuine, the common sense philosopher will, if at all possible, save whatever common sense beliefs belong to the initial data which lead to the *aporia*. Most importantly, if a common sense belief clashes with a *philosophical* theory or argument, the common sense belief is always given the benefit of the doubt. That is, it is always the philosophical theory or argument which must give way, and the common sense belief preserved.

As I say, this approach to philosophical problems is decidedly at odds with that commonly found in the work of most of the major philosophers in the history of the discipline. For most have treated a sub-set of the initial data leading to *aporia*, namely the views of the common man, as little more than a Wittgensteinian ladder, which once used can be kicked away. That is, while philosophers generally recognise that they must *begin* their reflections by considering beliefs that are widely shared and accepted by the common run of mankind – if only because these beliefs play a role in the emergence of the initial puzzlement – they feel no need to "save" these beliefs in their *final* account of the puzzle in question. In short, when a co-ordination problem can be solved by the rejection of a widely held and intuitively plausible belief, philosophers have generally shown themselves quite prepared to take this revisionist course.

It is on precisely this point that the common sense philosopher and the revisionist part company. And, says the common sense philosopher, if the account of philosophy sketched earlier is on the right track, then this most common of revisionist manoeuvres needs to be regarded with suspicion. For if the task of the philosopher is to remove tensions between pre-existing and otherwise *reputable* lines of thought, then the philosopher has no business rejecting any of the initial data except as a last resort. Rather, as Aristotle would have it, the philosopher ought to strive to *preserve* as many of the initial "reputable" or "common" opinions (*endoxa*) as possible, for these views come stamped with the authority of their respective domains, an authority which, as Ryle puts it, neither waits for nor fears the approval or disapproval of philosophers (1984, p. 7).

As for the relative authority of common sense and philosophy, the authority of philosophy is of a decidedly inferior rank to that of common sense, because any claim that a philosophical theory or argument might have upon us arises from its usefulness in solving *aporia*, that is, its usefulness in showing us our way around the complicated web of beliefs derived from the sciences, the truth-directed subjects of the humanities, *and* our pre-theoretical intuitions. Common sense beliefs, on the other hand, like all other endoxa, do *not* have to establish a claim upon us; their claim is felt immediately and is in part responsible for the emergence of philosophical reflection in the first place. A philosophical theory or argument, by contrast, has no immediate authority, but only after it has proved itself useful does it gain any claim upon us.

Both hierarchies are at play in Aristotle's terse discussion of methodology in the *Nicomachean Ethics*. He writes,

> We must, as in all cases, set the observed facts before us and, after first discussing the difficulties [i.e. *aporia*] go on to prove, if possible, the truth of all the common opinions about [the topic at hand], or, failing this, of the greater number and the most authoritative; for if we both refute the objections and leave the common opinions undisturbed, we shall prove the case sufficiently.
>
> (1145b0–7)

It is worth noting that this point regarding the relative authority of common sense and philosophy can be put in terms which even Quine could appreciate. While no defender of common sense, and certainly not shy of philosophical paradoxes, Quine argues nonetheless that although everything in principle is up for revision, one ought not to go in for revision for revision's sake, but only in order to solve a problem – say, to square a recalcitrant experience with one's overall belief system. Furthermore, when opting for revision, Quine insists that one ought to operate on the assumption that a "minimum of mutilation" is to be sought.[19] On the view of philosophy presented here, while what is saved and what is dropped will have to be decided on a case-by-case basis, *in all cases* one ought to strive to save as much of the initial data as possible. Since the philosopher's job is to solve philosophical puzzles, and not revision for revision's sake, if solution A saves more of the initial data than solution B, then A is to be preferred. But this entails saving as much of common sense as possible, because revisions here are not minimal by any means, but demand extensive and widespread changes to the entire Big Picture under construction. And more to the present point, abandoning a common sense belief will always be more revisionary than rejecting a philosophical thesis.

Note that it is not claimed that common sense beliefs should never be given up. The point is that one should not abandon a common sense belief on the strength of 'mere' philosophical arguments, since these arguments have a merely derived authority, an authority derived from their ability to accommodate and co-ordinate reputable opinions. But if one reputable opinion genuinely clashes with another, then clearly something has to give. Moreover, if a common sense belief genuinely clashes with newly discovered and reliable empirical information, then the common sense belief will have to give way. The important point here is that there is nothing sacrosanct about common sense beliefs and other endoxa which forever preserves their revision. But this account of philosophy suggests that philosophers ought to think far more carefully indeed about rejecting a common opinion than many have been wont to do, particularly if the only motivation to do so is pressure from a philosophical argument or theory.

The upshot of the discussion so far can be expressed as follows: The metaphilosophy of common sense insists that common sense beliefs are to be treated as default positions. That is, a common sense belief is to be accepted as true despite the fact that no deductive proof can be offered for it, and is to be abandoned only under considerable pressure. In practice this means that when a philosophical theory or argument contradicts a common sense belief, the benefit of the doubt must be given to "vulgar" opinion and the philosophical argument or theory viewed with suspicion if not entirely rejected.

According the status of default position to common sense beliefs also has another very important consequence for one's methodology. Treating common sense beliefs as default positions means that one has *shifted the burden of proof* onto the shoulders of those who would reject common sense beliefs, a point nicely expressed by Reid in the context of his discussion of human free agency:

> This natural conviction of our acting freely, which is acknowledged by many who hold the doctrine of necessity, ought to throw *the whole burden of proof* upon that side; for, by this, the side of liberty has what lawyers call a *jus quaesitum*, or a right of ancient possession, which ought to stand good till it be overturned. If it cannot be proved that we always act from necessity, there is no need of arguments on the other side to convince us that we are free agents.
>
> (*Essays on the Active Powers*, IV, vi, p. 620)

The point here is that if the burden of proof on the shoulders of those who would reject common sense beliefs is not discharged, then common sense wins the day by default, and no further proof of the common sense belief is required. Consequently, to establish or defend a common sense belief it is enough to show that the arguments of the revisionary philosophers fail to make their case.

Now it is this general set of metaphilosophical attitudes which forms the backdrop against which Aristotle, Reid and Moore, but also Ryle, Austin, Grice and Searle, carry out their philosophical researches. We can find explicit modern expression of these points in Ryle, who writes, "We possess... a wealth of information... which is neither derived from, nor upset by, the arguments of philosophers" (1984, p. 7). And in Grice we find the clearest possible expression of the caution with which philosophical conclusions are treated when these conflict with common sense:

> It is almost certainly (perhaps quite certainly) wrong to reject as false, absurd, or linguistically incorrect some class of ordinary statements if this rejection is based merely on philosophical grounds. If, for example, a philosopher advances a philosophical argument to show that we do not in fact ever see trees and books and human bodies, despite the fact that in a variety of familiar situations we would ordinarily say that we do, then our philosopher is almost (perhaps quite) certainly wrong.
>
> (1989, p. 172)

The common sense project

Adoption of this general metaphilosophy leaves the common sense philosopher with a philosophical project consisting of five principal tasks, tasks which will occupy us in the remainder of this work. These are as follows: (1) The common sense philosopher must provide some principled means of determining just what is to count as a common sense belief. (2) The common sense philosopher owes his or her philosophical brethren an argument justifying the view that common sense beliefs ought to be treated as default positions. (Something of an argument to this effect has been suggested here, and this topic will be taken up again at length in the next chapter.) (3) It is not sufficient to refute a philosophical claim simply to point out that it clashes with common sense. The errors which lead to the mistaken claim must be identified. The common sense philosopher thus has the ongoing and seemingly interminable task of exposing the errors in the arguments of philosophers which purport to overturn particular common sense beliefs, thereby providing an indirect defence of those particular common sense beliefs. (4) A further task is to provide a general explanation as to why it is that philosophers repeatedly end up denying what everybody knows to be true prior to beginning to philosophise (and what everybody continues to believe after the philosopher has presented his arguments to the contrary). (5) Finally, the common sense philosopher will need to provide, at the level of metaphysical description, an account of what is implicit in our everyday dealings with the world in such a fashion as to enable progression towards the completion of The Big Picture.

It is against the backdrop of these principal tasks that the continuity of the common sense tradition is most apparent, with different figures engaging with some but not necessarily all of these tasks. Reid, for example, made some attempt to justifying the view that common sense beliefs ought to be viewed as default positions. He also offered extensive discussion and criticism of the arguments of Hume, and the theory of ideas in particular. As for Moore, his interest in conceptual analysis stems from his work on the third, fourth and fifth of the principal tasks of the common sense philosopher.[20] It was Moore's general contention that arguments purporting to overturn common sense beliefs all rest on faulty analyses of the concepts on which the arguments turn, thereby providing his general answer to (4);[21] but equally he maintained that conceptual analysis would allow the philosopher to move beyond common sense beliefs to a clearer and deeper understanding of the nature of reality. Perhaps Ryle's great contribution to the common sense tradition was his introduction of the notion of a category mistake as a diagnostic tool. And Austin, Grice and Searle can all be seen to be developing philosophical theories consistent with common sense on a wide variety of topics from metaphysics to ethics. But perhaps the greatest figure of the common sense tradition is Aristotle himself. Having formulated the basic principles of the metaphilosophy of common sense, he also provided the most sophisticated metaphysical system developed to date which really does take our everyday dealings with the world as its point of departure.

What counts as a common sense belief?

The characteristic features of the common sense approach to philosophy and philosophical problems in general having been set out, it now falls to us to identify, at least in a preliminary way, those beliefs to be accorded the status of default position. I will close this chapter with an initial stab at this task, a stab constituting little more than a list of such beliefs as identified by Reid and Moore, with more to follow in the course of the next chapter. But again I must begin with a few preliminary remarks on this score to ward off possible misunderstandings.

If the metaphilosophy of common sense is not to be fundamentally misunderstood, it is important to recognise that the term "common sense" as I will employ here is something of a term of art. For example, it is important to realise that having a common sense belief is *not* about having "street smarts", or a general ability to deal with a tricky set of circumstances without proper preparation or warning, although in a looser, more colloquial sense this way of speaking is perfectly acceptable. This is Ryle's point when he insists that one does *not* display common sense in our strict sense when "dealing with a plausible beggar or with a mechanical breakdown when I have not got the proper tools" (2002, p. 3). Moreover, a common sense belief is not just any belief which happens to be accepted pre-theoretically by virtually everyone and challenged by virtually nobody, although common sense beliefs usually do fit this bill.[22] For example, the belief that cleaning one's teeth after every meal is generally a good idea, despite its near universality, does not constitute a common sense belief in the sense of interest to us. Common sense beliefs in the sense which I use the term here, and in which Thomas Reid understood the term, are those views regarding the nature of things which are *presupposed* by ordinary everyday beliefs and abilities. More precisely, common sense philosophers are interested in the fundamental elements, principles or cornerstones of the conceptual scheme lying behind the views and actions of the ordinary person. It is these "principles of common sense", as Reid calls them; that "massive central core of human thinking which has no history – or none recorded in histories of thought", as Strawson styles them (2006, p. 10) which are the common sense philosopher's main concern.

Several important points follow. First, many common sense beliefs can be given expression in terms no non-philosopher would ever use. In fact, the beliefs themselves may never have been consciously formulated by any non-philosopher. But this is not because common sense beliefs are obscure, or difficult, or arcane. Precisely the reverse is the case. It is precisely because they are so obvious that they ordinarily pass entirely unnoticed. These beliefs are assumed in virtually all our actions, and there is rarely, if ever, any need to think about them consciously and explicitly at all. Nevertheless, these beliefs, or close approximations to them, must be true if the sorts of things we commonly and consciously accept as true are true.

Second, as mentioned earlier, not all common opinions are philosophically interesting or worthy of defence. Many common opinions can stand or fall with no consequences for the metaphilosophy of common sense because their truth or falsity does not affect the viability of the underlying conceptual scheme. To continue our example, if it should turn out that cleaning one's teeth before every meal is *not* generally a good idea, this surprising turn of events will no doubt be significant for dentists and public health officials, but it is unlikely to have ramifications for the conceptual scheme underlying our everyday beliefs and actions.

Finally, it is also worth highlighting the fact that common sense does *not* have a view on all matters of philosophical interest. This is important when considering the oft-levelled allegation that common sense philosophers appear to think that answers to all philosophical questions are to be found simply by reviewing what everyone already knows. This is false on a number of scores. First, there are philosophical topics about which the philosophical laity has no view whatsoever because the issues are not encountered in ordinary day-to-day life. For example, it is highly unlikely that common sense would have anything directly to say about Frege's attempt to derive arithmetic from logic – it is simply not an issue that falls within the purview of common sense. There are also philosophical topics which are well known and of great interest to non-philosophers, but concerning which there is no settled view to be found amongst the philosophical laity. For example, Moore suggests that the existence of God is a topic on which common sense has nothing to offer because there is no near unanimity on this question. He writes,

> On the whole, I think it is fairest to say, that Common sense has *no* view on the question whether we do know that there is a God or not: that it neither asserts that we do know this, nor yet that we do not; and that, therefore, Common sense has no view as to the Universe as a *whole*.
>
> (1965, p. 17)

Another reason for insisting that common sense does not contain answers to all philosophical questions is that there are philosophical topics about which the philosophical laity has but a very incomplete view. For example, while it is no doubt a common sense belief that space and time are "real" in some important sense of the term, common sense has virtually nothing to say about the *nature* of space and time. For instance, all that common sense has to offer on space is that it is of such a nature as to allow objects to be at a distance from each other. True, any view of space which denies that objects are at a distance from each other falls foul of common sense. But this stipulation hardly tells us anything at all about the nature of space. One certainly cannot appeal to common sense to adjudicate between Newtonians and Leibnizians on the nature of space. As for time, common sense dictates that it must be of such a nature as to allow for change, which implies that events are able to happen one after the other in an ordered succession. But common sense goes no further than this. Beyond this lies the domain of the relevant specialists in the sciences and metaphysics.

With these preliminaries in mind I can now present examples of common sense beliefs as I intend to use the term. These have been gleaned mainly from the works of Reid and Moore. The first ten are found in Moore's first lecture in *Some Main Problems of Philosophy* entitled "What is Philosophy?"

1. There are in the Universe an enormous number of material objects (e.g. our bodies, other people, animals, plants, stones, mountains, rivers, seas, planets, tables, chairs, etc.)
2. Human beings have minds inasmuch as we have a variety of mental states, including acts of consciousness. We see, hear, feel, remember, imagine, think, believe, desire, dislike, will, love and so on.
3. All material objects are located in space inasmuch as they are located at a distance from each other.
4. Mental acts are attached to – contained within – certain kinds of bodies (human bodies and perhaps those of the higher animals).
5. Mental acts are ontologically dependent upon bodies.
6. Most material objects have no acts of consciousness attached to them.
7. Material objects can and do exist when we are not conscious of them.
8. There was a time when no act of consciousness was attached to any material body.
9. All objects and acts of consciousness are in time.
10. We *know* (1)–(9) to be true.

From Reid, the following set of beliefs can be extracted

11. I think, I remember, I reason, and, in general, I really perform all those operations of the mind of which I am conscious.
12. My well functioning memory is reliable if not infallible when concerned with recent events.
13. By attentive reflection a man can have a clear and certain knowledge of the operations of his own mind.
14. All the thoughts I am conscious of, or remember, are the thoughts of one and the same thinking principle, which I call myself, or my mind.
15. There are some things which cannot exist by themselves, but must be in something else, as qualities, or attributes.
16. In most operations of the mind there is an object distinct from the operation itself. I cannot see without seeing something.

17. We ought to take for granted, as first principles, things wherein we find a universal agreement, among the learned and the unlearned, in the different nations and ages of the world. (Among these he includes beliefs in material objects; that every effect has a cause; that there is a right and a wrong in human conduct; he also includes passages concerning the common structure of language as an indicator of commonly held beliefs.)
18. Moral judgements are true or false.

Points 11–17 are taken virtually verbatim from Chapter 5 of Reid's sixth essay in *Essays on the Intellectual Powers* entitled, "The First Principles of Contingent Truths", while 18 is taken from Chapter 7 of the fifth essay in *Essays on the Active Powers*.

These examples are meant to give an idea of the sort of thing that passes for a common sense belief. As one can see there is a degree of overlap, but the overlap is not complete, and it is possible that there is some disagreement on particular cases. I will be focussing on a range of beliefs that strike me as important and interesting, and which have in fact come in for serious criticism from philosophers in recent times. For the purposes of this study, the common sense beliefs that will receive most attention are as follows:

- That there is a real world that exists independently of us, of our thoughts, language and representations
- That human beings have direct, non-projective perceptual access to this world via the senses
- That causation is a real relation among objects and events in the world, a relation whereby one phenomenon, the cause, brings about another, the effect
- That statements are either true or false in virtue of states of affairs in the world
- That human beings have beliefs, desires, hopes and fears and other mental states to which one can appeal to in order to explain and predict human actions
- That human beings are responsible for their actions in certain specifiable circumstances, and so are proper objects of approval, condemnation, praise, blame and punishment
- That moral and evaluative statements, like other statements, are typically true or false depending on whether they correspond to how things are. That is, value exists independently of our language and representations.

The principal contention of this chapter is that any philosophical argument, thesis or system which is inconsistent with any of this set of common sense beliefs is almost certainly (perhaps quite certainly) wrong, and that no lasting philosophical achievement is to be expected if these beliefs are not accommodated within that philosophical effort. The defence of this contention is the business of the next chapter.

2
The "Evolutionary Argument" and the Metaphilosophy of Common Sense

Introduction

In the previous chapter an attempt was made to provide an account of the metaphilosophy of common sense, to present in schematic form what I called the common sense project, and to list a number of putative common sense beliefs. In this chapter I want to address the second of the principal tasks of the common sense project, namely, to provide an argument to justify the view that common sense beliefs ought to be treated as default positions. I have already argued, on what might be called "internal" grounds, that this distinctive approach to the business of philosophy makes sense given the nature of the philosophical enterprise. If strictly philosophical problems are co-ordination problems, then it behoves the philosopher to seek to resolve the tensions between reputable opinions while preserving as many of those opinions as possible. It also follows that common sense beliefs will have a greater claim on the philosopher than philosophical theories and arguments.

But what if one is unimpressed by this account of the nature of philosophy? What happens if it becomes impossible to secure widespread agreement on the nature of the philosophical enterprise? Is there anything else that can be offered in support of the common sense position? It is because worries of this kind are difficult to quell that I want to develop an additional line of support for the view that common sense beliefs ought to be treated as default positions.

I suggest, however, that we need to approach our problem afresh from an entirely different angle. For reasons that will become clear in due course, an "external" argument, an argument based on non-philosophical considerations, will be the focus of our efforts to develop an additional line of support for the metaphilosophy of common sense.

In particular, I revisit an old argument based on evolutionary biology and psychology which, its supporters allege, gives reason to suppose that our pre-theoretical intuitions, beliefs and concepts are at least approximately true or adequate. In its standard form this evolutionary argument (EA) faces many serious objections. But I will show that a revised version of EA, placed in a new context and employed to different ends, is not vulnerable to the standard criticisms levelled against arguments of this general type. And as we shall see, it lends crucial external support to the metaphilosophy of common sense.

Preliminary scene setting

Since I am now approaching matters from an entirely different perspective, some preliminary scene setting is in order. Consider the following two pairs of arguments:

A1

1. If Hume's epistemological principles are correct, then I do not know that this object in my hand is a pencil.
2. Hume's epistemological principles are correct.
3. I do not know that this object in my hand is a pencil.

(3), of course, is just one of the sceptical conclusions, or "philosopher's paradoxes", for which Hume is justly (in)famous. Now consider the closely related argument from Moore:

A2

1. If Hume's epistemological principles are correct, then I do not know that this object in my hand is a pencil.
2. I "do" know that the object in my hand is a pencil.
3. Hume's epistemological principles are false.[1]

Both arguments are equally valid from a formal point of view, and both share the central premise. At issue, of course, is the strength of our commitment to the second premise of each argument. How is one to choose between them? The question is clearly quite urgent given the significant differences in the respective conclusions to which they lead. And the urgency extends beyond this particular case, for stand-offs of this sort occur regularly in philosophy, stand-offs, that is, between those inclined to accept what they take to be "plain common sense" on the one hand, and those willing to forgo such intuitions in the light of sophisticated philosophical theories on the other. Examples abound, but I confine myself to one more recent case:

B1

1. If Quine's indeterminacy of translation thesis is correct, then there is no difference between my meaning "rabbit" as opposed to "undetached rabbit parts" or "rabbit stages".
2. Quine's indeterminacy of translation thesis is correct.
3. There is no difference between my meaning "rabbit" as opposed to "undetached rabbit parts" or "rabbit stages".

Again, this is just one of the many philosopher's paradoxes for which Quine is justly (in)famous. But again there is a philosopher to play the part of Moore, who argues

B2

1. If Quine's indeterminacy of translation thesis is correct, then there is no difference between my meaning "rabbit" as opposed to "undetached rabbit parts" or "rabbit stages".
2. There is all the difference in the world between my meaning "rabbit" as opposed to "undetached rabbit parts" or "rabbit stages".
3. Quine's indeterminacy of translation thesis is false.[2]

Again both arguments are equally valid from a formal point of view, and both share the central premise. How is one to choose between the respective second premises?

Of course the common sense philosopher wants to argue that (i) contrary to appearances, arguments A1 and B1 are *not* on all fours with arguments A2 and B2; (ii) the burden of proof lies with the upholders of arguments of the type exemplified by A1 and B1; (iii) until the conclusions of such arguments have been conclusively established, the upholders of arguments exemplified by A2 and B2 need bring no evidence at all. For ease of exposition I will apply the term "revisionist" and its cognates to both the arguments exemplified by A1 and B1 and the philosophers who uphold them, while "common sense" and variants thereof will apply to both the arguments exemplified by A2 and B2 and the philosophers who uphold these.

But how does one argue for such a position? If the argument forwarded in the previous chapter is unlikely to persuade everyone, what else can the common sense philosopher say in defence of his or her position? In fact this is a rather old and dusty question, a question that had its last proper airing during the early and middle decades of the last century when questions of methodology in philosophy enjoyed pride of place. We know, for instance, that the later Wittgenstein would simply dismiss the paradoxes of philosophers as the result of so many flies yet to be freed from their linguistic bottles.[3] But few now seriously maintain that *all* or even most philosophical paradoxes are the result simply of linguistic confusions. As for Moore, he would insist that he is far more certain, say, of the object in his hand than he ever could be about highly abstract and complex philosophical theories, and so plumps for (A2).[4] But Hume could and would respond to this differential certainty argument by agreeing that he is himself more certain of the object in his hand than of his own epistemological theories, since he accepts that the latter produce no conviction. But, Hume would continue, this just goes to show that our beliefs have more to do with custom and habit than with reason, for while sceptical arguments produce no conviction, they admit of no answer either.[5]

Not content to let matters lie, Moore and the Ordinary Language Philosophers are then likely to respond by saying that any philosophical analysis of a concept, be it knowledge, meaning and so on, is never self-evident and always stands in need of justification. Furthermore, they would contend, such analyses can be justified only after suitable testing by means of the search for counter-examples. If no counter-example is found then the analysis is confirmed; but if one is identified, then the analysis fails. Moore and company would then contend that (A2) and (B2) provide just such counter-examples to the analyses of knowledge and meaning at work in (A1) and (B1). But again a Hume or Quine is likely to meet this line of argument by insisting that while it is true that one cannot begin to provide an account of a concept without first taking into consideration particularly clear-cut instances of the concept's application (admitting that particular instances do have some sort of priority over the abstract philosophical account of concepts) nonetheless, unless one assumes that our pre-theoretical use of these concepts is entirely coherent and unproblematic (and, they would say, if they were entirely in order would these concepts be the subject of philosophical dispute?) there is no reason to assume that philosophical reflection will not reveal that even apparently paradigmatic instances of a concept's application may be infelicitous.

The result of these exchanges, at least as I read them, is a stalemate, with neither side gaining the upper hand.[6] But eventually, after much to-ing and fro-ing, the general consensus appears to have emerged that the so-called philosophers of common sense and Ordinary Language were unable to give a good reason to assume that our pre-theoretical use of language is entirely in order. Although the argument had not in fact been lost, siding explicitly with common sense in philosophical debate became increasingly unfashionable, and, if the sudden and dramatic death of Ordinary Language philosophy is anything to go by, the laurel of history appeared to have been handed decisively to those willing to let their philosophical reflections "cast them out of the garden in which the common man lives".[7]

But the tide may be turning. Now one increasingly finds appeals to what look like common sense principles and beliefs cropping up in respectable works in virtually all sub-branches of the discipline, although this move is usually employed quietly and with little fanfare, often cloaked in different terminology, and sometimes without complete conviction.[8] But while the common sense philosopher will welcome this trend, important questions remain unanswered. If a respect for common sense has been rekindled in the breast of at least some philosophers, what has *not* emerged in the interim is a systematic justification of this sort of appeal to common sense. The stand-offs between revisionists and common sense philosophers remain without a principled resolution. And as recent history shows, when left to our own devises we philosophers have proved unable to break these stalemates decisively.[9] Indeed it begins to look as though progress on this matter will be achieved only if an external arbiter is brought in.

It is precisely in order to break these sorts of stalemates that I look to draw upon resources from *outside* the field of philosophy. In particular, I turn to evolutionary biology and psychology, and call upon a version of EA which, properly understood and deployed, bolsters confidence in common sense intuitions simply in virtue of their being common sense intuitions, while rendering doubtful the reliability of the philosopher's abstract reflections precisely on the grounds that they are philosophical reflections. I will defend this version of EA against the standard criticisms raised against arguments of this general type, showing that this old argument, too quickly discarded by some, can be dusted off and, with proper handling, put to use in the service of the metaphilosophy of common sense.

The argument from evolutionary theory (I)

It has long been suspected that there are philosophical gains to be made on the back of the view that concepts, beliefs and belief formation systems are adaptations. Darwin himself felt the tug of this intuition.

In his notebooks he wrote, "Origins of man now proved. Metaphysics must flourish. He who understands baboons would do more towards metaphysics than Locke" (1987, D26, M84). And despite the fact that the difficulties facing EA are well known and well aired, the suspicion that there is philosophical gold in the evolutionary hills remains as strong as ever.[10] The difficulty, to continue the metaphor, has been to hit upon a viable process of extraction.

In the first instance it was thought that evolutionary theory provided as very straightforward and simple argument to the effect that our everyday, common sense beliefs and concepts are true or adequate, or at least approximately so. The gist of this early version of EA is as follows: Our ordinary, everyday, common sense beliefs, concepts and thinking strategies have proved their worth over the millennia in the work-a-day field of action. It is these beliefs, so the story goes, that made it possible for human beings to cope with the diverse and variegated ancestral environment in which our species first evolved. If these beliefs were not true, or at least approximately so, and these concepts not at least roughly adequate, then, we are told, human beings would have quietly slipped off this stage and into oblivion. The central claims here are that our belief formation systems and general cognitive apparatus are adaptive, and could not be so if their products, namely acts of perception, beliefs, concepts and thinking strategies were not at least approximately reliable, true, adequate and rational. And when used by evolutionary epistemologists, the conclusion drawn is usually rather strong, to the effect that natural selection more or less guarantees that *most* of our beliefs will be true, and *most* of our thinking strategies rational.

Very often the proponents of this version of EA are so confident of its virtues that they hardly bother to flesh it out any further. Indeed, the intuitive plausibility of the premises is felt to be so high that, as Stich (1990, p. 55–56) has complained, often very little in the way of argument is provided for them. Quine, for instance, appears quite happy to write, "creatures inveterately wrong in their inductions have a pathetic but praiseworthy tendency to die out before reproducing their kind" (1968, p. 126) and more or less leave it at that. In a similarly confident vein, Dennett writes that "natural selection guarantees that *most* of an organism's beliefs will be true, *most* of its strategies rational" (1987, p. 75).[11] And such confidence in evolutionary considerations is not confined to card-carrying naturalists like Quine and Dennett. Austin's famous claim that Ordinary Language deserves our respect because "our common stock of words embodies all the distinctions men have found worth drawing, and the connexions [sic] they have found worth marking, in the lifetimes of many generations" and that these are likely to be sound "since they have stood up to the long test of the survival of the fittest" is a clear case in point (1979, p.183).

However, while some have been only too sure of the argument's soundness, others have been quick to point out what they take to be its fatal flaws.[12] For example, many have noted that our belief formation systems are far from "optimal", a view backed up by numerous studies demonstrating that human beings are inveterately prone to making certain kinds of cognitive errors. The Wason 4-card test is a case in point. But the list of cognitively non-optimal behaviours is depressingly long.[13] This line of attack forces one to recognise just how fallible human cognition is *despite* it being an adaptation. In another line of argument, it is alleged that some false beliefs are in fact adaptive, and consequently there is no logically safe inference from a belief's being adaptive to that belief's being true (Sage, 2003). There are also fears in some quarters that EA leads to unpalatable conclusions, for example dualism in the philosophy of mind, or realism in metaethics. But perhaps the most pressing concern for philosophers has been the charge that EA begs all the interesting question because it assumes precisely what is at issue in most philosophical contexts (Quine, 1975; Rorty 1979; Clark 1987; O'Hear 1997; Wright 2002). It is with these objections in mind that I sketch a more fully worked out version of EA.

The argument from evolutionary theory (II)

One of Stich's complaints against the EA as presented above is that it is rarely more than sketched, sometimes only waved at, and its central assumptions rarely defended. It behoves anyone who wishes to employ this kind of argument to take note of these objections, and take steps to meet them. But a word of qualification is needed. Since the *empirical* assumptions of the argument are *not* the bone of contention between its defenders and detractors, I will not attempt to secure all of the steps in this argument, particularly those that involve either truisms in biology or assumptions motivating well-developed research programmes. I will rest satisfied if the empirical assumptions called on in the course of the argument are widely accepted in their respective scientific communities, and focus attention rather on the alleged implications of these findings. My intention here is simply to present a version of EA that brings its assumptions out into the open, that has no implausible premises, and which can serve my metaphilosophical purpose, namely breaking the stalemate in favour of common sense. I will argue in due course that this does not leave this version of EA open to the charge of circularity.

I turn now to the somewhat laborious step-by-step presentation of the version of the argument to be defended here. We can make a start by noting the following:

1. Organisms need to be able to cope with their environment if they are to be in a position to reach maturity and reproduce their own kind. Organisms that cannot cope with their environment die young, and do not pass their genes onto the next generation.

This is as close to a truism as one is likely to get in biological thinking, so I proceed to the following:

2. If the organism is an animal, "coping with one's environment" usually includes, among other things, being able to avoid predators while also being able to secure food, shelter, mates and other resource requirements.

Again there is no question of anyone baulking at this premise. All that is at issue here is the obvious point that different types of organisms have different environmental factors to cope with, and that the factors facing animals are of the general sort mentioned. Since we are interested primarily in beliefs, and no serious biologist believes that organisms other than animals have beliefs or belief-like states, our attention from now on will be exclusively on animals.

3. Coping is achieved in large part (but by no means entirely) by the performance of appropriate bodily movements, that is, an animal's engaging in appropriate behaviour and action.

At issue here is that most animals, as opposed to plants, are not fixed or rooted to any one spot, and their coping with their environment demands that they move themselves from location to location as the occasion warrants. Again, I doubt that anyone will seriously want to quibble with this premise, so I proceed to the following:

4. Successful bodily movement requires a reliable guidance system.

Again, at the risk of labouring the obvious, an animal is not likely to be able to find its way around in the world successfully without being able to tell where biologically relevant objects are located.

5. An animal's cognitive apparatus is such a guidance system.

This premise makes the obvious point that it is with eyes, ears, noses, radar systems, and so on, along with the central nervous system and brain, that animals detect extradermal objects and their properties, as well as their lay-out. However, the substantive claim is the following:

6. Action guidance is the evolutionarily primary function of mental states.

The claim here is that animals have cognitive systems and mental states *in order to be able to act*, and that a necessary condition of successful action is the having of cognitive systems and mental states. That action and cognition co-evolved in mutual inter-dependence is a central claim of this version of EA, a claim shared with a number of substantial on-going research projects.[14]

I now need to introduce a further substantive claim regarding biological functions, namely,

7. If a trait or structure x has a biological function y in organism o (i.e. if trait or structure x is a feature of o because it does y, and y is a consequence of x's being present) then, in an organism that is coping with its environment, x is usually performing function y adequately.[15]

Obviously I am relying on Wright's analysis of biological function. What is not so obvious is that I am *not* claiming that if x is performing function y in o, then x is "optimal". All that my argument requires is that natural selection be a satisficing rather than optimising force.[16]

I now return to the consideration of an organism's cognitive system.

8. Beliefs are one form of mental representation, and as such their evolutionarily primary function is the support of adaptive behaviour.

Since no parties to this particular dispute wish to bring anti-realist views regarding beliefs to bear on this argument, these concerns will be waved for now.[17] (I will, however, take up this particular anti-realist challenge in a separate discussion in Chapter 7.) But a further unfamiliar claim about beliefs is required at this point:

9. Beliefs are "decoupled representations".

Here I am relying on Peter Godfrey-Smith's (1991) and Sterelny's (2003) distinction between detection systems and belief systems proper. Godfrey-Smith and Sterelny characterise beliefs as cognitive states which "(a) function to track features of the environment and (b) are not tightly coupled functionally to specific types of response". Detection systems, like belief systems, function to track features of the environment; but, unlike belief systems, they produce or trigger in an animal one specific behavioural response. Examples here might include a frog's detection of a fly-shaped figure, a rabbit's detection of an eagle-shaped shadow or a Herring gull chick's detection of a mobile red dot on a medium-sized object. In each case the registering of a particular type of stimulus triggers one specific behavioural response. Things are otherwise with beliefs. Beliefs are mental representations that are decoupled from any particular response, and so can be put to service in a range of behavioural possibilities. Whether this can be taken as a complete analysis of the notion of belief or not will not delay us further here, for all surely recognise the distinction that Sterelny is drawing, and further refinements in the analysis of the notion will not affect the course of our argument. We are now ready for the entry of natural selection:

10. There is selective pressure in favour of cognitive systems able to produce decoupled representations if an animal's environment is complex.

This is the central plank of Godfrey-Smith's highly regarded environmental complexity hypothesis. The reasoning behind the claim is that beliefs, not being functionally tied to a narrow range of responses, allow for behavioural flexibility or plasticity, and the expansion of the organism's behavioural repertoire. Behavioural flexibility confers an advantage on an organism by allowing it to tailor its actions more precisely to suit the specific and often changing conditions in which it finds itself. Where a detection system produces woodenly the same set of behaviours, which may or may not be appropriate in a given set of circumstances, beliefs, or decoupled representations, give the organism a better chance of hitting upon the right course of action. I can now introduce a relatively unproblematic historical claim:

11. The environment in which human beings found themselves at the relevant stage in our evolutionary past was complex.

Again, no one is likely to take issue with this, so we draw the conclusion:

12. There was selective pressure in favour of decoupled representations in *Homo sapiens* and other hominids.

I can now state the other major premise of the argument.

13. Beliefs about the world that accurately represent those states of affairs in the world are, on the whole, better guides to action than are false beliefs.

Apart from being intuitively plausible, this premise explains why we value truth at all. If beliefs were *not* functionally linked to action we could reasonably ask, with Nietzsche (1966, p. 9), "Suppose we want truth: *why not rather* untruth? and uncertainty? even ignorance?" But the answer, obvious enough, is that we want our various projects to succeed, and so we give them every opportunity of success by generally seeking to ground those projects on true beliefs.[18] And despite the fact that some critics of the argument attack precisely this premise, alleging that false beliefs can also be adaptive, no one seriously doubts that a belief's being true goes a long way to explaining why it can play a role in the successful guidance of action.

 I will return to this premise in due course, but for the moment we can continue with the argument by noting that if Points 1–13 are true then it follows that

14. Natural selection will favour those animals with reliable sensory systems and belief formation systems *insofar as those sensory systems and beliefs have a direct bearing on the animal's ecological and social fitness*.

 I introduce this important qualification because we need to note that there is nothing to preclude the possibility that beliefs, and particularly belief formation systems, may in time be put to work in domains distinct from those for which they were originally selected. But if these new domains are not ecologically or socially sensitive, then there can be no legitimate expectation that natural selection will guarantee that the otherwise reliable belief formation systems will continue to be reliable in these new domains. This restriction is also entirely in keeping with the claims of the common sense philosophers, who never claim that common sense has a view on *all* topics, but rather tends to be confined to matters of practical significance. So it is no part of my argument that natural selection favours "...cognitive faculties [that] are reliable in the sense that they generate mostly true beliefs". Some opponents of evolutionary epistemology (e.g. Sage, p. 97) have found it easy to attack this excessively strong because of unqualified claim.

There is an important implication here regarding the application of EA, particularly with respect to science and its often counter-intuitive claims. First, common sense intuitions have a restricted sphere of competence for the reasons just outlined, and so common sense must give way to science on matters outside this limited sphere. But it is also important to realise that science and common sense do not come into conflict as often as one might think. For example, while it is true that physics employs counter-intuitive views of space and time, there is no conflict here with common sense. As mentioned in the previous chapter, common sense demands only that space and time be of such a nature as to allow objects to be located at a distance from each other, and for events to be sequentially ordered. It has nothing to say beyond this about the nature of space and time, in the same way that common sense has nothing to say about the chemical composition of water. These theoretical matters, while of the greatest scientific interest, had no ecological or social import in the ancestral environment, and are of no interest to common sense.

With this important qualification in mind we can then say,

15. It is not likely that human beings will be given to believing what is obviously false, or to missing what is obviously true, as long as those truths and falsehoods have a direct bearing on our ecological and social fitness.

The essential idea here is that error in these sensitive domains is simply too costly. This is important because if an organism is going to invest in expensive cognitive systems (as we certainly have), then a minimum requirement of such systems is that they get certain basic things right, otherwise the systems will not pay their way, and the organism will be selected against. False beliefs can be tolerated if the cost is not too high, for there is likely to be little selective pressure against systems that produce false but neutral beliefs. But as the old joke has it, what natural selection can and must guarantee is adequacy with respect to "the four Fs", namely, feeding, fighting, fleeing and reproducing. An organism that is not satisficed for the four Fs will not reproduce its kind.

At this point it remains for me to link these adaptive beliefs and belief-formation processes with those of common sense. This can be done quite straightforwardly as follows:

16. The obviously true beliefs adverted to in (15) are what the common sense philosophers have been identifying as common sense beliefs.

Indeed I would go so far as to claim that a common sense belief is nothing other than a belief required to ensure ecological and social fitness. This move would certainly tally with Reid's repeated insistence that common sense beliefs are crucial to our being able to act in our everyday world where gross error is simply too costly. It is only when one has the luxury of not having to act, that is, when one is not in the context in which beliefs are performing their essential function, that one can entertain alternatives to these common sense beliefs.[19]

Two additional points are needed before I can draw the desired conclusion:

17. There was no selective pressure, natural or sexual, for philosophical ability in the ancestral environment.

However, regrettable it may seem to some of us, human beings were simply not built for philosophical reflection, and philosophical reflection has never been the proper function of our cognitive apparatus. Philosophical ability is at best a by-product of belief formation systems which themselves were selected for reasons having little or nothing to do with philosophical concerns. A corollary to this is that neither philosophical ability nor philosophical incompetence per se influences positively or negatively one's biological and social fitness. The consequence is clear.

18. There is no reason to expect that human belief formation systems will be reliable in the domain of philosophical research and reflection.

I now proceed to the desired conclusion.

19. If (1)–(18) are true, and the inferences drawn are valid, then in stand-offs between paradoxical and common sense arguments the burden of proof lies with those upholding paradoxical arguments.

It is important to note that the conclusion is *not* that common sense beliefs are always to be preserved at the expense of paradoxical conclusions even in their restricted domain of competence, but merely that it is reasonable to assume that common sense beliefs are *more reliable* than their philosophically sophisticated alternatives in their domain of competence.

Responses to the standard objections

It is now time to consider whether this version of EA falls to the standard objections raised against arguments of this general type. Let us take the objections in turn.

One common line of objection can be expressed as follows: There is no argument from evolutionary theory that allows one to assume that any traits or features of organisms are optimal. So there is no reason to assume that because natural selection was the chief formative cause of the emergence of our cognitive systems that they can be relied upon to produce mostly true beliefs. Moreover, there are good empirical grounds for asserting that human beings are not particularly efficient processors of information. All of this suggests that one ought to be stressing the inherent fallibility of human cognitive capacities despite their being adaptations rather than trying to establish their reliability on these flimsy foundations.

This line of objection is best met by pointing out that it contains nothing inconsistent with our version of EA. The version of EA presented here does not claim that our cognitive systems are optimal, or that they produce mostly true beliefs. It merely claims, quite plausibly, that our cognitive systems are satisficed. As a consequence, our cognitive systems are only as reliable as they have to be to ensure that we can cope with our environment, both ecological and social. In fact it is part of my claim that we must *not* place too much trust in our cognitive abilities, particularly those that have little adaptive value, such a philosophical theorising.

Another line of attack is that EA overlooks the fact that there are false but adaptive beliefs. The point here is that one cannot conclude on the basis of a belief's being adaptive that it is true. The objector then usually points to particular examples of allegedly false but adaptive beliefs. Sage

(2003) presents three types of allegedly false but adaptive beliefs, namely beliefs about colour, false-positives concerning the presence of predators (i.e. the belief that a predator is in the vicinity when in fact no such predator is present) and religious beliefs.

There are two kinds of response to this line of attack. First, one can raise questions about the alleged examples of false but adaptive beliefs. Are the alleged beliefs really false? Are they really adaptive? A second response is to insist that established cases of false but adaptive beliefs are not the threat to EA the objector imagines them to be. Let's consider this second response first.

The objection that there are cases of false but adaptive belief, and that this undermines EA, overlooks an important feature of arguments concerning natural selection, namely their statistical or probabilistic nature.[20] The claim of this version of EA is that *on the whole* a greater proportion of beliefs with a direct bearing on biological and social fitness will be true rather than false because *on the whole* error in such domains is too costly. This claim is perfectly compatible with there being instances in which false beliefs are not maladaptive or neutral, but positively adaptive. EA as presented here does not assume or seek to establish that there is a *logical* connection between adaptivity and truth, so that there could be a logically safe inference from a belief's being adaptive to that belief's being true. EA seeks to establish only that there is a statistical connection between adaptivity and truth. But this is all that is required to establish the point that a belief's being adaptive is a good reason to proceed on the assumption that it is true, particularly if there is no strong evidence to the contrary, since we have reason to believe that *most* adaptive beliefs will be true. To undermine EA on the basis of false but adaptive beliefs one would have to show not that there are particular instances of false but adaptive beliefs, but the much stronger claim that *most* of our adaptive beliefs are in fact false. But no one seriously maintains this. At best we get interesting instances of false but adaptive beliefs.

With this response in mind we can afford to pass over the alleged examples of false but adaptive beliefs with a few brief comments. All I wish to point out here is that the alleged instances are all highly controversial. It is sufficient for present purposes to note, for example, the controversial and contested nature of the claim that beliefs about colour are in fact false. The allegation assumes that it has been established that colour is not a real feature of objects themselves, but a product of the perceiver's "mind-spinning". But a cursory survey of the state of play both within philosophy and within the science of vision community reveals that highly respected figures continue to argue forcefully for the view that colours are in fact genuine properties of objects. Consequently allegation in this instance is anything but established, and so, at least as yet, there is no case to answer. Frank Jackson's (2000, Ch. 4) "primary quality" theory of colour is a good example of colour realism from within the philosophical profession, while Thompson, Palacios and Varela's (1992) present an authoritative view from within the scientific community. While the latter argue that a more nuanced approach to colour vision is required than is usually found within philosophical discussions, they nonetheless insist that the ecological importance of colour vision is enough to suggest that colour cannot simply be a matter of "mind-spinning". They insist "... colour is a property of the extra-dermal world understood as the animal's environment". Their primary complaint against the view that colour vision is about the "recovery" of "mind-independent, distal properties" (as the naïve colour realist might have it) is that this ignores the co-evolution of colour vision and various aspects of the world, for instance fruit in the case of fruit-eating animals or flowers in the case of certain insects. It is not that fruits and flowers are not really coloured. The point is that fruits and flowers have the colours they do at least in part because of their interactions with certain organisms, and in this non-troubling sense their colour cannot be seen as entirely mind-independent.[21]

What can be said in response to the allegation that false positives are adaptive? Again my comments are brief, not because these allegations do not require serious treatment, although one cannot help but feel that they are overstated, but because I here advert to work already carried out by others. Stevens (2001) has already shown that the "better-safe-than-sorry argument" has a very narrow band of applicability. And this result should not be surprising if we recall that organisms have other imperatives in addition to avoiding predation, like securing food and mates. This serves to remind us of what ought to have been pretty obvious from the start, namely that too many false positives will be positively maladaptive since they will prevent to organism from engaging in other essential activities. Hiding in one's burrow all day in the false belief that a predator is lurking just outside may keep one alive in the short term. But neurotic organisms do not feed well, nor do they tend to secure high-quality mates (or any mates at all).[22]

What then of the allegation regarding religious beliefs? Religious beliefs perhaps present the most interesting of the allegedly false but adaptive beliefs. But without writing a separate treatise in the philosophy of religion, I will have to confine myself here to pointing out the very real difficulties involved in establishing that religious beliefs are false but adaptive. In the first place, there is real disagreement within the religious studies community as to what counts as a religious belief. Some, like Hudson (1977), insist that a belief counts as religious only if it has some relation, more or less direct to the concept of God. Social anthropologists tend to agree with this sort of analysis at least to the extent that they make some specifically religious subject matter, the determining criterion of religious belief. However, social anthropologists are likely to extend the scope of religious beliefs to include (a) belief in other non-physical entities in addition to God, (b) the belief that a non-physical component of human beings survives death, (c) the belief that certain human beings are more likely to receive communications from supernatural forces than others and (d) the belief that rituals performed correctly can bring about changes in the natural world (Boyer, 1994).[23] However, this analysis does not fit all religions well. It is far from clear, for example, whether Buddhism, usually numbered as one of the five great world religions, would count as a religion on this view. So other philosophers of religion have contended that what makes a belief religious is not the subject matter of the belief itself but the role played by the belief in the believer's life, and the degree and nature of the believer's "commitment" to the belief. For example, Paul Griffiths (1999) contends that a set of beliefs is religious if that set (a) provides the believer with a comprehensive account of things, which (b) is of central importance in the believer's life and (c) is not capable of being subsumed or surpassed by any other account. A belief then counts as religious if it is a member of such a set.

This conceptual difficulty concerning the criterion of religious belief is no idle matter. Until we know what to count as a religious belief it is impossible even to begin to set about the task of assessing whether they are false and adaptive. But even if this definitional issue is waved, the difficulties facing our objector would not be at an end. For it is a commonplace in both philosophical and theological circles that religious beliefs are neither true nor false, and so could not be both false and adaptive. This is the Wittgensteinian inspired view that religious beliefs are part of a discreet "language game", and that to construe religious beliefs as on all fours with ordinary statements is simply wrongheaded.[24] And on the other front, many evolutionary psychologists would simply not accept that religious beliefs are adaptive, so again religious beliefs could not be both false and adaptive. For example, Scott Atran has recently argued that, far from being adaptive, religious beliefs are very costly, demanding time, energy, material wealth, and sometimes even the sacrifice of one's life. In fact his project is to explain precisely how such a *maladaptive* set of beliefs and mindset could emerge in an evolutionary context.[25] In short, given that even the established existence of false but adaptive religious beliefs would not damage EA in any case, I will not waste further time on issues best left to treatises on the philosophy of religion.

Science, philosophy and the charge of circularity

I want to conclude by considering a set of questions regarding the propriety of employing scientific ideas in the treatment of this metaphilosophical debate. The most pressing objection against EA is that it simply begs all the interesting philosophical questions. For if one is willing to question that one really knows that an object in one's hand is a pencil (to return to our first example), then one is hardly likely to concede any claims drawn from the natural sciences. This most common of charges has been made in one version or another by many, including Quine (1975), Rorty (1979), Clark (1987), O'Hear (1997) and Crispin Wright (2002), to name only a few. Even Stewart-Williams (2005, p. 796), who is sympathetic to EA, concedes that justifications relying on EA are circular.[26] But the charge of begging the question will not fly in the context in which I have placed this version of EA. In fact to level this charge in this context is itself to beg the question.

To recall, our starting point was the philosophical stalemate exhibited by the stand-offs of the type illustrated by arguments A1 and A2, and B1 and B2. Our operating assumption was that neither side had any philosophical advantage over the other, and at issue was how to break this stalemate. I implied, following Reid, that the stand-off could be overcome if the burden of proof could be shifted onto one or other of the parties. I then argued that EA allows us to do just that. But it was no part of my design to justify any particular common sense belief, and certainly no part of my design to justify common sense beliefs to the satisfaction of philosophers upholding paradoxical arguments. But to insist that such a justification is required in order to break the stalemate is in fact to assume that there is no stalemate at all because one is assuming that the standards of proof required by those upholding paradoxical arguments are the philosophically correct standards. But it is these very standards which are at the heart of the metaphilosophical debate. That is why it was necessary to go to an independent third party, in this case an evolutionary biologist or psychologist, for another perspective on this question. And just as it is illegitimate of philosophers upholding paradoxical arguments to dictate the terms of engagement to their philosophical brethren, it is also illegitimate to impose these terms on evolutionary biology and psychology. The upshot is to stipulate in advance that no appeals to scientific theories are to be allowed in this context because such appeals beg the question is itself an attempt to beg the question. The only recourse the upholder of paradoxical arguments has at this point is to appeal to their own external third party, or to throw doubt on the merits of EA of the sort that would impress an evolutionary biologist *qua* evolutionary biologist.

But if no questions have been begged by the use of EA in this discussion, one might still wonder whether the argument establishes what it seeks to establish. For one could argue as follows: "The basis for your favouring common sense over philosophy is not common sense but a set of scientific theories. But given that there were no selective pressures in favour of the emergence of scientific abilities in the ancestral environment any more than there was for philosophical ability, one is left wondering how this type of argument could warrant the favouring of science over philosophy, and so your decision to favour commonsense over philosophy on the basis of EA is left blowing in the wind."

I believe this argument has little force. It is most likely true that there were no evolutionary pressures in favour of scientific abilities, and so science and philosophy are on all fours in this respect. But the scientist is in a position to test his or her theories and discover his or her errors in a way that the philosopher is not. Despite the currency of the Quine–Duhem hypothesis, and not wanting to over-simplify the nature of scientific experimentation, it is widely recognised that scientists are able to discover their errors through the process of falsification, while philosophers are notoriously unable to rid their discipline of theories centuries if not millennia old. This might at first blush seem a reason to favour philosophy over science, for if science has always (eventually) discovered that its theories are in fact false, then it appears that we have good reason to be cautious about current scientific theories, however venerable, since they too are likely to be overturned. And if this is the case, then perhaps the philosopher ought to privilege philosophical theories over science. But this would be a grotesque mistake. This apparent weakness of science is in fact its greatest virtue, for the scientist can lay false theories to rest and move on to new and as yet unfalsified theories. But the philosopher is never able to be sure either that his or her theories are true or false in anything like the relatively clear-cut fashion enjoyed by the scientist. So while it is true that science and philosophy are in the same boat evolutionarily speaking, nonetheless it is better to side with mature science than philosophy if only because error in the sciences will be discovered, whereas a false philosophical path may never be revealed as such.

Finally, some will wonder whether science really can come to the defence of common sense since it is widely recognised that many scientific theories are counter-intuitive themselves. Have not the sciences forced us to give up what many have taken to be plain common sense? Does this fact not make one suspicious that focussing entirely on evolutionary biology and psychology to the exclusion of other sciences has not given an unrepresentative picture of the relation between the sciences and the common sense?

I have already said something in response to this line of questioning in my remarks about the range of applicability of EA. But we can also point out first that many if not most of the particularly striking examples of counter-intuitive scientific results stem from sciences that tell us little or nothing about human brains/minds and how they work, and since the issue for us here has been to determine which cognitive tasks human brains/minds are best able to cope with, a context in which the strange results of quantum mechanics, say, have no relevance whatsoever, it is not surprising that our attention here has been on sciences that do claim to have something to tell us about the human mind. It is also worth noting that few of science's counter-intuitive results actually threaten the sorts of beliefs common sense philosophers have been keen to uphold.

Conclusion

In this chapter I have been at pains to provide what the common sense philosopher has always lacked, that is, an argument to support his or her gut intuition that philosopher's paradoxes should be taken as a sure sign that errors having entered our thinking. I have tried to show that such an argument can be constructed on internal grounds by adverting to the nature of the philosophical enterprise. Here I have tried to provide additional external support for the metaphilosophy of common sense by drawing on the resources of evolutionary biology and psychology. I have presented a version of EA that does not fall to the usual objections levelled at arguments of this general type, and which, when properly construed, gives the common sense philosopher something he or she has always lacked, that is, a justification of the view that common sense beliefs ought to be treated as default positions.

Finally, it is worth emphasising that we have also received an answer to one of our pressing questions, namely what counts as a common sense belief. The suggestion made here is that a belief counts as a common sense belief if it is reasonable to assume that it was necessary to ensure ecological or social fitness in the ancestral environment of hominids and early humans. And as we have seen, EA provides the rationale for giving such beliefs the status of default position. This is a notable advance upon former accounts of common sense beliefs. The common sense philosopher no longer has to maintain that a common sense belief is one that is found to be obvious by the vast majority of people, or is psychologically necessary, or one that appears early in childhood, or one for which we can simply no longer remember the evidence. The obvious problem with these accounts was that they provided no good reason to assign common sense beliefs the status of default position. That situation has now been rectified. But our solution does impose certain unfamiliar burdens. The common sense philosophers will now have to familiarise themselves with evolutionary theory, and with accounts of hominid evolution in particular. But this, I would suggest, is no bad thing.

3
Towards a Taxonomy of Philosophical Error

Introduction

If the burden of the previous chapter was to deal with the second of the five principal tasks facing the common sense philosopher, namely, justifying the claim that common sense beliefs ought to be treated as default positions, then the object of this chapter and the next is to broach the third of these tasks, that is, to provide a general account of what Moore took to be the most striking fact about the work of many philosophers. Moore writes,

> It seems to me that what is most amazing and most interesting about the views of many philosophers is the way in which they go beyond or positively contradict the views of Common Sense: they profess to know that there are in the Universe most important kinds of things, which Common Sense does not profess to know of, and also they profess to know that there are not in the Universe (or, at least, that, if there are, we do not know it), things of the existence of which Common Sense is most sure.
>
> (1965, p. 2)

And as the list of philosophical extravagances provided at the outset of this book suggests, it is not just the odd one or two philosophers who have parted company with common sense. On the contrary, this seems to be a general tendency within mainstream Western philosophy.

Moore noted that this tendency takes three distinct forms. A philosopher could, first and foremost, simply deny that a certain common sense belief or set of beliefs is true or is known to be true. This route is taken by sceptics, for example, who notoriously deny that we do in fact know what we commonly think we know. It is also taken by those who maintain that the world is significantly or perhaps even radically other than common sense takes it to be. We will have occasion to discuss several examples of this kind of departure from common sense in Chapters 5–9. Secondly, a philosopher might go beyond common sense by claiming to establish the truth of claims or the existence of entities undreamt of by common sense. For example, Moore thinks that philosophers who postulate the existence of God or life after death are adding to but not contradicting common sense (ibid., p. 17–18). Plato's postulation of the realm of the Forms would also serve as a clear example of a philosopher's going well beyond common sense. Finally, the third possibility is to combine the first two, that is, to both deny certain common sense beliefs while also going beyond common sense in the manner just described. Berkeley is a good example of a philosopher working in this vein since he denies that there are material objects in the ordinary sense while asserting the existence of God.

Now the philosopher's tendency to go beyond common sense is not in and of itself particularly surprising. It has already been noted that common sense does not have a complete view of the universe, and that it is one of philosophy's goals to provide a complete account of all that is. Consequently, it is only to be expected that philosophers will have made claims that go beyond common sense in the sense Moore identified. Even common sense philosophers will go beyond common sense in this respect when trying to provide a complete metaphysical description of what is implicit in our everyday dealings with the world. Taking leave of common sense in this fashion is thus perfectly harmless and entirely in order as long as one's additions do not contradict common sense beliefs and their status as default positions. My point then is that the truly amazing and most interesting fact about the work of many philosophers is simply their tendency, explicitly or implicitly, to deny common sense beliefs. And at some point the common sense philosopher will want to provide an explanation of this curious fact. That is, at some point, we will want an answer to Searle's question, expressed in his characteristically direct and pungent language: "Why is it that when we start studying philosophy, we are almost inexorably driven to deny things we all know to be true?" (1999, p. 9).

There are at least three reasons for attempting to answer this rather depressing question. The first is simply to address our natural curiosity on this issue. Is it not interesting in and of itself that such a brilliant collection of thinkers would maintain such a bizarre collection of theories? Secondly, providing an explanatory account of this amazing and most interesting fact will go some way to convincing those who remain unconvinced that errors have in fact been made. A brute fact, however unwelcome, is always easier to accept when an explanation can be provided for it. And as we shall see, when we look into this matter closely, it becomes only too easy to understand how it is that philosophers come to make mistakes. In fact, one may begin to think the amazing fact in need of explanation is rather that philosophers ever manage to say anything sensible at all. Thirdly, an answer to Searle's question will presumably help would-be philosophers from making the same mistakes. Forewarned is forearmed.

Now Searle's question, arresting as it is in its current form, requires and deserves careful handling. To address it systematically, it must be posed at at least three different levels. At the most basic level, one needs to ask: What are the technical or mechanical first-level errors to be found in the arguments of errant philosophers? A philosopher, one assumes, reaches paradoxical conclusions at least in part because he or she has inadvertently made some sort of error (logical or otherwise) in the course of his or her argumentation. What we need then is an inventory of the *kinds* of technical errors to which philosophers *qua* philosophers are prey in the course of developing their arguments. These errors identified, we can then answer Searle's question at one level by saying, "Well, philosophers are prone to making these sorts of technical mistakes which, in the right circumstances, lead to paradoxical results."

Now as important as this aspect of the question undoubtedly is, one is not likely to be satisfied until answers are provided to two follow-up questions. For instance, we will want to know why it is that philosophers are prey to these sorts of technical errors. Is there perhaps something about human cognitive capacities, or the nature of the discipline itself, that makes it so difficult for us to philosophise well? Or are there perhaps higher level errors that contribute to the committing of these mechanical first-level errors? Finally, one ought also to ask perhaps the most perplexing question of all: Once a philosopher has arrived, for whatever reason, at a philosophical paradox, why does he or she tend to seize upon it as an exciting discovery rather than as evidence of error? The force of this question can be brought out by considering a passage from Reid. When discussing whether philosophy must always end in Cartesian scepticism, a worrying possibility since Descartes and his followers had been unable to avoid it, Reid insists that we should not give in to despair. His grounds for optimism on this score are drawn from his comparison of the philosopher with a wayward traveller:

> A traveller of good judgement may mistake his way, and be unawares led into the wrong track; and, while the road is fair before him, he may go on without suspicion and be followed by others; but, when it ends in a coal-pit, it requires no great judgement to know that he hath gone wrong, nor perhaps to find out what misled him.
>
> (2005, p. 103)

Unfortunately, it would seem that Reid's optimism was misplaced. Indeed, it would seem that many philosophers do *not* have the good judgement of Reid's lost traveller, for philosophers repeatedly mistake coal-pits for the right track. Understanding this fact is the final element of an answer to Searle's question.

Now it seems to me that we need answers to all three of these subsidiary questions in order to fully comprehend the plight of the philosopher and to address the third of our principal tasks. And it is more than likely that the causes behind any one philosopher's paradox will be multifaceted and inter-connected. But on the assumption that it is usually much easier to notice something when one knows what to look for, we can also expect answers to our three questions to serve a practical as well as a theoretical purpose. In particular, we can expect these answers to provide the common sense philosopher with something of a tool kit, a checklist to consult when carrying out specific researches aimed at addressing the second of the principal tasks, namely, identifying the errors in the particular arguments philosophers have used to overturn common sense beliefs.[1] In fact, it is rather odd that this sort of study has not been conducted before in any systematic fashion. It is of course true that many philosophers have hinted at or perhaps even developed answers to parts of Searle's question; but these scattered reflections have not been carefully gathered together and distinguished in an attempt to provide a comprehensive account of Moore's most amazing and most interesting fact. Philosophers, it seems, have satisfied themselves with elements of answers to our leading question, or, perhaps, have taken these partial answers for the whole. But however that may be, in this chapter I intend to take the three subsidiary questions as the principle of organisation for the scattered and tangled reflections to be found in the works of many philosophers and to begin constructing something of a taxonomy of philosophical error. I propose to start with the first of our subsidiary questions, namely, what are the technical first-level errors that philosophers tend to commit in the development of their arguments?

Mechanical first-level errors

Identifying the sorts of technical errors philosophers are prone to committing is in one way perfectly straightforward, and in another way, very difficult. On the one hand, it is perfectly clear, for example, that philosophers use arguments of various types – deductive and inductive arguments, arguments to the best explanation, transcendental arguments, arguments from analogy, arguments based on dilemmas and so on. Moreover, the typical ways in which these sorts of arguments can fail are well documented in textbooks on formal and informal logic. We know that arguments fail for one of two broadly construed sorts of reasons: Either the premises of the argument are false, or dubious, or in some other way inadmissible; or the logical form of the argument is such that its premises do not lend support to the conclusion. Introducing students to these sorts of arguments, and teaching them to be on the alert for the typical ways in which they can go wrong, is an important element of any sound philosophical education. But what is usually missing from the textbooks is a discussion of the particular kinds of errors that philosophers *qua* philosophers are prey to in the course of their work. It is of course true that philosophers make the same sorts of errors that non-philosophers make;[2] but there are mistakes that seem to be more like occupational hazards, hazards that non-philosophers are not exposed to as frequently simply because they are not engaged in thinking about philosophical topics. These mistakes are far more elusive and difficult to pin down precisely, and the reasons for this particular difficulty are worth noting.

In the first place it is important to realise that paradoxical conclusions are rarely the result of one error in one argument. Paradoxical conclusions, like any conclusion, emerge as a result of what one might call a mindset, that is, an inter-connected set of beliefs and accompanying conceptual framework, as well as hidden assumptions, attitudes, interests and agendas. More often than not, it is a disorderly mindset as a whole, one containing false beliefs or assumptions as well as conceptual confusions, that leads to perplexity on the part of the thinker. In such cases, one is likely to find that a philosopher has made several mutually re-enforcing errors at different levels on the way to his or her paradox, making it difficult if not impossible to identify the one false step on the road to disaster. Part of the difficult task of diagnosing the source of a philosophical paradox then is the initial disentangling of the various false threads that make up the fabric of a disorderly mindset. Secondly, it is not always clear just what error has been committed even in the case of an argument that appears to be largely separable from a wider conceptual framework. The ontological argument is an interesting case in point. While there is a general consensus that the argument fails to establish its intended conclusion, no one diagnosis of that failure has gained universal acceptance. The literature is replete with suggestions on this score, each offering a different account of where the fatal flaw really lies.[3] A further source of difficulty is that one and the same error can be described or construed in different ways. There may be cases where there is agreement on where the false step occurs in an argument without there being agreement on the characterisation of that false step. For all of these reasons, then, it is difficult to generalise safely about the mechanical errors encountered in the arguments of philosophers. Nonetheless, the task is not entirely hopeless.

First, we need to acknowledge the simple point that philosophers often fall into error because they begin with false premises. However valid one's reasoning, if one begins with false premises one's arguments are worthless, and they will often end in philosophical paradoxes. Of course, this is not a particularly philosophical error in and of itself, for each and every one of us is libel to believe what is false. However, there are particular reasons why philosophers in their efforts at philosophical theorising are prone to accepting what is false as the starting point of their reflections. Most of these are best discussed in the next section, but one particularly important reason can be noted immediately. If philosophical problems are co-ordination problems, that is, problems emerging from perceived tensions in otherwise attractive lines of thought generated in other disciplines, then the philosopher is always and unavoidably at risk, for the philosopher is always having to accept his or her premises in good faith on the authority of some other discipline or domain of enquiry. The philosopher's arguments are then only as good as the premises supplied to him or her by others.

Unfortunately false premises are only the beginning of the philosopher's troubles, for philosophical problems are rarely of a purely factual nature. Philosophical problems as a rule arise from conceptual confusion. And while in normal circumstances, we can usually think and talk sense *with* concepts, our footing is far less sure when it comes to thinking and talking *about* concepts. This second-order thinking is something we find particularly difficult and somewhat unnatural. But since philosophical problems are by and large conceptual in nature, philosophers constantly have to fight their battles on ground for which they are not particularly well suited or equipped by nature and so perpetually prone to error.

Conceptual errors can take different forms. One common source of error, noticed and insisted upon by Moore, is the faulty conceptual analysis. Although Moore was not as precise as he could have been about what counts as a piece of conceptual analysis,[4] at a minimum, one can say that a faulty analysis of a concept implies a faulty understanding of that concept, which usually entails a faulty grasp of the necessary and sufficient conditions of its application. But we can set aside these niceties for the time being and simply note Moore's conviction that philosophers arriving at paradoxical conclusions were almost certainly working with a faulty analysis of the key concept or concepts on which their arguments turned. Indeed, it is worth recalling that Moore's interest in conceptual analysis stems in no small part from his belief that *all* philosopher's paradoxes could be accounted for in this fashion, and that conceptual analysis is thus the philosopher's principal weapon in the defence of common sense.[5]

While I think it highly unlikely that all philosophical paradoxes can be explained by reference to only one type of mistake, this kind of diagnosis does appear to apply in many cases. By way of illustration consider a famous example: In his "The Refutation of Idealism" Moore argues that the key premise of all forms of idealism, namely that *esse est percipi*, is false, and that idealists had failed to notice its falsity because they had adopted or unconsciously assumed a faulty analysis of perception. Idealists, Moore maintains, fail to distinguish between what is perceived and the perception of it, between, blue, say, and the perception of blue. Failure to make this distinction results in the conflation of objects of perception and the perception of those objects, which, not surprisingly, leads quickly to the claim that one does not find existence apart from some perception. But it is also worth noting that this conflation of *esse* with *percipi* is all the more likely to occur if one has adopted or unconsciously assumed a faulty analysis of a further concept, in this case, the concept of relations. If one has accepted the view, characteristic of many forms of idealism, that there are no purely external relations, that is, that no terms of a relation are ontologically independent of any of the relations in which they stand to other terms, then, even if one recognised a *conceptual* distinction between blue and the perception of blue, one would not grant that this distinction is mirrored in the ontological status of the referents of these terms. The points for present purposes, however, are (a) that faulty conceptual analyses lead to error and (b) mutually re-enforcing but faulty conceptual analyses are often at work in the generation of a philosophical paradox.

An interesting point to notice about the forgoing discussion of idealism, whether one agrees with Moore's diagnosis or not,[6] is that an allegedly faulty analysis of a concept can be, and often is, the result of a *failure to notice important distinctions*. For example, Grice famously pointed out that the failure to distinguish the meaning of a linguistic item from the use to which that item is put was responsible for many faulty conceptual analyses.[7] In fact, it is probably safe to say that if there is a primary source of mechanical philosophical error, it is the failure to notice a salient distinction of some sort or another. Failure of this sort is widespread, and it occurs in many forms. There is, for example, the failure to distinguish between the various senses a word might bear, a failure that can easily lead to arguments that fail due to equivocation. This is particularly likely to happen when a philosopher uses an established word with an established sense in a new and unconventional fashion. It is easy in such cases to slide between two distinct senses of the same word without noticing, particularly if the philosopher is only dimly aware that he or she is extending or stretching the sense of the established word. But it is also common to find philosophers confusing the properties of words or concepts with the properties of the referents of those words or concepts. This leads to the familiar mistake of confusing use and mention, but it is also involved in the confusion of the distinct realms of thought and reality. If, for example, I believe that my concept of God includes the property of existence, I might be tempted to conclude that God exists extra-mentally as well if I fail adequately to distinguish the realms of thought and existence.

Finally, it is also easy to fail to distinguish adequately between things, be they objects, actions, events or properties.[8] No doubt this is due at least in part to the fact that, in our efforts to render the world intelligible to ourselves, we tend to look for the connections and similarities between things, for we understand the unfamiliar by means of the familiar. As a consequence, there is a natural tendency to overlook or fail to notice significant distinctions in words, concepts and things, particularly when it comes to theorising. It is this point about human cognition that lies behind a range of phenomena noted by Austin. He attributes "typically scholastic" or "philosophical" views to "oversimplification, schematization, and constant obsessive repetition of the same small range of jejune 'examples' ", describing these failings as "far too common to be dismissed as an occasional weakness of philosophers" (1964, p. 3). But the point we must notice is that philosophers often fail to note that things are much more diverse and complicated than is generally admitted precisely because theorising demands simplification and schematisation. There is thus an ineliminable tension between our desire to understand the world as it is in itself while doing full justice to its diversity and complexity.

This inevitable failure to take on board the full diversity and complexity of things leads to a further common diagnosis of philosophical error: the faulty analogy. When theorising about a relatively unfamiliar topic, or on a familiar topic which has for whatever reason given rise to perplexity, a thinker is likely to fish around for models or analogies to guide his or her thinking. It is, of course, of the very essence of intelligence to be able to see such analogies that aid understanding; but analogies are not always wisely chosen, and at times, they can be pressed further and harder than is appropriate. By way of illustration, it is worth noting that Reid claims to have identified such a faulty analogy as the source of two prejudices that lead directly to the acceptance of the theory of ideas.[9] The two prejudices are (a) that in all mental operations, there must be something with which the mind is in immediate contact in order to allow one to act upon the other (there is no action at a distance) and (b) that in all operations of the understanding, there must be an object of thought. These two prejudices lead to the postulating of an inner realm of ideas or representations because (i) the extra-dermal objects of which one may form a conception are at a distance from the conceiver, and so cannot be the immediate objects of thought, and consequently some *tertium quid* must be introduced between mind and world and (ii) since one can form conceptions of things which do not exist extra-dermally – a centaur for example – but cannot think without an object of thought, there must be some internal image contemplated by the mind in such cases. Both prejudices, argues Reid, are arrived at by faulty analogical reasoning. It is falsely assumed that since other kinds of operations presuppose an agent and an object acted upon – for instance, a carpenter who makes a chair out of wood could not make the chair unless there were wood for him to act upon – it must similarly be the case with mental operations: One cannot think or conceive of x without there being an x to be the object of this thought. But Reid maintains that there is in fact no need to accept this analogy, and so no need to sign up to the two prejudices. While mental operations are operations of a sort, on the face of it, they appear to be significantly different from other kinds of operations. Again, it is not my point here to comment on the merits of this particular diagnosis, but merely to provide an instance, albeit alleged, of error resulting from the uncritical use of analogies.

A further type of conceptual error needs to be noted. Ryle, no less than Moore, argued that philosophical error had its source in conceptual confusion, particularly in what he famously called category mistakes. Ryle claimed to find such errors lurking behind the arguments of many philosophers on a wide range of issues. The idea here is that philosophers must work with a set of ontological categories, with each category associated with a range of category specific properties. The trouble begins when a thinker places an entity in an inappropriate category, and then goes on to attribute category specific properties to the entity that it cannot in fact take.[10] For example, Ryle argues that philosophers have posited the existence of sense data because they have mistakenly treated sensation as though it were on all fours with observation. Since observation is always of some observed object, so, if sensation is a form of observation, there must be a corresponding object of sensation. But finding that ordinary language contains no words or phrases for entities playing the role of sensible object, philosophers have felt the need to introduce the necessary terminology, hence the talk of "sense data". This philosopher's mythical entity is entirely due, says Ryle, to philosophers not realising that sensation is not observation.[11]

No doubt this is an incomplete account of the sorts of mechanical errors that philosophers are particularly prone to in their distinctively philosophical moments. But as said at the outset, I am keen at this point only to identify those errors that seem to be the particular preserve of philosophers *qua* philosophers. So bearing in mind that an error can be described in different ways, and that more than one error is likely to be involved in the production of a philosophical paradox, we can summarise our findings by saying that five types of first-level technical error have been identified. In addition to the garden-variety errors that all arguments are prone to, a philosopher's argument may fail because

(a) It contains a false premise or premises (the source being endoxa);
(b) It fails to take account of an important distinction (either between senses of the same word, between a word or concept and the referent of the word or concept, or between things themselves);
(c) It is based on a faulty analysis of the concept or concepts on which the argument turns;
(d) It is based on a faulty analogy;
(e) It turns on a category mistake.

It is reasonable to suggest that the master error at this level of analysis is the failure to notice important distinctions. It is not altogether unreasonable to suggest that faulty analyses, faulty analogies and category mistakes all involve a failure to recognise a relevant distinction of some sort, and that they are merely different species of this genus. The status of (b) as master error might also be enhanced if we consider that (a–d) are also common causes of the adoption of false premises.

Why is philosophy so difficult?

Having identified at least some of the mechanical first-level errors that lead philosophers down the garden path, let us now move on to consider our leading question at the next level of abstraction. In particular, it is worth pausing for a moment to consider why it is that philosophy proves so difficult to carry out successfully. Why are we prone to making the sorts of mechanical mistakes we noted in the previous section? Answers to this question fall into two general categories: The first set focuses on certain objective features of the discipline itself; the second highlights our own cognitive shortcomings and failures. Let us take these in turn.

We should note immediately the subject matter of philosophy itself as a source of difficulty in its own right, the mastery of which requires both an extraordinary breadth of knowledge and frequently a detailed acquaintance with developments in the various sciences. The breadth of the discipline is second to none, encompassing metaphysics, epistemology, logic, philosophy of mind, ethics, political philosophy and aesthetics, each branch containing its own sub-disciplines and topics. This is bad enough; but it is an impossible intellectual challenge to master the big picture while maintaining an adequate grasp of the particular facts and theories that make up the data of the various domains. A consequence of this is an unavoidable ignorance on the part of the philosopher, an ignorance which explains why it is relatively easy for even the most careful philosopher to accept false beliefs as premises.

There are other objective features of the discipline that also prove taxing. If it is true, as it appears to be, that human beings learn best by trial and error, then philosophy is a discipline that poses particular problems for human beings. A great difficulty facing philosophers is precisely that there is no straightforward manner in which errors can be detected because there is no straightforward manner in which to verify or falsify philosophical theories or conclusions. To return to the image of the wayward traveller, Reid's optimism was misplaced because there are no obvious coal pits to alert us to the fact that we have lost our way.

Philosophical problems are of such a nature as to be amendable to different and often contradictory solutions, the relative merits of which are often far from clear because there is no *coercive* evidence forcing the adoption or rejection of any given solution.[12] How a philosophical problem is to be handled is thus a matter of professional judgement about which there is room for rational disagreement. The upshot of this is that a philosopher can never be sure that he or she has made an error simply in virtue of having reached a paradoxical conclusion. And lacking that certainty, he or she will often have little or no incentive to re-examine his or her arguments for the sorts of errors identified in the previous section, particularly if he or she is fond of his or her paradoxical conclusion.

A closely connected difficulty facing philosophers is that there is no consensus on philosophical method. Scientists employ clearly defined and articulated research methods and are able to teach these methodologies to their students. No such methodology exists in philosophy and probably never will. Searle underlines this point when he cheerfully confesses that he will use any and every stick he can find to beat a philosophical problem as long as it leads to results. So the lack of coercive evidence noted in the previous paragraph is compounded by a lack of *coercive* methodological constraints on philosophical theorising, which only exacerbates the problem of detecting errors once they have been committed. An unfortunate but probably inevitable consequence of this lack of constraint is that philosophers are particularly prey to intellectual fashions. Intellectual fashions, while not epistemologically or methodologically coercive, can often be psychologically coercive because it is more comfortable psychologically, as well as professionally expedient, to work in a climate of general agreement, where one knows that one's work is likely to receive a warm welcome because it falls in line with the expectations of one's peers. Unfortunately, the merits of too many intellectual fashions are simply psychological and professional rather than philosophical.

If these are the sorts of objective facts about the disciple that would make philosophy intellectual challenging for any conceivable finite mind, we must also consider our own shortcomings which make the philosophical enterprise more difficult than it objectively needs to be. The first set of such shortcomings I want to draw attention to includes various species of the same general error: the application or employment of something outside its sphere of competence.

The first version of this general type of error has been stressed at some length in the previous chapter, namely, that human cognitive capacities were not designed for this kind of intellectual challenge. While Kant is probably right when he suggests that our cognitive capacities make it impossible for us not to ask philosophical questions,[13] it remains the case that there were no selective pressures at work in our evolutionary past that encouraged the development of philosophical abilities for their own sake. This fact suggests that the form of Kant's general explanation of philosophical error was correct. It was Kant's claim in the *Critique of Pure Reason* that philosophers fall into error when they seek to apply a faculty outside its sphere of competence. His point was that, given the way we are constituted, human beings cannot adequately conceptualise that which falls outside the range of sensory experience, and that this is what philosophers are attempting to do when engaged in old-fashioned metaphysics.[14] Evolutionary psychology now offers a similar explanation: Our cognitive capacities were selected to cope with a range of quite specific tasks likely to be encountered repeatedly in the Pleistocene. Philosophical problems were not in this range, and so when human beings attempt to philosophise, it is not at all surprising that we have difficulties. As Aristotle suggested long ago, when human beings philosophise, we are in a similar position to bats attempting to navigate by the light of day.[15] We are doomed to ask questions we are not properly equipped to answer. This accounts for the frequency and ease with which we commit the conceptual errors discussed in the previous section.

A second version of this type of error also needs to be noted. It would seem that philosophers are prone to employing inappropriate methodologies adopted from other disciplines. I noted above that there is no generally accepted philosophical method. But this has not stopped philosophers from occasionally thinking that this want of method can be remedied by adopting the methodologies of mathematics or logic or the sciences or even literature. In these cases, a methodology is applied outside its sphere of competence, the result being a serious distortion of philosophy by the misguided attempt to make it fit the dictates of another discipline. Descartes is probably the most famous philosopher to have committed this error. He quite self-consciously applied the methods of geometry to philosophical questions, seeming not to notice that philosophical questions are of an entirely different order from geometrical questions. When Descartes insists that he will not accept any belief that is not in itself clearly and distinctly perceived to be true (as is the case with the axioms of geometry) or seen to follow from such a belief (as is the case with the theorems), he is applying a method adopted from outwith philosophy.[16] This is a second-order category mistake. And as Reid noted, the adoption of this geometrical approach leads to a curious result: Since common sense beliefs are not clear and distinct in the Cartesian sense, and since they do not follow from clear and distinct beliefs, the Cartesian will either reject outright or at least begin to doubt a common sense belief simply because it cannot be made to conform to the norms of Euclidian geometry.[17] But of course, Reid is merely repeating a point Aristotle himself was at pains to stress. Aristotle argued that it is a want of philosophical education which leads people to demand a proof when none is required, thinking all questions are mathematical in nature, and, conversely, to accept a belief without argument precisely when an argument is required.[18]

But in addition to being poorly designed for philosophy, being deprived of an adequate methodology, and using the wrong tools for the job, many have argued that we are further hampered by our naïve use of language. It has been widely claimed that philosophers are "bewitched by language", and that language seems to have been designed specifically for the purpose of confusing philosophers. This idea spawned the hope that by escaping the snares set by language philosophising would be made much easier if only we would be free of certain confusions. Some went so far as to claim that all philosophical problems would disappear once the workings of language had been properly understood. This kind of explanation has a certain historical pedigree as well, for philosophers throughout history have complained about the ambiguities of natural languages.

This account of the difficulties language poses to philosophers has been so widely discussed that there is little need to elaborate on it here. However, I would like to draw attention to two points regarding this kind of explanation. First, one interesting feature of this explanation is that similarities of grammatical form are taken to be a cause of philosophers missing or overlooking certain important distinctions. To take a simple example, the grammatical form of subject/predicate sentences is the same whether or not the subject term has a referent. If one also thinks that the meaning of a subject term is its referent, then, when faced with a putatively meaningful sentence with a subject term that denotes nothing in the empirical realm, one might very well be tempted by the similar surface grammar to posit a realm of subsisting by non-existent entities in order to secure a referent for the subject term. Misleading surface grammar has often been accused of giving birth to false analogies.

The second point is that one might very well wonder if the difficulties due to language are simply another case of something being applied outside its sphere of competence. As Ryle once noted, ordinary language does not lead anyone astray when they are not philosophising.[19] And it seems fairly clear, Chomsky and others notwithstanding, that language has developed in order to aid communication between speakers who have to cope with the exigencies of practical life. If language is a tool designed for these purposes, and is reasonably competent for these purposes, then we can see the way clear between the Ordinary Language philosophers and those bent on developing ideal languages. If one is interested in philosophical issues lying close to daily life, then perhaps it is wise to pay close attention to "what one would ordinarily say in such circumstance"; conversely, ordinary language must be used with extreme care when one is philosophising on topics only distantly related to daily life.

One final human failing need be noted if only for the sake of completeness. It is often the case that philosophers allow themselves to be "gripped" by a particular theory or insight, a grip that can lead to at least two types of errors. To be "in the grip" of a theory is to not be able to recognise or accept that one's pet theory contains serious falsehoods, or has a limited sphere of application. If one is in the grip of a false theory, then it is not unusual, in the course of drawing out its implications, to arrive at paradoxical conclusions which would repel any but the most fervent supporter of the theory in question. One might point to Ayer's now widely rejected verificationist theory of meaning, which provided the premises for a number of paradoxical conclusions, or Ayer's descendent Dummett, whose sophisticated verificationism in the form of semantic anti-realism has led to the rejection of realism with respect to the past. Quine's infamous indeterminacy of translation thesis is perhaps another good illustration. It is now widely recognised that behaviourism is untenable as a theory of mind. Nonetheless, this widely rejected theory clearly influenced Quine's views in the philosophy of language, on the back of which he arrived at strikingly counter-intuitive ontological claims. In all these cases, the paradoxical conclusions reached were found acceptable when viewed in the favourable light cast by the gripping theory.

To summarise the findings of this section, I have suggested that we are prone to making the kinds of mechanical errors identified in the previous section for two sorts of reasons: objective features of the discipline itself and our own cognitive shortcomings. The objective features of the discipline identified as contributory causes were

(a) The breadth and depth of knowledge required to engage in the philosophical enterprise at an advanced level. It was noted that this

makes it almost inevitable that the philosopher will incorporate false beliefs or inaccuracies into his or her reflections.
(b) The lack of coercive evidence that might allow one conclusively to verify or falsify philosophical theses. This is due to the very nature of philosophical problems. This means there is no way to know with certainty if one has made an error.
(c) The lack of consensus on methodology.

The human shortcomings that make philosophy more difficult that it otherwise needs to be were

(a) The fact that our cognitive faculties were not selected to deal with philosophical problems. This goes some way to explaining why we commit the conceptual errors identified in the previous section.
(b) The fact that methodologies appropriate to other disciplines are adopted by philosophers to deal with philosophical matters where they have no valid application.
(c) The fact that natural languages can be used in a naïve fashion by philosophers when theorising about matters only distantly related to practical concerns.
(d) The fact that philosophers often allow themselves to be gripped by a particular theory or insight.

Discoveries or *reductios*?

I turn finally to our most perplexing question. Once a philosopher has arrived at their philosophical paradox, why is it that they take them for exciting discoveries rather than the basis of a *reductio ad absurdam*? One reason for this has already been canvassed, namely, that there is no clear-cut evidence one can appeal to conclusively verify or falsify a philosophical theory. This means a philosopher can never be sure that he or she has in fact made a mistake. But this is only one possible explanation. There are several other possible answers to this question that need to be considered.

The first, and most obvious, is that the philosophers in question sincerely believe that they have lighted upon an important discovery because they also sincerely believe that the argument, or line of thought, that leads to the surprising result is irrefutable (at least as far as they have been able to determine) or at least as strong as arguments to the contrary. The point to notice for present purposes is that, rather endearingly, philosophers are the sort of people who place great faith in arguments, and in their ability to identify a good argument when they see one. But we should not forget Moore's canny observation about the power arguments often exercise over clever people in particular. He wrote "The pity is that some of the best minds are the most likely to be influenced by theories – to think that a thing is right, because they can give reasons for it. It is something important to recognise that the best of reasons can be given for *anything* whatever, if only we are clever enough" (1991, p. 195). Now if Moore is right about the allure arguments have for "the best minds", then an explanation for our surprising fact is in the offing: The great philosophers were, and most professional philosopher are, on the whole, rather clever people. Clever people as a rule tend to be attracted to, and often seduced by, abstract arguments and ideas. Clever people also take perhaps undue pride in their own intellectual abilities and thus tend to stand resolutely by the products of their own ratiocinations, even if those products are paradoxical. As ever in great tragedies, the protagonist's outstanding virtue is also his Achilles' heel.

This is at least a charitable explanation for our surprising fact, and it is the explanation I believe applies in most cases. It also provides a very clear lesson. If the "best of reasons" can be given for anything whatever (as long as one is clever enough) then the "best of reasons" can seduce one into error. Arguments are thus double-edged swords and need to be seen as such. On the one hand, they are the bread and butter of philosophical activity; and, like moths to flames, philosophers find them hard to resist. But philosophers need to have a healthy degree of suspicion about these alluring creatures because, like flames, they can be treacherous.[20]

There is another charitable explanation for our surprising fact stemming from the nature of philosophical problems themselves. Perhaps, the philosopher finds it easy to accept paradoxical results because it is thought that, philosophical problems being what they are, only paradoxical solutions are available. If, as I suggested in Chapter 1, philosophical problems are co-ordination problems which emerge as a result of perceived tensions between reputable lines of thought, one could think that *any* solution to such a problem is likely to involve the rejection of some belief found highly plausible by a great number of people. This appears to be Searle's primary answer to his own question. Philosophical questions arise, says Searle, because of perceived tensions between default positions. If two default positions genuinely clash, then something which appears to most people as true will have to be abandoned. Searle's answer to his own question then is that philosophers tend to opt for the second of the four ways of coping with a co-ordination problem outlined in Chapter 1 because the logic of the situation demands it.

I am inclined to think that Moore and Searle have offered plausible suggestions regarding our surprising fact. Philosophers do become enamoured with their own theories, and the logic of co-ordination problems does lend itself to revisionary solutions (although, as we saw, this need not always be the case). Unfortunately, these charitable views do not exhaust the field of likely explanations. For it frequently arises that, while a philosopher sincerely believes that a paradoxical result stands firm, he or she does not always arrive at this belief on the basis of argument alone. There may be other non-rational factors that mitigate in favour of acceptance of a paradoxical result that have nothing to do with the philosophical merits of the case. For example, human nature being what it is, we tend to find extraordinary occurrences and paradoxical claims far more captivating than the ordinary and humdrum (in much the same way that news of fresh disasters will always receive greater coverage in the media than positive yet modest developments). And there is, at some level at least, a desire that these surprising results be taken seriously if only because life in general, and philosophical activity in particular, becomes far more alluring. The ironic parallel here with Hume's rightly disparaging remarks about human credulity in respect of miracles will not be lost on anyone; for what Hume says on that score applies equally to philosophical paradoxes, of which Hume was a notable propounder. He writes, "The passion of *surprise* and *wonder*, arising from miracles, being an agreeable emotion, gives a sensible tendency towards the belief of those events, from which it is derived. And this goes so far, that even those who cannot enjoy this pleasure immediately, nor can believe those miraculous events, of which they are informed, yet love to partake of the satisfaction at second-hand or by rebound, and place a pride and delight in exciting the admiration of others" (*Enquiry*, p. 117).

It is a basic human weakness, from which philosophers are by no means exempt, to be attracted to the novel, the unusual, the startling and the extraordinary, and, conversely, to be displeased with the wet blanket who insists on living relentlessly in the realm of the ordinary. For real life, like war, is comprised of lengthy periods of crushing boredom punctuated by relatively short bursts of sheer terror. Who then can grudge the philosopher his harmless frisson of paradox?

However, this universal human weakness is exacerbated in the case of philosophers because, at least since Parmenides if not earlier, philosophers have generally assumed that there is a real distinction between reality and appearance, and that it is of the essence of philosophical activity to rip through the veil of quotidian appearances to reveal a hitherto concealed and unfamiliar reality. On this view, it is part and parcel of the philosopher's job description to show that what normally passes for reality is mere appearance and illusion, and so there is every *expectation* that a philosopher's conclusions will be paradoxical – quite literally beyond belief – if he or she is doing his or her job correctly. This expectation is reinforced by the young and aspiring philosopher's education, which will have undoubtedly included a continuous diet of the most extraordinary claims made by the most illustrious figures in the history of the discipline.

No doubt there is room to draw a real distinction between appearance and reality in the ordinary course of life. No doubt, it is possible, for example, to take a forged bank note for the genuine article; no doubt, many have taken the shrewdly disguised stick insect for a twig, a copy for the original, a decoy for the real McCoy, a deceiver for an honest broker. There is no doubt, that is, that much of our natural and social environment is epistemologically opaque, particularly when it comes to dealing with other life forms and other humans. But these are *not* the sorts of appearance/reality mistakes that have generally excited the imagination of philosophers. The philosopher has often urged that appearance/reality mistakes can persist even after one has followed the normal procedures usually felt necessary to safely distinguish appearance from reality (like taking a closer look).[21] This can easily lead imperceptibly to the view that appearances are *never* a guide to reality. The roots of this particular philosophical fantasy will be discussed in the next chapter. But for the time being, it is enough to note that there is indeed much more to the world than that meets the eye; nonetheless, the easiest and most economical explanation for an object *appearing* to be such and so is that it genuinely *is* such and so.

There is a further explanation for our perplexing fact floated by Searle in his *Mind, Language and Society: Philosophy in the Real World* which relies on the notion of Bad Faith. Searle suggests that there is a degree of self-deception and will to power behind many paradoxical claims, particularly those associated with philosophers who wish to deny that there are any mind-independent facts out there in the world which constrain our thought and action. "It just seems too disgusting somehow", Searle suggests, "that we should have to be at the mercy of the 'real world'. It seems too awful that our representations should have to be answerable to anything but us" (1999, p. 17).

Again I think Searle has a point. There are some thinkers for whom brute facts appear to be nothing more than an inconvenience when they tell against a favoured view or opinion. But it is the connection between knowledge and power in particular that lies behind much current anti-realism. This is particularly so in the case of the so-called "post-modern thinkers" who repeatedly insist upon the links between (if not the identity of) knowledge and power. Motivated by the morbid *fear* that objectivity and claims to knowledge necessarily go hand in hand with oppressive political and social power, these thinkers see claims about the "real world" as cynically employed tools of repression. Aside from its intellectual incoherence, the deep moral problem with this attitude is the fact that ontological and epistemological issues are decided not on the basis of evidence and argument, but on the basis of a thinker's political and social ideology, that is, on the basis of what he or she *would like* to be the case, or at least what he or she would like us to believe to be the case. Whatever one's views about the relations that can appropriately obtain between one's desires and one's beliefs – even if one were to agree with William James, for example, that there are occasions when it is appropriate to let one's desires determine what one believes – letting one's political and social agenda determine one's picture of the world while flagrantly ignoring the relevant evidence is both philosophically and morally dubious.[22]

It is also worth noting in passing that Searle's will-to-power explanation connects with the previous explanation in the following way. One way to achieve the "disarming" of objectivity so longed for by post-modernists is to insist not on the ontological claim that there are no mind-independent facts, but to retreat to the weaker epistemological claim that objective facts might well exist but that knowledge of them is impossible because the appearance/reality distinction can never be overcome. If we have no access to reality, but are acquainted only with our subjectively bound appearances, then it is clearly impossible to forward any objective knowledge claims. And there can be little doubt that scepticism has served many who wish to defend certain cherished beliefs from threats posed by either philosophy or science.

One final explanation ought to be considered. Perhaps part of the explanation for the fact that philosophers take paradoxical results seriously is that they quite literally can afford to do so.[23] To conduct research in philosophy is ridiculously cheap compared to the costs of research in the natural sciences. This economic fact is significant. If I am to pursue serious scientific research I will need to obtain not insubstantial financial backing to secure the necessary equipment and laboratory facilities and other necessary resources. Unless I am independently wealthy, I will need to persuade someone (usually a non-scientist) or some institutional body (manned no doubt by non-scientists) to invest, usually rather heavily, in my research. People are generally wary about their investments, and, erring on the side of caution, investors in scientific research tend to be scientifically conservative rather than radical. The upshot is that it is unlikely that a scientist will be able to pursue top level scientific research if his leading ideas cannot grab the imagination of the shrewd non-scientist – he simply will not be able to afford it.

The economic situation is significantly different for philosophers. A philosopher needs time, a library, writing materials, and access to other philosophers; but that is about the extent of his or her requirements. In this economic context, *any* idea can be pursued because there is no effective economic constraint. Furthermore, because the philosopher does not need to persuade a non-philosopher of the value of his or her research project, the philosopher can afford to disregard entirely the views of the non-philosopher, and to cut his or her links to the real world as no scientist can.

Let us now summarise our findings so far. Four distinct explanations for our most perplexing question have been canvassed. A philosopher many cling to an obviously paradoxical conclusion for the following reasons or combination of reasons:

(a) Sincere belief in the merits of the paradoxical conclusion due to the philosopher's inherent weakness for the allure of a subtle argument;
(b) The expectation that paradoxical conclusions are the norm within philosophy and so no cause for alarm. This expectation is grounded in (i) the logic of co-ordination problems, which lends itself to revisionary solutions and (ii) the acceptance of the appearance/reality distinction;
(c) The desire to believe in one's paradoxical conclusion for non-rational reasons (e.g. bad faith, or for the reasons canvassed in Hume's "On Miracles");
(d) The lack of economic or social constraint on the adoption of paradoxical conclusions.

This completes my first attempt to impose some order on the disparate views to be found in the literature regarding our particular question. But it remains only an initial stab, one confined to gathering the insights of others and organising them in some systematic fashion. In the next chapter I want to continue this discussion by adding my own contribution by way of a study of Hume's problem of induction. In the course of this study it will emerge that there are at least two more types or sources of philosophical error. I will look at the misuse of thought experiments in philosophy, and suggest that these have their origins in our largely forgotten intellectual history.

4
Theology's Trojan Horse

Introduction

In the previous chapter I began to gather reflections on the aetiology of philosophical paradoxes, with a view to imposing some sort of order upon them. I suggested that in any particular case, there are likely to be numerous factors operating at different levels that together make up a "mindset" out of which paradoxical conclusions eventually emerge. Unfortunately, some of these factors are unavoidable (e.g. the lack of coercive evidence, the lack of agreed methodology, the breadth of the discipline, the nature of coordination problems, the nature of our evolutionarily endowed cognitive capacities). Others have their origin in avoidable but particularly philosophical thought patterns (e.g. category mistakes, mistaken or faulty analogies, failure to recognise relevant distinctions, faulty conceptual analyses, inappropriate application of the appearance/reality distinction, employing a method outside its realm of competence). I also noted that certain non-rational factors were likely to be a feature of a disordered mindset (e.g. there were what we might call "Humean weaknesses", bad faith, the clever person's propensity to place too much store in pet arguments).

I now want to consider a further concatenation of factors that lead to a peculiar handling of certain modal concepts. In particular, I want to examine the tendency to conflate *logical* necessity and possibility with *physical* or *natural* necessity and possibility. This tendency, rather common in post-Cartesian philosophy, is peculiar not just because it can lead to philosophical paradoxes but also because its roots lie in the acceptance of certain quite specific assumptions which make sense only within a particular *theological* context. Our discussion of this set of aetiological factors, which I collect under the banner of "Theology's Trojan

Horse", begins with a re-examination of Hume's notorious problem of induction; but, as we shall see, the theologically motivated assumptions at work in this particular case are by no means confined to this one philosophical paradox. In fact it is my contention that "the spirit of modernity", thought to have been ushered in by Descartes, is itself a product of these same theological commitments, commitments no philosopher *qua* philosopher is duty bound to honour. My claim then is that much of post-Cartesian philosophy, with its emphasis on epistemology, the quest for certainty and the challenge of scepticism, is guilty of a fundamental error, namely, the application of the assumptions and methods of one discipline, in this case theology, outside their area of competence. In a word, post-Cartesian philosophers have often erred because they have been operating as theologians and not as philosophers.

Hume's problem of induction

It is best to approach this set of claims via a close examination of a particular case, and Hume's problem of induction is admirably suited to our needs. On the one hand, the problem of induction is highly paradoxical, seemingly intractable and particularly embarrassing, especially for empiricists. For if Hume cannot be answered, and we are forced to concede that it is indeed unreasonable to rely on inductive arguments, then, as Russell memorably put it, the distinction between sanity and insanity will be lost.[1] Perhaps less dramatically, it is not unreasonable to assume that, pace Popper, the very possibility of the natural sciences depends on the reliability of induction.[2] So in virtue of its own paradoxical nature, the problem deserves the attention of the common sense philosopher. But a close examination of Hume's problem of induction will also tease out the assumptions that lie behind the problem, permitting us to then run them to ground.

For the sake of simplicity of exposition, I will confine my attention to enumerative inductive arguments, that is, arguments employing the following rule of inference (or some equivalent):

From: (m/n of) all observed A have been B
To infer: (m/n of) all A are B

The problem of the justification of induction is then taken to be the attempt to show that this rule of inference is truth-preserving most of the time. Of course, it is widely thought that Hume succeeded in showing that no such guarantee can be given. The crux of Hume's argument is that no finite set of observations logically entails the corresponding universal generalisation, so it is always possible to accept the premise(s) of an inductive argument while denying the conclusion without contradiction. Indeed, it is precisely this feature which most clearly distinguishes inductive from deductive arguments. It is then argued that because no guarantee of the principle of induction is available, it is, strictly speaking, irrational to rely upon it. But since it is psychologically impossible for us to abandon it entirely (if at all), Hume can claim to have discovered something interesting, but highly unwelcome, about human psychology, to wit, that our beliefs have little to do with reason and rationality and more to do with custom and habit.[3]

Unsurprisingly, this result rankles with philosophers and scientists who pride themselves above all on their rationality. Their challenge then has been to show that reason and rationality still have much to do with the fixation of our beliefs, despite the fact that Hume has identified a genuine problem. Now much (perhaps too much) ink has already been spilt in the attempt to deal with this challenge.[4] Fortunately, there is no need to discuss the many approaches found in the literature. For according to the view to be defended here, all these attempts make a common fatal mistake, namely, letting Hume set the terms of the debate. At best, the traditional approaches offer what might be called "sceptical solutions", since, with the exception of Ayer (who decided the problem must be a pseudo-problem because he could see no way to solve it), everyone has assumed that Hume has identified a genuine problem and that the issue is to determine how to live with its consequences. But, like Ayer, I am not convinced that Hume has identified a pressing philosophical problem because Hume's problem rests on certain unforced assumptions regarding the nature of necessity and possibility.

The crucial step in Hume's account of the problem of induction is the undoubtedly correct claim that it is logically possible to accept the premises of an inductive argument but still reject the conclusion, for it is this feature of inductive arguments which gives rise to questions about their rational acceptability. But while philosophers of an empirical persuasion have seen this insight as pregnant with implications, I suggest that on its own it is not terribly interesting. The rationale for this claim is quite simple: For all Hume has shown so far, there may well be *other* types of constraint at work in any given situation, constraints above and beyond those imposed by logic. So while Hume correctly points out that it is always *logically* possible for the conclusion of an inductive argument to be false while its premises are true, we have as yet no reason not to suppose that in many cases it may be *physically* impossible (in this world at least) for this circumstance to arise. In a word, what the laws of logic permit, other types of necessity may rule out. And if it could be established in a given case that non-logical constraints *are* in play, then (other things being equal) there would be no rational bar to accepting appropriately formed inductive arguments which trade on those non-logical constraints, since these constraints would provide the "guarantee" Hume thought to be lacking. (In due course, I will suggest how this might be done.) If this is on the right track, we might then say that good inductive arguments track physical relations, while valid deductive arguments track logical relations. If this view is adopted, one is no longer tempted to judge inductive arguments by deductive criteria, necessarily finding the former to be defective.

I am suggesting then that Hume's problem of induction has a bite only if a case can be made for at least one of the following assumptions:

(a) There is no necessity but logical necessity (a metaphysical claim that either does away with or conflates natural necessity with logical necessity)

or

(b) It is unreasonable to believe that there is any form of necessity in addition to logical necessity (an epistemological claim – scepticism about causal necessity).[5]

If either (a) or (b) could be established, then Hume's problem of induction would emerge as a genuine problem. And, of course, many will insist that Hume has in fact argued persuasively for (a) and a fortiori for (b). One of the aims of this chapter is to justify the denial of *this* claim precisely.

My threefold strategy is as follows:

(1) In accordance with the metaphilosophy of common sense, I begin by shifting the burden of proof. We remind ourselves that any philosophical viewpoint commends itself to our attention by its ability to organise features of our experience and to solve co-ordination problems not capable of solution in any other manner. But as Russell and others have recognised, the rejection of the principle of induction is extremely counter-intuitive, creating more problems and solving none. This fact alone should be enough to raise our suspicions that a serious mistake has entered our thinking. It is also worth pointing out that any early human living in the ancestral environment that refused to operate with the principle of induction would have quickly come to grief in the real world, for such a person would have been unable to learn anything from exper-

ience. (The fitness consequences of being unable to learn are obvious enough. For example, my reproductive success will be severely restricted if, despite having noticed that people suffer from flatulence, intestinal cramps, diarrhoea, nausea, vomiting and often death after eating certain berries or mushrooms, I remain unmoved by these observations and decide to eat them anyway since, after all, there is no logical guarantee that the berries or mushrooms will poison me on this occasion just because they have poisoned others in the past.) Consequently, I believe it is fair to say that the burden of proof with respect to assumptions (a) and (b) rests squarely on Hume himself. If the arguments Hume brings forward in defence of (a) and (b) can be defused, and shown to be at best inconclusive if not entirely worthless, then this invites one of two conclusions, one tempting but unwarranted, the second less exciting but sound. In a rush of blood, one might be tempted, first, to conclude that there really is no problem of induction. The wiser conclusion, and the one to be defended here, is that there is a problem with enumerative induction, but it is not the problem identified by Hume, nor is it insurmountable.

(2) Now because it is difficult to accept that thinkers of the stature of Hume, Russell, Reichenbach, Strawson, to name only a few, could be entirely wrong about such a well-worn chestnut as the problem of induction, some explanation for their collective failure to undo this Gordian knot would lend credibility to my central claim regarding the problem of induction. It is here that I will advert to the history of certain theologically grounded assumptions and their impact on philosophy. I suggest that this history goes some way to explaining the ease with which (a) and (b) tend to be accepted, assumptions that need to be in place before Hume's problem can emerge. No thorough historical study of these matters can be carried out here; but the bare bones of the case can be laid out nonetheless.[6]

(3) Finally, I will tie up some loose ends. Having claimed that there remains a surmountable problem with enumerative inductive arguments, I end with a brief characterisation of the problem and a possible approach to its solution.

Hume's arguments for (a) and (b)

> Outside logic all is accident.
>
> (Wittgenstein, *Tractatus*, 6.3)

> A necessity for one thing to happen because another has happened does not exist. There is only logical necessity.
>
> (Wittgenstein, *Tractatus*, 6.37)

The denial of physical, natural or causal necessity has been an entrenched dogma of empiricism ever since Hume.[7] Wittgenstein was simply voicing widespread assumptions when he confidently claimed that, indeed, until Kripke's *Naming and Necessity* and Marcus' ground-breaking work in modal logic, the passage of time had seen only the strengthening of this dogma, anti-necessitarianism having been extended in some quarters to include the denial of even logical necessity itself. Perhaps not surprisingly then, very little if any attention has been paid to the original arguments Hume used to impugn causal necessity. But Kripke and Marcus have changed the philosophical landscape. For present purposes, we can set aside the ongoing debate concerning the metaphysical import of the now widely recognised fact that natural language proper names are rigid designators.[8] It is enough to note that the notion of non-logical necessity (and its common bedfellow essentialism) has regained some semblance of philosophical respectability, and are the focus of much serious debate.[9] This philosophical sea change should enable all of us to return to Hume's original arguments with new eyes, not simply those who have adopted the metaphilosphy of common sense.

So just what are Hume's arguments against causal or natural necessity, and are they sound? As one would expect, Hume employs his familiar two-pronged attack. On the one hand, he tries to show that there is no impression to which the notion of causal necessity can be traced and on the other that reason itself reveals the notion to be incoherent. Since he takes these arguments to be difficult if not impossible to refute, Hume commits the sophistic and illusory notion to the flames. Let us revisit these arguments in order.

There is no impression of causal necessity

This is by far the most familiar of Hume's arguments against the notion of a necessary connection obtained between causes and effects.[10] Hume submits the common sense notion of causation to analysis and finds that one of its key ingredients, namely, the necessity of the connection between cause and effect, cannot be traced back to a corresponding impression. On the basis of the theory of ideas adopted from Locke, Hume then concludes that the common sense notion of causation includes an illegitimate projection of our expectations onto the world. He suggests that this notion ought to be abandoned and replaced by the weaker notion of constant conjunction. On this revised view, a cause (or set of causes) is constantly conjoined with its effect, but (a) there is no necessary connection between the two or at least (b) we are not justified in believing that there is (depending on whether one reads Hume as a content or a justification empiricist).[11]

Let us consider the conclusions (a) and (b) separately, beginning with the out-and-out denial of the existence of a necessary causal connection. Not to put too fine a point on it, it is difficult to see how this strong conclusion could be warranted without appealing to a highly dubious metaphysical assumption, which Hume nowhere defends. This is particularly surprising coming from Hume, since he is keen to eschew excessive metaphysical speculation. For the denial of the existence of causal necessity would follow only if in addition to the theory of ideas one also accepted Berkeley's dictum that *esse est percipi*. Now Berkeley's reliance on theological commitments to make this claim remotely plausible is too well known to require a separate discussion here. It is enough simply to note that these commitments are not available to Hume, and that nothing Hume has offered so far goes anywhere near to justifying this claim. It certainly receives no support from the theory of ideas on its own. For even if we agree that all mental content, and all knowledge of matters of fact, stem from sense experience – so that one cannot speak or think about that which has never been, or is not reducible to, an object of sense experience – there is still no warrant to say that if something is not an object of sense experience it cannot exist. So Hume has as yet no warrant to assert (a).

If the strong metaphysical claim does not receive any support from Hume's reflections so far, what of the weaker epistemological claim? Perhaps Hume hopes to defend (b) by accepting that while there may be necessary connections between causes and effects, we would, nonetheless, never be in a position to know this since we have no impressions of this necessity. Let us concede that Hume is right in his assertion that we have no impression of a necessary connection between cause and effect, for this does appear to be phenomenologically accurate. He then wishes to infer from this that we have no warrant to believe in the existence of necessary connections between causes and effects. But notice that Hume goes further than this. For he then quite naturally infers from the claim that we have no warrant to believe in the existence of causal necessity that we can assume that causal connections are contingent, despite the fact that causes and effects are constantly conjoined.

But this argument will not do. The phenomenological facts in question do not support Hume's desired conclusion, or more accurately, they also support precisely the opposite conclusion in equal measure. Hume ought to have noticed that we have no sense impression of modal facts *of any sort.* To speak loosely, while it can be agreed that we do not have impressions of events *having to happen* as they do, it is just as important to recognise that we do not have impressions of things *just happening to happen* either. Our sense impressions are blind to modal facts of any sort, including contingency. To conclude, as Hume seem to have done, that all relations between causes and effects are contingent because we have no impression of necessity is simply unwarranted because one can run an equally powerful version of his own argument in reverse: Since there is no impression of the contingency of the connection between cause and effect, there is no warrant to assume that these connections are contingent; so, by parity of reasoning, we must assume that the causal connections are necessary. Running Hume's argument in reverse reveals that appeals to the phenomenology of impressions cannot decide the matter. Whether beliefs concerning modal facts are justified is a question that will have to be decided on other grounds, for the phenomenology of impressions provides no decisive leverage one way or the other.

Now if Hume's phenomenological fact does not support his argument anymore than my reverse argument, leaving his case for (b) still unmade, further considerations simply exacerbate matters for the Humean. It is now widely recognised even amongst empiricists that many indispensable terms embedded in our most well-established scientific theories are of unobservable entities and processes. Furthermore, no attempt to reduce these terms to observable phenomena has been remotely successful. One need only mention subatomic particles and fields of force to remind ourselves of the cost of accepting even this weaker form of the theory of ideas which insists simply that we cannot have justified knowledge of an entity if we have no impressions of it. Not only do we have the ideas of these unobservable entities and processes but also they are integral components of a set of *justified* beliefs insofar as they are part of an empirically adequate theory with wide cosmological role, the posits of which offer the best available explanation of observable phenomena. Only an excessive concern for certainty born of an obsession with the bogey of scepticism would lead one to deny that the acceptance of the atomic theory of matter is rationally justifiable. But if we can have justified beliefs about entities and processes of which we never have any impressions, what is to stop us from having justified beliefs regarding the connected notions of physical necessity and contingency? These notions, I would suggest, are deeply embedded in any effort to understand the natural world, deeply embedded in our scientific theories, and are as justified as the theories of which they are a part.[12] We need to posit physical necessities and possibilities, and in particular necessary connections between causes and effects, in order to account for the regularities that all parties agree are observed in the natural world. It would be a cosmic coincidence of unimagined proportions if the regularities we observe in nature had no grounding in the very nature of things. If there are no necessary connections between causes and effects, no physical, chemical or biological constraints placed on what can flow from what, then every observed regularity in nature becomes miraculous and beyond comprehension.[13] To argue that the possibility of cosmic coincidence has not been conclusively ruled out is to fall prey again to the siren song of scepticism. True, this theoretical possibility remains alive; but it remains no more than a theoretical possibility, and one we have no reason to take seriously.

We can conclude then that this prong of Hume's attack on the notion of physical or causal necessity has failed. The fact that we have no sense impression of any necessary connection between a cause and its effect provides no warrant to conclude that there is no such connection. Nor does this phenomenological fact allow us to conclude that no belief in such a connection is ever justified, for the fact cuts equally in both directions. Indeed, as the analogy with scientific theoretical entities and processes suggests, there is good reason to believe that the belief in causal necessity is justified. So there is no warrant as yet for (a) or (b). We need then to proceed to the second prong of Hume's fork to see if it is any more successful.

The principle of separability

The second prong of Hume's fork aims at establishing the claim that reason on its own cannot be the source of the idea of a necessary connection between cause and effect. We can now agree with Hume that this may very well be the case; but this is no longer a pressing concern. It is far more likely that modal notions arise as part of our attempt to rationalise our experience of the world – in Hume's terminology, modal notions arise when reason is brought to bear upon our impressions, with neither impressions nor reason on their own being sufficient to produce them. So if Hume is to get anything out of this wing of the attack, he must show more than the obvious point that reason without recourse to sense experience can suggest nothing about the causal implications of a given object or event. (Why would we expect anything else? The implications in questions are of a physical, not logical, nature.) Hume must show that reason itself can cast doubt on the very coherence of the notion of causal necessity granted that the notion already exists.

Such an argument can be gleaned from some of Hume's more familiar passages. In the *Treatise*, Book I, Part III, Section XIV, he writes,

> The mind can never possibly find the effect in the supposed cause by the most accurate scrutiny and examination. *For the effect is totally different from the cause, and consequently can never be found in it ... every effect is a distinct event from its cause.* It could not, therefore, be discovered in the cause, and the first invention or conceptions of it ... must be entirely *arbitrary.* (emphasis added)

Of course, this passage speaks to the question concerning the *origin* of the notion of causal necessity, an issue we have put aside. But it alludes to a further argument which challenges the coherence of the notion of causal necessity itself. It is worth reproducing Hume's argument here:

> As all distinct ideas are separable from each other, and as the ideas of cause and effect are evidently distinct, "twill be easy for us to *conceive* any object to be non-existent this moment, and existent the next, without conjoining to it the distinct idea of a cause or productive principle. The separation, therefore, of the idea of a cause from that of a beginning of existence, is plainly possible for the *imagination*; and consequently the *actual* separation of these objects is so far possible, that it implies no contradiction or absurdity; and is therefore incapable of being refuted by any reasoning from mere ideas without which it is impossible to demonstrate the necessity of a cause." (again, emphasis added)

Before commenting on this argument, it is worth stating clearly its essential premise and its implications. The argument assumes the principle of separability, namely, the rule that if "A" and "B" are "distinct" concepts, then A and B are "separable", that is, A and B are able to exist independently of each other. But if A and B are separable in this sense, then (a) there can be no necessary connection between them, and if there is no necessary connection between A and B then a fortiori (b) there is no certain or necessary knowledge of such a connection that would allow one to infer the existence of the one from the existence of the other. The notions of cause and effect are "distinct" in precisely this sense, therefore...

It is this argument I believe which lies behind Hume's confident rejection of the notion of causal necessity. But it has a number of difficulties, some serious, one fatal. First, the notion of conceptual "distinctness" is not entirely unproblematic. But for the sake of argument and simplicity, let us assume that conceptual distinctness is connected to the notion of analyticity. Let us assume, that is, that two concepts are distinct if neither is analytically "contained" within the other. This would at least agree with Hume's insistence on the point that "the mind" cannot "find the effect in the supposed cause by the most accurate scrutiny and examination". Moreover, let us wave for the moment any complaints one might harbour against the notion of analyticity itself. For even if we grant Hume the benefit of the doubt on these issues, there remains a serious problem with the argument in that he assumes that conceivability is the mark of the logically possible.[14] This is no longer accepted by any current thinker, as far as I am aware. As Marcus has pointed out,[15] the notion of conceivability is always relative to a conceiving subject, in the sense that a proposition p is deemed conceivable by A if p is believed by A to be consistent with the rest of A's beliefs. Thus, Hume's "conceivability" coincides with what we might call "epistemic" possibility. But a logical possibility or necessity has no such relation to anyone's beliefs inasmuch as it is perfectly intelligible to imagine a situation where a proposition is deemed inconceivable (or conceivable) by all who entertain it while remaining logically possible (or impossible) for all that. What makes a statement about the conceivability of a proposition true or false are facts about some particular psychology; whereas, no one's psychological state can be that in virtue of which a proposition is logically possible or impossible. The point for present purposes is that there is no warrant to assume that p is logically possible or impossible simply on the grounds that one can or cannot conceive of p.

But I will not press this point here, for there is a more important and indeed fatal flaw in Hume's argument. The damning charge is that Hume has conflated logical and natural necessity, and so has begged the question at the outset. For even if one accepts the principle of separability, and we grant that the concepts of cause and effect are "distinct" in the requisite sense, all that would legitimately follow is that it is *logically* possible for causes and effects to exist independently of each other. But Hume goes beyond the realm of the logically possible, the realm of the "imagination", to make claims about what can *actually* happen in the physical realm. As he says, "The separation, therefore, of the *idea* of a cause from that of a beginning of existence, is plainly possible *for the imagination*; and consequently the *actual* separation of these *objects* is so far possible." But this move from the realm of logic and the imagination to the realm of the natural world (the move, that is, from "p is logically possible" to "p is physically possible") is illegitimate unless one assumes that the only necessity is logical necessity. But of course this is precisely what was in question. So yet again, Hume has failed to discharge his burden of proof with respect to (a), and so no proof has been offered for (b) either. And since these two prongs exhaust all of Hume's arguments for (a) and (b), we can conclude that no case has been made for either. The upshot of this is that we have as yet no reason to take Hume's problem of induction seriously.

Theologico-historical background

So far I have claimed that Hume's problem of induction arises only if certain background assumptions concerning causal necessity are credible. I have shown that Hume has not provided sufficiently plausible arguments to warrant our acceptance of those assumptions. Given the well-known counter-intuitive consequences that follow on the rejection of the principle of induction, I suggest this is a result to be welcomed. But we are left with a puzzle: If these assumptions are so poorly supported, why has Hume's problem of induction been taken as seriously as it has been?

It is worth digressing for a moment to try to explain just how enumerative induction came to be seen as a problem in the first place. I would suggest that the historical question requiring an answer in this regard is the following: Why does the problem of induction go unnoticed until Hume?[16] No doubt, part of the answer will be Hume's philosophical brilliance. And no doubt, many will subscribe to the common view that the problem of induction emerged as the consequences of empiricism were slowly recognised, first by Berkeley and then by Hume himself. But this cannot be the whole story, for empiricists of no slight philosophical sophistication and logical acumen existed long before the arrival of the British empiricists. And the slogan, "There is nothing in the mind that was not first in the senses", the essential point of Locke's theory of ideas, was a commonplace in scholastic thinking. So if we must look with some suspicion on the view that the problem of induction is simply a corollary of empiricism, what other factors might have been in play?

There is a history to the principle of separability worth recounting at this point as it throws light on the mindset in which Hume and other early modern philosophers are working. The crucial point to bear in mind here is that the principle of separability *can* be put to work in the way Hume requires *if* there is a legitimate means of sliding between the logically possible (Hume's realm of imagination) and the physically possible. There is in fact such a means, but it involves an appeal to the Judeo-Christian–Islamic God, in whom, to modify Dante only slightly, intellect, power and will are one. The theologically grounded rationale for what appears to be a conflation of logical and natural necessity was the claim that if some state of affairs is *logically* possible, it is also *physically* possible because God's omnipotence allows Him to bring about *any* state of affairs, save those that violate the principle of non-contradiction. Acceptance of God's omnipotence thus precludes the possibility of natural or physical necessity because these forms of necessity, were they to exist, would place limits on His unlimited power, which is a contradiction.

The point for present purposes is that if one accepts God's omnipotence as part of one's conceptual scheme then a novel inference pattern become available, a pattern that crops up in a number of important philosophical arguments. The pattern is the following:

If p is conceivable (by us), then p is logically possible. And if p is logically possible, then, because God's power is limited only by the principle of non-contradiction, p is physically possible as well.

This is precisely the rule of inference Hume requires to plug the logical gap in the second prong of his attack. But note also that it is precisely the rule that was used explicitly by Descartes in his argument for the real distinction between mind and body. The following passage from Descartes' *Principles of Philosophy* is worth quoting in full, for it establishes beyond doubt that this theologically loaded inference pattern was consciously employed by the father of modern philosophy. He writes,

LX ... Real distinction between two or more substances ... is discovered from the mere fact that we can clearly and distinctly conceive one without the other. For when we come to know God, we are certain that he can do whatever we distinctly understand. For example, our having the idea of extended or corporeal substance, though not enough to assure us that any such substance in fact exists, is enough to assure us that it can exist; and further, that if it does, any portion of it delimited by us in thought (cogitatione) is really distinct from other parts of the same substance. Again, each of us conceives of himself as a conscious being, and can in thought exclude from himself any other substance, whether conscious or extended; so from this mere fact it is certain that each of us, so regarded, is really distinct from every other substance and from every corporeal substance. And even if we supposed that God has conjoined some corporeal substance to such a conscious substance so closely that they could not be more closely conjoined, and had thus compounded a unity out of the two, yet even so they remain really distinct. For however closely he had united them, he could not deprive himself of his original power to separate them, or to keep one in being without the other; and things that can be separated, or kept in being separately by God are really distinct.

(Descartes, pp. 193–194)

It is important to note that Descartes is fully cognisant of the fact that the principle of separability cannot be employed without reference to God. He does not argue that one's being able to clearly and distinctly perceive A to be distinct from B is the ground of A's ability to exist without B, or that the fact that A and B really are distinct entails that they could ever exist apart *without the intervention of God*. What he claims is that in our clear and distinct perceptions, we recognise what God could do with respect to A and B if he so chose. This is important for the defence of the metaphilosophy of common sense. We have already noted that Descartes' overarching intellectual project was essentially that of the Middle Ages, namely, seeking the reconciliation of theology and philosophy. Now we see that an important inference pattern on which he relies to generated support for some of his most characteristic theses is itself grounded explicitly in certain specific theological assumptions. In fact, as we shall see, the quest for certainty and the obsession with the challenge of scepticism, hallmarks of the spirit of modernity, are traceable to precisely this same set of theological assumptions.

Further historical facts about the history of the principle of separability require attention. For example, it is important to note that Aristotle would have rejected Descartes' argument for the real distinction precisely because he did not accept the principle of separability. As though anticipating Descartes' argument, Aristotle insists that "the other parts of the soul are not separable, as some assert them to be, *though it is obvious that they are conceptually distinct*" (*De Anima*, II, Chapter 2, 413b 27–29). Aristotle's rejection of the principle of separability is not particularly surprising, given that he lacked the required means of sliding between logical and natural necessity. However, philosopher/theologians begin to employ the principle in the West after 1270 and 1277 as a result of ecclesiastical pressure. The ecclesiastical powers of the day felt, with some justification, that the rise of Aristotelian physics and metaphysics posed a real challenge to the authority of the Church. Many began to fear that Aristotle represented a dangerously impressive alternative view of the world and its workings which could eventually compete with the Church for the hearts and minds of philosophers and theologians. One way of combating the growing influence of Aristotle was to categorically condemn any of his teachings that conflicted with received theological doctrine and to forbid anyone from teaching such things in the Universities. Although there were many condemned teachings, those that directly concern us most have to do with the notion of natural necessity, for natural necessity was deemed incompatible with omnipotence of God. Bosley and Tweedale write,

In December of 1270 Etienne Tempier, the Bishop of Paris, condemned thirteen propositions concerning the necessity of events, the eternity of the world and limitations upon divine power and knowledge. Further steps were taken to fight positions held by Aristotle, Avicenna, and Averroes, as well as positions of the Latin Averroists Siger of Brabant and Boethius of Dacia. On March 7, 1277 Bishop Tempier condemned [a further] 219 propositions.... One effect of the condemnation[s] is to expand an account of God's power.... It is fair to say that the Condemnation of 1277 is a signpost of the road ahead.

(1999, p. 52)

The Condemnations had two particular effects on the contemporary philosophico-theological community. First, a sea change concerning the understanding of very nature of the cosmos had been on the cards ever since the widespread acceptance of Christianity in the West. In the ancient world, the notion of natural necessity was accepted as a matter of course. For example, Aristotle expected no adverse reaction when he wrote that:

We all suppose that what we know is not even capable of being otherwise; of things capable of being otherwise we do not know, when they have passed outside our observation, whether they exist or not. Therefore the object of scientific knowledge is of necessity. Therefore it is eternal; for things that are of necessity in the unqualified sense are all eternal; and things that are eternal are ungenerated and imperishable.

(*Nicomachean Ethics*, Book vi, Chapter 3)

But with the arrival of an omnipotent God, one who had created the world out of nothing, it was only a matter of time before the natural world came to be viewed with significantly different eyes. In a Christian and Islamic context, the course of nature must be seen as radically contingent, for the laws of nature operable in this world could be altered at a whim if God chose to do so, for God is not bound by His own creation. The Condemnations thus encouraged the recognition of this decidedly un-Aristotelian metaphysical implication of the doctrine of creation ex nihilo. And the belief that the course of nature is radically contingent gets carried well into the modern era. Indeed, it was a calling card of Protestant scientists like Newton and Boyle who styled themselves "Christian virtuosi".

The second and closely related effect of the Condemnations is a corollary to the metaphysical thesis just discussed. If the order of the natural world is radically contingent, if, for example, there is no necessary connection between a cause and its effect, then one cannot safely infer the existence of the one from the existence of the other. This new form of reasoning, reminiscent of many a passage of Hume, leads to a new form of scepticism found in William Ockham and Nicolaus Autrecourt. The sceptical implications of the Condemnations are perhaps most starkly evident in passages from Autrecourt's *Certitude and the Principle of Non-Contradiction*, which clearly illustrate the connection between the theologically motivated assumptions regarding the nature of necessity and epistemological issues. He writes,

> From the fact that some thing is known to be, it cannot be inferred evidently, by evidenceness reduced to the first principle [the principle of non-contradiction] that there is some other thing.
>
> (Bosley and Tweedale, p. 495)

Hume himself could have written this line. And Nicolaus' reasoning is precisely that employed by Hume:

> In such an inference in which from one thing another thing would be inferred, the consequent would not be factually identical with the antecedent, nor with part of what is signified by the antecedent. It therefore follows that such an inference would not be evidently known with the aforesaid evidentness of the first principle.
>
> (Ibid., p. 495)

Bosley and Tweedale's gloss on this is that "Any real distinction implies separability. And across the potential gap between the separable there in no completely safe inference" (ibid., p. 493). For Nicolaus, the consequences of this view were clear:

Aristotle in his entire natural philosophy and metaphysics possessed such certainty of scarcely two conclusions, and perhaps not even one....I have an argument that I am unable to refute, to prove that he did not even possess probable knowledge.

(Ibid., p. 497)

Note how high the bar has now been raised before one can claim to know anything. Only that which can be known with the evidentness of the first principle is truly known. Frede did not fail to notice the importance of this new kind of reasoning:

What is... important is that one can see in Nicolaus how this medieval background gives a certain shape to the problem of scepticism which, though not entirely alien to ancient scepticism altogether, is not in the spirit of either Pyrrhonism or the Academic scepticism of Arcesilaus or Carneades, but rather close to the problem of scepticism as Descartes or Hume came to see it.

(1988, p. 67)

Indeed, we have here the beginnings of the Cartesian "spirit of modernity" that Reid found so pernicious. Even the roots of Descartes' infamous Evil Demon argument can be found in the Condemnations of 1277. Condemned proposition 69 reads as follows: "That God cannot produce the effect of a secondary cause without the secondary cause itself" (Bosley and Tweedale, p. 54).[17] In effect, the ecclesiastical authorities were insisting that God *can* bring it about that, for example, we have visual experiences of a world even if there is no world to cause those visual experiences. The reason for this claim is that there is nothing in logic to rule out this possibility. And, more to the point, any claim to the contrary was seen as a violation of God's omnipotence, and not to be tolerated by the faithful. Here is how Ockham puts it in his sixth *Quodlibet* where he asks if it is possible to have a visual experience (intuitive cognition) of an object that does not exist:

[B]y God's power there can be an intuitive cognition of an object that does not exist. I prove this, first, through the article of faith, "I believe in God the Father Almighty". I understand this to mean that whatever does not involve an obvious contradiction is to be attributed to the divine power. But it does not involve a contradiction that the effect in question should be brought about by God....On the basis of this proposition I argue as follows: Every effect that God is able to produce by the mediation of a secondary cause he is able to produce immediately by himself. But he is able to produce an intuitive cognition of a corporeal thing by the mediation of a [corporeal] object. Therefore, he is able to produce this cognition immediately by himself....Furthermore, every absolute thing that is distinct in place and subject from another thing can by God's power exist when that other absolute thing is destroyed. But the vision of a star in the heavens – both the sentient vision and the intellective vision – is of this sort. Therefore, etc.

(*Quodlibetal Questions*, p. 506)

Now if one becomes accustomed to the thought that what one sees might not in fact be there, but could be a figment of one's imagination produced by God's direct intervention in one's mental life, then one is well on the way to the Cartesian nightmare scenario familiar to all first-year philosophy students. Because I cannot know with the evidentness of the first principle that my visual experience of a tree, say, is not caused directly by God, I cannot know that there is a tree before me. It is with these considerations in mind that Bosley and Tweedale make the following observation:

[W]hile meaning to strengthen the understanding of God's omnipotence and filter out of philosophical thought neo-Platonist assumptions, the condemnations helped renew *skeptical* procedure; in effect *a Trojan Horse* was introduced into philosophical practice.

(Ibid., xx, emphasis added)

What is the point of all this history? The point, I believe, is that it has long since been forgotten, and was forgotten, or perhaps never recognised, by Hume himself. The scholastic philosophers were fully aware of the fact that the principle of separability cannot be used without theological support, as was Descartes himself. But the same cannot be said of Berkeley. In the course of his famous attack on Locke's theory of abstraction Berkeley says, almost as an aside:

To be plain, I own myself able to abstract in one sense, as when I consider some particular parts or qualities separated from others, with which though they are united in some object, yet it is possible they may really exist without them. But I deny that I can abstract one from another, or conceive separately, those qualities which it is impossible should exist so separated.

(*Principles of Human Knowledge*, Introduction, Section 10)

The importance of this passage is twofold. First, Berkeley is very matter-of-fact about the employment of the principle of separability. He clearly expects no opposition to this use of it. Second, there is no mention of the need for God's omnipotence to justify the use of the principle anywhere in this work.[18] And as we have seen, Hume, a great admirer of Berkeley, uses the principle of separability in the second prong of his attack on causal necessity without any reference whatsoever to God's omnipotence, and without betraying any awareness of the need for a functionally equivalent substitute. The upshot is that Hume continued unwittingly to employ an inference pattern whose proper ground lies in an intellectual context Hume has himself repudiated.

How might this have come about? It has been said of Ockham that he is "a philosopher who is constantly reminded by the theologian in himself that he must not call any truth necessary unless it can be shown that its denial implies a logical contradiction" (Ockham, 1990, p. xxii). I suggest that Hume is a philosopher who has so internalised the voice of the theologian that he no longer recognises its theological provenance. My suspicion is that by Hume's day anti-necessitarianism and the accompanying threat of scepticism are so well entrenched in philosophical consciousness generally that neither are thought to require any real support by way of argumentation (hence the feebleness of Hume's arguments for (a) and (b)). Hume does not really expect there to be any natural or causal necessity, and so is unjustifiably impressed by his arguments which suggest there could not be any. When this is combined with the epistemological obsession with scepticism to which the denial of causal or natural necessity gave rise, the inevitable result is the belief that only logically water tight guarantees are rationally acceptable, guarantees that are now in principle impossible concerning matters of fact. The stage is then set for the emergence of the problem of induction, as we know it. If I am right, we are then faced with an historic irony: The problem of induction owes less to Hume's empiricism than it does to the theologically motivated Condemnations of 1277. The enlightenment's greatest atheist bequeathed to philosophy a problem that makes sense only in a theological context. The problem of induction is quite simply a theological hangover.

Three points follow from this discussion. First, we must now suspect that the spirit of modernity as exemplified by Cartesianism is itself a product of medieval theological concerns, and that metaphysics and epistemology as they have been practiced since the early modern period have been conducted according to the rules appropriate to a medieval theologian. This suspicion provides further support for the common sense philosopher's refusal to accept the spirit of modernity (although on grounds that would not have been particularly welcome to Reid). But we should also notice a more general point about the aetiology of philosophical paradoxes, namely, that historical ignorance and intellectual inertia can allow certain assumptions and thought patterns to remain operative long after the support for them has evaporated. This suggestion has obvious parallels with Anscombe's comments in "Modern Moral Philosophy" concerning Hume's remarks on the problem of deriving an "ought" from and "is" (another of Hume's legacies to modern philosophy). Anscombe writes, "The situation, if I am right, was the interesting one of the survival of a concept *outside the framework of thought that made it a really intelligible one*" (*Collected Papers*, Vol. III, p. 31, emphasis added). This observation applies even more clearly in the case of the principle of separability. Finally, we need to notice the highly problematic nature of a standard philosophical tool, namely, the thought experiment. Philosophers often engage in armchair speculations and let themselves be taken away by flights of fancy, the idea being that what we can conceive or imagine in strange and exotic circumstances is a guide to how things really are or really can be. For the reasons just outlined, we must regard this as a particularly hazardous exercise.

The real problem of induction

So far I have sought (1) to establish that Hume's understanding of induction is misguided and (2) to provide some explanation for how this error has managed to go unnoticed by empiricists. But if Hume's version of the problem should no longer concern us, there remains a real problem with induction nonetheless. For even if we avail ourselves of the notion of causal or natural necessity, as I think we should, we are still left with the task of distinguishing between universal laws and accidental generalisations. How does one decide if the conclusion of an inductive argument is to be taken as instantiating a universal law rather than a simple accidental generalisation with no basis in the nature of things? It is worth pausing if only for a moment to consider how the scholastics handled this problem, for their approach is particularly informative.

Recall that the working assumption has been that if it can be established in a given case that non-logical constraints *are* in play, then there is no rational bar to accepting appropriately formed inductive arguments which trade on those non-logical constraints. But how does one determine whether such non-logical constraints are in play? The scholastic answer, and the answer accepted both by common sense and the natural sciences, is to appeal to the notion of natural kinds and the accompanying metaphysical doctrine of essentialism. If an essential feature of gold, to take an old example, is that it has the atomic number 79, then we can be confident that *all* samples of gold will have the atomic number 79. If a substance does not have the atomic number 79, then it is not gold, whatever other superficial similarities it may have to gold. Furthermore, an object's being of a certain kind can be the ground for the claim that there is a causal connection between its non-essential properties. Marcus uses the example of the relations between being gold, being immersed in aqua regia, and dissolving.[19] While being immersed in aqua regia and dissolving are both accidental or non-essential properties of some samples of gold, it is *not* accidental that a sample of gold dissolves when immersed in aqua regia. The claim is that this happens to samples of gold because of the essential nature of gold itself. If this claim can be substantiated, then we can safely infer that all samples of gold will dissolve when immersed in aqua regia even though this universal generalisation goes beyond all possible experience.

The suggestion then is as follows: suitably formulated inductive arguments that trade on the essential properties of natural kinds are to be viewed very differently from those that do not. The former invoke a form of non-logical necessity in a way which warrants a degree of confidence in the truth of the conclusion which is unavailable in the case of inductive arguments without these features.

If this is the basic strategy to be employed, we are then left with a substantive question: How do we know when we are homing in on a natural kind and its essential properties? And again the Scholastics have a straightforward answer in line with empiricist, albeit Aristotelian, principles: By the examination of an object's "constitutive activities" over a suitably lengthy period of time. Of course, we will want to know if an object's observed causal behaviour is "constitutive" of that object and not merely a temporary aberration. But Duns Scotus provides an unlooked-for answer to this sort of worry. He writes,

Whatever occurs for the most part by a cause *that is not free* is the natural effect of that cause . . . . A *non-free* cause cannot produce unfreely for the most part an effect opposed to the effect to which it is naturally directed, or to which it is naturally directed by its form . . . . Consequently, nothing which frequently produces an effect is a chance cause [of that effect], and thus *if it is not free* it will be a natural cause [of that effect]. But this effect occurs through this cause for the most part. This we learn from experience, because we observe such and such a nature with sùch and such accidents and then with such and such other accidents, and we discover that, no matter how diverse the accidents it is with, such and such an effect always follows on that nature. Therefore, this effect follows not because of some accident belonging to the nature but rather because of that nature itself.

(*Ordinatio* I, dist. 3, pt. 1, qu. 4.)

The point to be noticed here is that, although an empiricist, Scotus does *not* assume that the natural order is *in and of itself* radically contingent. If the order of the natural world is contingent, it is so only because God can intervene in its workings if He so chooses. There is no suggestion that the natural world, when left to its own devices, has any tendency or capacity to deviate from the path marked out for it. Consequently, the only way in which a cause could produce an effect contrary to its nature is if it were a *free* agent. Since the Scholastics are not given to seeing the natural world as populated by free agents any more than we are, Hume's problem of induction simply does not arise. The sun will rise tomorrow and bread will continue to nourish because neither is a free agent capable of doing anything else.

These are the bare bones of the common sense approach to the "real" problem of induction, the problem, that is, of distinguishing universal laws from accidental generalisations. But while this approach might appeal to the philosophical layperson, many philosophers will find it unsatisfactory, or at least harbour grave misgivings. "This 'solution'", many are likely to say, "assumes that natural bodies have essences. But essentialism, for reasons Quine pointed out, is a thoroughly dead doctrine." It is worth ending this chapter with a brief look at Quine's argument because it perfectly illustrates the principle of separability at work well into the twentieth century.

I noted above that the principle of separability sanctions the following inference pattern:

If p is conceivable (by us), then p is logically possible. And if p is logically possible, then, because God's power is limited only by the principle of non-contradiction, p is physically possible as well.

But this inference pattern can be reformulated as follows:

Because God's power is limited only by the principle of non-contradiction, if "A is B" is not analytically true, or true a priori, then "A is B" cannot be physically necessary.

These inference patterns are two sides of the same coin. The first states that if p is logically possible, then ṗ is physically possible, while the second states that if p is not logically necessary, then p cannot be physically necessary. Both require acceptance of an omnipotent God or some functional equivalent. And the second formulation of the rule in particular is frequently appealed to in modern philosophy;[20] in fact, Quine employs it in his argument against Aristotelian essentialism.

Quine (1953) begins his famous attack on Aristotelian essentialism by pointing out, unproblematically, that if E were essentially true of x (i.e. if E were the essence of x), then "x is E" would be a necessary proposition. This is an accepted ingredient of any version of essentialism. But Quine then states that if "x is E" is necessary, then "x is E" is analytic. He then argues that we find "x is E" analytic or not depending on how *we* refer to x, and depending on how *we* conceive of x. Consequently, " 'x is E' is necessary" will be true or not, not in and of itself, but only depending on how one conceives of and refers to x. Likewise essences themselves become observer relative, the implication being that x cannot have an essence in and of itself as the Aristotelian maintains.

We can now see quite easily where this argument goes wrong. It unjustifiably assumes that the only necessity is logical necessity, which is why he states that "x is E" cannot be necessary unless "x is E" is analytic. In fact, how we refer to x or conceive of x is entirely irrelevant to whether x has an essence. If x has an essence, it will be in virtue of the fact that it is what it is independently of our representations of it, which is entirely in line with common sense.

5
Metaphysical Realism as a Pre-condition of Visual Perception

Introduction

So far in this book I have been at pains to address, or at least begin to address, three of the five principal tasks of the common sense philosopher as they were set out in Chapter 1. I have explained what counts as a common sense belief and have provided an argument to back up the intuition that such beliefs ought to be treated as default positions (tasks 1 and 2). I have also attempted in Chapters 3 and 4 to provide a general explanation as to why it is that philosophers so often end up denying what we all know to be true (task 4). Now, in the remainder of this work, I turn to the third of the principal tasks, namely, the piecemeal, laborious and seemingly endless job of dealing with particular challenges to particular common sense beliefs mounted by highly respected and respectable philosophers. In order to illustrate the methodology and approach of the common sense philosopher in action, I have chosen to examine a number of recent challenges on topics ranging from metaphysics to ethics.

I begin, in this chapter, with an examination of the claims of Kant and other neo-Kantians, regarding the ontological status of the external world and the nature of our perception of it. In the course of this chapter I will present a transcendental argument based on the findings of cognitive psychology and neurophysiology which invites two conclusions: First and foremost, that a pre-condition of visual perception itself is precisely what the common sense philosopher maintains, namely, the mind-independent existence of a *featured*, or *pre-packaged* world; second, this finding, combined with other reflections, suggests that, contra Kant, McDowell and other neo-Kantians, human beings have access to "things as they are in the world" via *non-projective perception*.

98

These two conclusions taken together form the basis of common sense, or Aristotelian, metaphysical realism and a refutation of the neo-Kantian "two-factor" approach to perception.[1]

The denial of metaphysical realism

Kant is famous (or infamous) in philosophical circles for having maintained that external objects as we know them do *not* exist independently of us but only in virtue of our imposition of concepts and a spatio-temporal setting upon what he argued must be a phenomenal chaos received via sensation.[2] This revolutionary claim was in large part a response to Humean scepticism, itself a direct descendent of Locke's representative realism – which acknowledged a gap between what is perceived (allegedly an internal sense impression or sense datum) and the object of knowledge (the object in the external world) – combined with "the spirit of modernity" exemplified by Cartesianism. To speak somewhat loosely, to close this gap and eliminate the possibility of scepticism, Berkeley brought the external world into the mind, thereby adopting a form of idealism. Kant rejected this approach to the problem and instead took the mind out into the world, thus acknowledging an external world populated by physical objects, but at the cost of rendering its features dependent upon the ordering mind.[3]

In the twentieth century, representative realism has become less and less popular as a theory of perception. This is in no small part due the heavy criticism levied at the arguments traditionally used to support the existence of sense data.[4] There are also few takers for Berkeley's brand of idealism. But Kant has fared substantially better. There are many contemporary metaphysical anti-realists who take their inspiration from Kant: Kuhn (1970), Putnam (1981),[5] Feyerabend (1991) and McDowell (1994a) to name just a few. Their views represent varieties of "constructivism", which, following Devitt, we can take to be the view that:

> The only independent reality is beyond the reach of our knowledge and language. A known world is partly constructed by the imposition of concepts. These concepts differ from (linguistic, social, scientific, etc.) group to group, and hence the worlds of groups differ. Each such world exists only relative to the imposition of concepts.
>
> (1997, p. 234)

When applied to perception constructivism results in claims like the following from McDowell, perhaps the most prominent of the current neo-Kantians:

> It is essential to the picture I am recommending that experience has its content by virtue of the drawing into operation, in sensibility, of capacities that are genuinely elements in a faculty of spontaneity. The very same capacities must also be able to be exercised in judgments, and that requires them to be rationally linked into a whole system of concepts and conceptions within which their possessor engages in a continuing activity of adjusting her thinking to experience.
>
> (1994a, p. 46)

And lest anyone be unclear on how to read these claims, McDowell is explicit about the "demanding interpretation" of the terms "concept" and "conceptual" to which he, along with most other constructivists, is committed. He writes,

> It is essential to conceptual capacities, in the demanding sense, that they can be exploited in active thinking, thinking that is open to reflection about its own rational credentials. When I say that the content of experience is conceptual, that is what I mean by "conceptual".
>
> (1994a, p. 47)

The Kantian inspiration behind constructivism is clear enough, and its popularity in philosophical circles and beyond is undoubted. Nonetheless, for all its popularity as a philosophical thesis, the common sense philosopher cannot ignore the fact that neo-Kantian constructivism is diametrically opposed to the realist intuitions of common sense. And, for precisely those reasons outlined in Part I, I take it that any philosophical thesis, however venerable its origin, is seriously compromised if it is at odds with robust common sense. Nonetheless, even if the common sense philosopher is right to be suspicious of the neo-Kantian claims, it is still incumbent upon him or her to produce an intellectually cogent and compelling response to them. It is the finding of these cogent and compelling responses to particular challenges that constitutes the third principal task of the common sense philosopher.

Perhaps the chief means to this end is to point out the weaknesses of the arguments used to defend positions at odds with common sense. Once these weaknesses or errors have been identified, the common sense position then wins by default, requiring no further proof. One way of going about this in this particular case would be to show that the problems that Kant and the neo-Kantians hope to address by appealing to constructivism can be dealt with without resorting to counter-intuitive theses. The neo-Kantian position would then be superfluous as well as counter-intuitive. A more radical line of response, a line supported on the grounds sketched in Chapter 4, would be to suggest that the real problem lies not in the Kantian solution to the problem, but the acceptance of the assumptions crucial to the emergence of the problem itself. For example, it could be argued that overcoming Cartesian scepticism is not the proper business of philosophy, and that it has been this misguided endeavour of post-Cartesian philosophers which has led, unnecessarily, to so many counter-intuitive claims. It could also be pointed out that Cartesian scepticism rests on certain theological commitments that no philosopher is bound to respect.

While these approaches to the challenge of neo-Kantian constructivism are perfectly possible, they can be complemented by a more direct approach. The approach to be explored here is to argue that the neo-Kantian "two-factor" theory of perception, so central to the constructivist's case, is simply empirically inadequate. If this can be established then there would be no need to delve deeply into our taxonomy of philosophical errors in order to identify the false steps taken on the road to metaphysical anti-realism. For as I argued in Chapters 1 and 2, a necessary condition of a philosophical theory's being worthy of serious consideration is that it be consistent with the best available scientific theories on the relevant topics. It is not the business of philosophers *qua* philosophers to seek to compete with scientists on scientific matters, and philosophy must give way to science when the two come into conflict. Only when this approach to the relationship between philosophy and science is adopted will the philosopher be able to set about his legitimate task, namely, the attempt to provide "the Big Picture" in the fashion described in Chapter 1.

The burden of this chapter, then, is to show that the best available science tells against neo-Kantian constructivist theories while sitting easily alongside the intuitions of the common sense realist. In particular, I will show that the best available science indicates that a precondition of visual perception (at least in vertebrates) is precisely what the common sense realist maintains but which the constructivist denies, namely, the *mind-independent* existence of a *featured*, or *pre-packaged* world of persisting middle size solids and their various properties.[6] This conclusion, when combined with other plausible assumptions defended in Chapter 2, gives us a good reason to believe that visual systems in vertebrates receive the world *as featured* via *non-projective perception.* Together these arguments tell against all versions of neo-Kantian constructivisms (although McDowell will serve as my primary example) and provide support for the two defining components of metaphysical realism. The upshot of this excursion into the science of visual perception is the conclusion that neo-Kantian constructivism poses no real threat to common sense intuitions in this domain, and should simply be set aside as a historical curiosity.[7]

Preliminary remarks

Unfortunately a few preliminary remarks about the philosophy of perception in general are required in order to prevent possible misunderstandings of the position to be defended here. Perception is an extraordinarily complicated topic, but mutual understanding is made more difficult than it has to be by the fact that there is no common set of assumptions that all bring to the table. I begin then by stating explicitly the assumptions that motivate the position taken here.

All theories of perception are embedded in a wider web of metaphysical commitments

I take it as axiomatic that perception is a relation between a perceiver and that which is perceived. Consequently, all theories of perception are deeply embedded in, and inseparable from, a wider web of metaphysical commitments regarding both relata. It goes without saying then that a theory of perception is only as good as the metaphysics of which it is a part. Since this is equally true of the common sense approach to perception it would be useful to specify precisely at the outset what common sense metaphysical realism amounts to.[8] In particular, it is advisable to distinguish this version of metaphysical realism from that discussed by Putnam in his famous "brains-in-a-vat" scenario. For present purposes, common sense, or *Aristotelian metaphysical realism* (hereafter, MR) can be defined as the conjunction of two sub-theses, namely ontological realism (OR) and epistemological realism (ER). *Ontological realism* is the thesis that there is an extra-linguistic reality whose nature or structure is independent of our representation of it. *Epistemological realism* is the thesis that human beings in full possession of their properly functioning cognitive faculties are capable of ascertaining the nature (at least in part) of this independent reality in thought and non-projective perception. ER distinguishes Aristotelian from Cartesian forms of MR, since the latter maintain, while the former denies, the coherence of epistemological jeopardy.[9]

The term "two-factor theory" must be disambiguated

There are various senses in which a theory might be called a "two-factor" theory of perception. It is worth taking the time to distinguish these various senses in order to clarify the nature of our quarry, for only in certain senses is a "two-factor" theory incompatible with MR. Most of these senses are mentioned here only to be dropped from further consideration as not relevant to our present purpose.

In a trivial sense, *all* theories of perception are "two-factor" theories. Since perception is a result of interaction between a perceiver and that which is perceived, it will be impossible to understand perception without coming to terms with both relata, since each will have their part to play in the determination of the relation. But there are nontrivial senses in which a theory can be called a two-factor theory without it being at odds with MR. Indeed, the Aristotelian theory is a prime example. When the Scholastic Aristotelians state that extra-linguistic reality is perceived *in the manner of the perceiver*,[10] they are stating what is uncontroversially true, namely, that *what* one perceives is determined by what there is to see on the one hand, and one's perceptual apparatus on the other. But this position is not at odds with MR, for neither OR nor ER is compromised by the fact that each sensory modality only responds to, or picks up, a particular band of stimulation. The fact that an organism's perceptual systems do not pick up or respond to *all* of reality does not imply that what they do pick up are not objective features of an extra-linguistic reality. At issue here, and throughout this chapter, is Crispin Wright's so-called "Euthyphro Contrast", one of his four criteria for a realist discourse: Does the perceptual system track *pre-existing* features of the world, the presumed source of the sensory stimulation, or are these features *imposed* by structuring principles internal to the perceiver?

The same consideration applies to the family of theories according to which, what one sees is a function of one's *interests, ideology* or the *perspective* from which one views the world. Again, all of this is consistent with MR. One's interests, ideology or perspective no doubt determine what one *notices* (or fails to notice), for perception is a form of attention; but this does not compromise the ontological independence of what is attended to or perceived. It is only if one takes what one notices to exhaust reality (*esse est percipi*), or as the defining feature of reality, that the various forms of "perspectivism" begin to have ontological implications. But clearly these additional assumptions need not be taken on board. No one need deny that knowledge and interests are intimately related. But it is very easy to slide from this uncontroversial point into the unwarranted conclusion that all knowledge claims are thoroughly subjective.

If the types of two-factor theory discussed above can now be safely dismissed for the purposes of our discussion, there remains a final group of benign two-factor theories to be considered. Most orthodox theories of perception assume a disparity between sensation, the brute irritations of our sense organs, and the way the world actually looks to us in cases of normal vision. The received view has been that sensation is "impoverished" vis-à-vis our actual perceptions of the world, in the sense that we allegedly "see more" than is contained in the sensations themselves. The task of the visual theorist has then been to identify the mechanisms whereby "thin" sensory input is transformed by the perceiver into "thick" percepts. The *innatists*, who drew the fire of Berkeley's *New Theory*, held that the mind is furnished with concepts which, in conjunction with sensation, allow the perceiver (unconsciously) to draw inferences concerning the nature and structure of the external world. Berkeley, Helmholtz and other *associationists* reject innatism and its appeal to concepts, but still insist that thin sensations must be augmented, this time by past experiences contained in memory.

The key point of agreement between the innatists, associationists and contemporary computational theorists like Marr is that sensation must be processed in some way by the perceiver in order to close the gap between what is given in sensation and the "constructed" final product, our actual perception of the visual world. But despite appearances, these positions are compatible with MR. Most importantly, they do not deny that the world is received as featured. Indeed, as in the case of the dispute over distance perception, it is assumed that there are cues *within* the stimulus that allow the perceiver to work out what is going on (albeit unconsciously). This is an important point, for what can these cues be if not *features* of the sensory stimulus? And as mentioned above, the origin or source of these features is of first importance, an issue to which we shall return below. They still insist, no doubt, that internal processing must be carried out on this stimulus, and that this processing is in some sense "conceptual". But this processing is not conceptual in the demanding sense explicitly adopted by McDowell, as he himself is keen to point out (1994a, p. 53). And there is reason to wonder whether this processing should really be called conceptual in any sense.[11]

Things are altogether different in the case of the neo-Kantian two-factor theorists. This is due to the claim that the brute stimulus received by the sense organs is more than simply "thin"; by definition, sensation is *featureless*, *unstructured*, or *without content* because it has yet to be organised by the mind. On some accounts, sensation is at best an "indiscriminate porridge". On others, sensation presents a "kaleidoscope of impressions", which suggests not something totally unfeatured, but perhaps a blooming, buzzing confusion of, at least temporarily, bounded splashes of colour. On this weaker view, sensation actually contains many features, but remains devoid of "object meaning". We can distinguish these versions of the Kantian position, calling the first account *strong* Kantianism, and the second *weak* Kantianism. But what unites both versions of the neo-Kantian two-factor theory is the view that the structure of the visual world, complete with "object meaning", is the result of the imposition of Kantian-type categories and concepts upon what one might call "object free" stimulus. It is not unusual to find this view expressed in more colourful language as follows: "each one of us...*creates for himself the world* in which he has his life's experiences" (Ittelson, p. 19). This notion of creation is usually taken to be *the* defining feature of two-factor theories of perception.

I maintain that the only two-factor theories of perception that are really at odds with MR are strong and weak Kantianism. Strong Kantianism is clearly at odds with MR since it can be truly said to maintain an extreme version of the thesis at the heart of the two-factor theory, namely, that the perceiving subject *creates* his world. Weak Kantianism also falls foul of MR in its insistence that, despite the presence of semi-featured stimulus, the visual world awaits object meaning until the projection of Kantian categories (or some equivalent).

Differing assumptions concerning the task of a theory of perception and the different senses of "seeing"

In addition to differences in metaphysical "background-commitments", philosophers often differ on the issue as to what theories of perception are meant to accomplish. Traditionally, philosophers of perception have set themselves the task of providing rational justifications of *human* perceptual *beliefs*. Now this task demands a particular view of the nature of perception. Because many find it natural to assume that beliefs are impossible without concepts[12] it is also natural to assume that if perception is to play any role in the rational justification of beliefs (and not simply a causal role in their production) then there must be a conceptual component to perceptions themselves.[13] It is then only a short step to the conclusion that one cannot perceive an X unless one has the *concept* of X – one cannot see a fork, for example, unless one sees it *as* a fork, or sees *that* it is a fork.[14] The point for present purposes is simply to note that there is internal pressure within the traditional approach to perception with its intention to justify human perceptual beliefs to hold that perception is thoroughly imbued with concepts. In effect we find a philosophical agenda determining what perception "must" be like.

No doubt seeing that a fork is a fork, or seeing a fork as a fork presupposes that the perceiver has the concept FORK. And if this is the only form of seeing, then the common sense philosopher is in trouble. For if one cannot perceive without concepts, and concepts are essentially linguistic, social or cultural constructs, then we are driven to one of the two unpalatable conclusions: Either there is no mind-independent reality (because perception is of what is, and perception is thoroughly constructivist); or there is such a mind-independent reality, but we have no access to it. Neither is acceptable to the common sense philosopher, the first being a form of metaphysical anti-realism, the second a version of Cartesian MR.

But there is reason to believe that by focussing primarily on the senses of "seeing" found in the expressions "seeing that" and "seeing as", this theory of perception fails adequately to distinguish seeing from believing, the former being taken for a species of the latter.[15] This is to commit at least two further errors. First, it is to overlook the fact that, to continue with the example, one might well see a fork, in some sense of "see", without seeing *that* it is a fork, or seeing it *as* a fork. One might not know what a fork is; but as Dretske rightly points out, ignorance does not make us blind.[16] This ought to alert us to the fact that there is, as Dretske has argued, a more primitive "non-epistemic" form of seeing which does not involve the perceiver having any beliefs whatsoever.[17] Dretske's analysis of this form of seeing is that:

S sees$_n$ D = D is visually differentiated from its immediate environment by S.[18]

Awareness of this sense of "seeing" allows one to avoid a second mistake consequent upon the conflation of seeing and believing. Depending on one's theory of belief, the conflation of seeing and believing can lead to the denial of the obvious fact that animals perceive their environments, insofar as we say that they see, hear and smell predators, prey, mates and other aspects of their surroundings. This follows if one assumes what Ruth Barcan Marcus has called a language-centred theory of belief as found in Donald Davidson and others (Marcus, 1993, p. 235). Since on this popular view beliefs presuppose a language, and most are unwilling to attribute anything more than a proto-language to other animals,[19] it follows that non-human animals do not have beliefs. And if seeing is not distinguished from believing, one quickly arrives at the conclusion that animals do not perceive their environments. This is non-sense, for it is as obvious as anything can be that animals visually differentiate objects from the surrounding environment. This forces either a revision in the account of "belief"[20] or "concept"[21] on the one hand, or the recognition that there are other senses of "seeing". McDowell is not able to take any of these routes, although he does acknowledge the "discomfort" of his position (1994a, p. 65). But the best he can do to alleviate himself is to claim that human perception is significantly different from animal perception, in that animals do not require concepts in order to see, but humans do. Why this should be the case is left somewhat mysterious, and there seems to be no good empirical reason to think it true. I will return to this point below.

As a matter of fact, the common sense philosopher, and most natural scientists for that matter, takes perception to be attributable to all members of the animal kingdom,[22] recognising that seeing, even in humans, does not presuppose belief. Now if one adopts this non-epistemic sense of "seeing" as one's point of departure, then the task of a theory of perception changes dramatically. Rather than seeking to justify human perceptual beliefs, what the common sense philosopher and many scientists hope to explain via a theory of perception is how an organism copes with its environment, its "proper adjustments of oriented *activity*" with respect to its "resource requirements" (Turvey, Shaw, Reed and Mace, p. 241, 244).

All the above senses of "seeing" are legitimate in my view. But it is not unreasonable to assume that the successful completion of the common sense project, with the emphasis on the primitive form of seeing and its role in oriented activity, is a precondition for the successful understanding of the other forms of seeing. For if human perception is a form of animal perception (as it surely is) then it is reasonable to assume that understanding animal perception in general is a prerequisite for the understanding of human perception, since the latter is but a variation on a theme (whatever additional features or refinements it may display).[23] Since the antecedent of this conditional seems undeniable in a post-Darwinian climate (more on this in below), I feel free to advert to studies carried out on both humans and other animals in our subsequent discussion. In any case, it is the primitive form of "seeing" that will be the focus of our attention as our argument unfolds.

A transcendental argument for common sense in the domain of sense perception

With these remarks in mind we can return to our main concern. What can be said in favour of the common sense alternative to the neo-Kantian two-factor theory of perception, apart from the fact that it cannot be ruled out a priori? In this Section, I want to present and defend the following argument:

(1) Without a pre-structured world there is no visual perception.[24]
(2) But visual perceptions are commonplace.
(3) There is a pre-structured world.

I will assume that no one would care to challenge the second premise, so I will concentrate on defending the first. The first premise follows from two essential points: (a) the necessity of a structured optic array for vision, and (b) the source of the necessary structure. The evidence in favour of (a) comes from the natural sciences, so it will be necessary to summarise briefly some experimental results which show that stimulation of the retina by light is not sufficient for vision.

The experimental results that concern us first came to light in the early 1950s, and they have become commonplaces in cognitive psychology and neurophysiology. Metzger (1953) found that if a subject is presented with an illuminated field which is homogeneous in every respect and in all directions (a field known as a "Ganzfeld"), the light cannot be focused and no retinal image can be formed. In such cases subjects report that they see nothing, despite the fact that the eye is stimulated by the incoming light.[25] Gibson makes the point as follows:

> Consider an observer with an eye at a point in a fog-filled medium. The receptors in the retina would be stimulated, and there would consequently be impulses in the fibres of the optic nerve. But the light entering the pupil of the eye would not be different in different directions; it would be unfocusable, and no image could be formed on the retina. There could be no retinal image because the light on the retina would be just as homogenous as the...light outside the eye. The possessor of the eye could not *fix* it on anything, and the eye would drift aimlessly. He could not look from one item to another, for no items would be present. If he turned the eye, the experience would be just what it was before.... Nothing he could do would make any difference in what he could experience, with this single exception: if he closed the eye, an experience that he might call brightness would give way to one he might call darkness. He could distinguish between stimulation of his photoreceptors and nonstimulation of them. But as far as *perceiving* goes, *his eye would be just as blind when the light entered it as it would be when light did not.*
>
> (Gibson, 1979, Chapter 4)

Gibson's point about blindness in a fog-filled medium is well taken; but in fact he has exaggerated the extent to which fibres in the optic nerve respond to homogeneous light. Since Kuffler's work in the 1950s, it has been a commonplace amongst those working on the physiology of vision that cells at various levels of the visual pathway do *not* respond to diffuse or homogeneous light (Kuffler, 1953). Hubel writes,

> The usual consequence of stimulating [the ganglion cells of the retina] with a large spot of light or, in the extreme, of bathing the retina with diffuse light, is that the cell's firing is neither speeded up nor slowed down – in short, nothing results.
>
> (Hubel, p. 28)

The same is the case for cells in the visual cortex. Indeed, what Hubel and Weisel discovered, along with countless other researchers,[26] is that cells along the visual pathway are highly selective in terms of the light to which they respond. Cells in the retina, lateral geniculate bodies, and visual cortex respond to various aspects found in the *pattern* of light reaching the retina. These physiological results fit nicely with Metzger's experiments on the Ganzfeld. What is lacking in a Ganzfeld is precisely what cells in the visual pathway require, namely differences in the pattern or structure of the light reaching the retina.[27]

The conclusion drawn from these (at the time) unexpected experimental results is that stimulation by light is a necessary but not sufficient condition for vision. Only some types of light, that is, structured light, permits visual perceptions. In order to cope with this result it became necessary to differentiate between what some have called *radiant* light and *ambient* light, and their correlates, *stimulus* and *stimulus information* (The terms used for these distinctions are of no particular importance; the distinctions themselves are what matter).

The importance of structured light for vision can also be established by experiments carried out on subjects whose visual systems have been deprived of exposure to structured light. Hubel and Weisel found significant and irreparable disruption to cell physiology and histology in young animals whose eyes had been sutured shut before the visual system was fully developed. They were also able to establish that the disruption was not due simply to light deprivation.[28] The results of these experiments show not only that visual systems respond only to structured light, but also that visual systems require structured light if they are to develop properly at the cellular level. Similar results were found by Blakemore (1974, 1978), Rauschecker and Singer (1981) and Mitchell (1988).

With this background in mind a supporting argument for our first premise can be formulated with relative ease. At the risk of labouring the point, the implications of the experimental results can be spelled out as follows. As established above, visual systems (at least in vertebrates) do not respond to brute stimulus; such systems only respond to *differences* in the optic array, that is, to the stimulus information. So we can assert

(4) Without a structured optic array, there is no visual perception.

The next step in the argument concerns (b), the *source* of this structure. Now I assume that

(5) Since recognition of the distinction between unstructured radiant light and structured ambient light has been forced upon us by the experimental evidence, we cannot merely accept the presence of structure without further explanation (as the weak Kantian might wish). It is natural to ask *why* light is structured in some cases and not in others.

So how does the optic array get structured? The strong Kantian maintains, of course, that in perception the visual system is presented with an "indiscriminate, that is, unfeatured, porridge" out of which the *perceiver* "constructs" a world. But,

(6) The visual system of the perceiver *is not* the source of the structure in the optic array.

If the perceiver were the source of the structure, we would not expect visual impotence in the Ganzfeld, which is what we find. For if perceivers contained structuring principles within themselves, as the strong Kantian maintains, unstructured light ought to pose no difficulties for visual perception since the perceiver makes up for this deficiency by providing the structure itself. But the experimental results noted above show that this cannot be done. If the light entering the eye is not *already* structured, the observer remains effectively blind. Now,

(7) If the perceiver is not the source of the structure, then that source is external to the perceiver.

I take this to be self-evident. Furthermore, two-factor theorists will not balk at the assertion that

(8) The structure is not imposed on the optic array by God, a Cartesian demon, or any other third party.

There is simply no reason to take these suggestions seriously, and in any case they would involve the rejection of the *two*-factor approach. So by process of elimination we are left asserting that

(9) An external, *pre-structured* world is the source of the structure found in optic arrays.[29]

Finally, given (4) and (9), we can assert

(10) Without a pre-structured world there is no visual perception (QED).

Given that few would care to deny that visual perceptions are commonplace, and the assumption that some explanation is required for the fact that light is structured in some cases but not in others, I conclude that there is a featured, pre-structured world which is received as featured in perception.

Neo-Kantian responses

Let me address immediately a concern that is likely to have occurred to many. Some will suspect that this argument simply begs the question against the neo-Kantian. Some, for example, might ask whether the neo-Kantian two-factor theory is the sort of theory that could, even in principle, be open to empirical refutation. It could be suggested, implausibly in my view, that what the neo-Kantians offer is really a kind of conceptual analysis of our notion of perception, not an empirical hypothesis concerning the nature of things. If this is the case, then no amount of empirical evidence gathered from the natural sciences could possibly upset it.

But if we are to take this response seriously, and assume that the two-factor theory is simply an analysis of the notion of perception, or worse, an account of perception tailored to suit the requirements of a certain philosophically motivated agenda, then so much the worse for the neo-Kantian two-factor theory of perception. It can be safely ignored by those interested in the independent scientific investigation of perception. However, some might further the following subtler version of the same complaint, for one could argue as follows:[30]

> The Kantian assumes that the categories of the understanding are imposed upon the unstructured and unfeatured stimulus impinging upon our sensory organs. Furthermore, we can also attempt to approach the study of the mind empirically. But in such a study we necessarily apply the mind's categories to itself, and so we cannot assume that such a study give us access to some external, mind-independent reality. To assume that it does is to beg the question against the Kantian. But this is what you do in the argument you have just forwarded.

In response to this objection, let me note first that if it were to succeed it would place the neo-Kantian in a particularly awkward position, for again it implies that this two-factor theory of perception is not open to empirical refutation, and so its credibility as a contribution to the scientific study of perception is damaged. But in fact my argument does not beg the question against the neo-Kantian by assuming that empirical studies give us access to mind-independent reality. All my argument assumes is what any neo-Kantian should readily admit, namely that perception and empirical studies give us access to what they would call the phenomenal world of sense experience. The point of my argument is precisely that empirical studies have shown the *phenomenal* world not to be in line with Kantian expectations. If our perceptual experiences have the content they do in virtue of the mind's imposition of the categories of the understanding, then, since the mind takes its categories with it wherever it goes, the phenomenal world should never present us with unstructured, unfeatured, contentless visual experiences. But, on occasion, it does just that. And as I explain above, this shows that the mind is *not* the source of the features found in perception.

There is another possible neo-Kantian response to my transcendental argument that needs to be considered. If the argument of the previous section is sound, then neo-Kantian two-factor theorists like McDowell will have to accept that pre-structured light entering the eye is necessary for visual perception, and that this fact counts very much in favour or OR. But, the neo-Kantian could argue, it is still an open question whether the structure of ambient light is *sufficient* for visual perception. For all the argument of the previous section has shown, it is still possible that this structure is too jumbled or confused to allow for perception *without* the imposition of a conceptual component by the perceiver. It is here that projectivists might see their chance.

So is more "structuring" than is provided by the ambient optic array necessary for visual experience? The following considerations suggest that the structure found in the optic array is sufficient to the purpose. No doubt neural processing of the information contained in the optic array is required as the purely physical characteristics of the patterns in the optic array are translated into neural states. But we have every reason to believe that this processing is entirely neuro-physiological, and occurring entirely at the "sub-personal level". Furthermore, I will suggest that the process of "translation" is precisely that, one of converting information from one form to another – not a process of augmentation or enrichment.

In what follows I rely on two key assumptions. First, I assume that OR has been established. More precisely, I assume there is a pre-structured world existing independently of our experience of it, and that this structure is ontologically privileged since it is pre-linguistic and pre-conceptual. Second, I assume that for vision to aid oriented activity within this pre-structured world the content of an organism's visual perceptions must be (roughly) structurally identical to that of the external world. If this rough structural identity is not assumed it becomes very difficult to explain how perception allows an organism to cope with its environment. With these two assumptions in place we can then pose the following question: How does the required structural identity of visual perceptions and extra-linguistic reality arise? I suggest that the common sense theory of perception affords a credible answer to this question, whereas the neo-Kantian perspectives do not.

Let us consider the common sense option first. In short, the common sense philosopher maintains that the required structural identity arises because what we see *just is* the external, extra-linguistic, mind-independent world or environment as it is in itself. The visual world and the external world are one and the same, and so structural isomorphism is guaranteed from the outset. The simplicity of this view commends itself, but there are other considerations in its favour, namely the argument presented and defended at length in Chapter 2. If we assume, as I think we must, that organisms and their perceptual systems, including human perceptual systems, have evolved within a pre-existing and pre-structured environment in roughly the manner described by the synthetic theory of evolution by natural selection, then it is difficult to avoid the belief that our perceptual systems have evolved to their current state because they allow organisms to *track* the structure of this environment. If organisms were not able to keep in touch with the surrounding environment *as it is in itself* their biological viability would be seriously compromised. The idea that perceptual systems are "built" with a specific environment in mind also helps to mitigate the challenge of radical scepticism with respect to the reliability of sense experience. If sense perception were not generally reliable, we would not be here (or at least not in this form).[31]

Now in such a context a creative, constructivist or projectivist visual system, that is, a system which projects structures not already there, makes little sense. The only structure that is biologically relevant is that found in the external world itself, for this is where organisms live and make their way, not in a world of their own devising. So rather than there being evolutionary pressure to develop projectivist perceptual systems, precisely the reverse appears to be the case. Selective pressures would certainly encourage the development of more *discriminating* visual systems, not all aspects of the environment being of equal interest in terms of the organism's resource requirements; but there is little incentive to suggest that these pressures would encourage a truly creative visual system. So rather than having to supplement the information contained in the optic array with additional structure, it makes more sense to hold that perceivers actually come to discriminate and differentiate between aspects of what is already there, "to respond to variables of physical stimulation not previously responded to" (Gibson and Gibson 1982, p. 320). In this context, increased capacity for differentiation, not enrichment, is the order of the day.

I would submit that the plausibility of this common sense account stands in marked contrast to that of the projectivist. The projectivist must maintain that the required structural identity between the visual and extra-linguistic worlds arises not because perceptual systems pick up or track what is there to be seen (because this is what is excluded ex hypothesi) but because the visual system's structuring principles generate representations which are structurally identical to that of the pre-existing but untracked structure of the external world. In order to avoid what would otherwise be a fantastic coincidence, let us assume, in keeping with our Darwinian framework, that natural selection favours those organisms whose perceptual systems generate visual perceptions which happen to correspond structurally more closely to that of the environment itself. In any event, the picture on offer is of visual systems imposing an order on jumbled or confused (but somewhat structured) stimulus, thereby creating a visual world the structure of which nonetheless answers to the structure of the environment.

I would suggest that this answer suffers from more than a whiff of implausibility. For once OR has been granted, developing a perceptual system which tracks the pre-existing structure of the environment will be "the best move in design space".[32] But the following consideration also counts against projectivism. We might ask if such creative visual systems can properly be said to count as projective systems at all. For if the essence of Kant's Copernican Turn is that the phenomenal world is made to conform to the structures of our minds rather than the reverse, then such systems are decidedly *not* Kantian. For on the present hypothesis, human beings and other animals have the visual perceptions they do because our visual systems have evolved in accordance with the constraints supplied by the physical structure of an independent, extra-linguistic reality. But this effectively reverses the Copernican Turn. Since extra-linguistic reality *determines* which structures will be projected, thereby determining which objects will be seen, very little room for meaningful "creativity" is left to the mind. In such circumstances the distinction between projecting and tracking has been lost, with projecting collapsing into a form of tracking.

If projection makes little sense in this context, what of the alleged necessity of concepts in visual perception? As pointed out above, it is reasonable to assume that human perception is a form of animal perception, whatever variations it might display. Furthermore, there is every reason to insist that non-human animals do in some meaningful sense perceive aspects of their environment, and that they share roughly our sorts of perceptual experiences. (The visual worlds of non-human vertebrates, although different in some important respects, must be roughly identical in structure to our own given that their oriented activities are carried out in the same extra-linguistic reality as our own.) Against this background it seems that only a philosopher's prejudice could lead one to maintain that perception requires the employment of concepts if only because the perceptual capacities of non-human vertebrates vastly outstrip any conceptual capacity one might be willing to attribute to them.

The point to stress here is that no substantive *conceptual* processing in McDowell's demanding sense need take place for perception to occur in the rest of the animal kingdom. But is there any reason to think that human perceptual systems are radically different from those of non-human animals in this regard, as McDowell suggests (1994a, p. 65)? Certainly evolutionary biology gives us no reason to expect such a radical difference.[33] Moreover, this line of thought is independently supported by Warrington and Taylor's work in clinical neurology. They found that human subjects with serious language impairment as a result of left parietal lesions could nonetheless convey that they correctly perceived an object's shape even though they could not name the viewed object or state its purpose or semantics (1973). Marr concludes on the basis of this evidence that human beings can pick up or notice objects "even when the object [is] not recognized in the conventional sense of understanding its use and purpose" (1996, p. 35). This strongly suggests that concepts are not required for visual perception in humans either.

These considerations speak in favour of the common sense approach to perception, while sitting very uncomfortably with the neo-Kantian two-factor theories. If there is a pre-structured world, a world in which we have evolved and in which we must make our way, surely it is this ontologically privileged structure which is ultimately responsible for both our visual systems and our visual perceptions. Indeed, once OR has been granted one is almost inevitably drawn to a form of non-projective perception, if only because we ought not to multiply structuring principles without necessity. If philosophers are to put any store in the findings of the life sciences then common sense metaphysical realism must be given the laurel at the expense of neo-Kantian constructivisms.

Concluding remarks

By way of conclusion I would like to ward off a predictable response to the position defended here. Some might wearily remark that this chapter is simply another vain attempt to resuscitate a thoroughly discredited myth, the Myth of the Given. But this would be seriously to misunderstand my purpose. As is evident from my account of the proper business of philosopher, an account developed in Chapter 1, I do not share the epistemological concerns that give rise to the anxieties the Myth of the Given evidently arouses in McDowell and others. This is best seen by consideration of McDowell's project. He wishes to acknowledge an external constraint on our thinking while avoiding the Myth of the Given. But why should we be concerned to avoid the Myth of the Given? Because, says McDowell, we will not be able to credit experience with a *rational* bearing on empirical thinking if that experience is not already in some sense conceptual – otherwise it will offer "at best exculpations where what we need is justifications" (1994a, p. 46). McDowell envisages the neo-Kantian position as the only solution to the fruitless oscillation between a coherentism that cannot acknowledge an external constraint on our thinking, and a foundationalism that provides only exculpations.

The point to notice here is that there is nothing wrong with the notion of the Given per se. McDowell's complaint is that the notion of the Given does not suit the needs of philosophers with an agenda like his. But I am happy to accept mere exculpations from visual perceptions and forego justifications because I am not playing the same philosophical game as McDowell, a game that has animated philosophy since the days of Descartes. Descartes' epistemological turn, taken with the intention of addressing radical scepticism, put philosophy on a course that ends in something like the neo-Kantian position. But as I sought to show in Chapters 1 and 4, the concern with scepticism is misplaced. Consequently the common sense philosopher is not looking for a way off the foundationalist/coherentist merry-go-round. The common sense philosopher never got on it.

6
Semantic Anti-Realism and the Dummettian Reductio

Introduction

In the previous chapter I had occasion to deal with a challenge to common sense metaphysical realism from a version of neo-Kantian constructivism. I now want to examine another threat to common sense stemming from another quarter, in this case the philosophy of language. I want to discuss an argument put forward by Michael Dummett, an argument which, if sound, would have quite radical implications. Dummett's manifestation argument takes the form of a reductio and has for a striking conclusion the denial of the principle of bivalence, that is, the claim that each and every well-formed statement is either true or false.

In order to see that the blanket rejection of the principle of bivalence is radically revisionary, consider the common sense position. Common sense realism would have it that statements are true or false in virtue of the way the world is. A statement is true if what it maintains about the world is mirrored or matched by states of affairs in the world, otherwise it is false. What is more, a statement is either true or false even when we do not know its truth-value and perhaps could never know it. Another way to put this is to say that a statement's truth-value is independent of our ability to tell whether the statement is true or false. The rationale behind these intuitions is the belief that the world is in some particular state or another, a state that has nothing to do with us, and a sentence is true or false in virtue of what those states happen to be. An example will help. Consider the hypothesis that the mass extinctions of the late Ordovician were caused by the loss of shallow water habitat area. Consider also the very distinct possibility that, given the time that has elapsed since the events in question (around 450 million years), there is no clear-cut evidence still available that allows palaeontologists and geologists to decide in favour of this kill mechanism as opposed to other possibilities, global cooling, say, or oceanic anoxia. The question is "undecidable" because conclusive proof is simply not available for any of these theories. Consider, finally, a geologist willing to stick his neck out and say that the mass extinctions in question were caused by the loss of the necessary habitat area. Now the common sense realist, when brought up to date on the niceties of the debate, would say that *something* caused the mass extinctions, but the geologist's categorical claim is a bit rash since we cannot be sure what that cause was. The geologist's claim might be a good working hypothesis, but it is no more than that. Nonetheless, common sense would not even begin to doubt that the hypothesis does at least have a truth-value. That is to say, common sense would not doubt that the geologist's hypothesis is either true or false because we are wont to assume that the world is in one and only one definite configuration at any one time, and the relevant configuration was such that either the extinctions were caused by the loss of the necessary habitat or they were not, and this definite config-uration is that in virtue of which the hypothesis is true or false. What is more, this remains the case despite the fact that no one will ever be in a position to know what the truth-value of the hypothesis actually is.

Now our geologist is not likely to draw much comfort from the common sense concession. "Of course my hypothesis is true or false!", he will say indignantly. "At issue is whether it is true, as I maintain, or whether it is false, as some of my colleagues would have it." But Dummett would argue that the common sense philosopher has already conceded too much. For if the manifestation argument is sound, a state-ment gets a truth-value only when we are in a position to tell that it is true or false. Undecidable statements, such as our geologist's hypothesis, are neither true nor false, but indeterminate. According to Dummett, it is not the case that the extinctions were caused by a loss of shallow water habitat area but nor is it the case that it is not the case that the extinctions were caused by the loss of shallow water habitat area. Contrary to common sense, says Dummett, the principle of bivalence does not apply to undecidable statements. But if Dummett is right, then large sections of the remote past are indeterminate – in no particular state at all. But since being a determinate something or other has been a criterion of existence since at least the time of Aristotle, Dummett's claim is tantamount to denying the reality of the past, as he all too readily admits. It is the reasoning behind his striking claims that will be the focus of our attention in this chapter.

Naturalism and mentalism in semantics

A brief digression into related matters in the philosophy of language is necessary before the Dummettian reductio or manifestation argument can be intelligibly discussed. In particular, a few words concerning the debate between what may be called "naturalists" and "mentalists" in semantics are necessary in order to present the context out of which the manifestation argument emerges.

In the twentieth-century analytic philosophy of language, there seems to have been widespread agreement on certain fundamental points about language, the process of language acquisition and the nature of meaning. Following the lead of thinkers as diverse in character as Wittgenstein and Dewey, many philosophers of language have been attracted to what Quine (1968) refers to as "naturalism" about language. This naturalism is favoured over past theories of meaning that are decidedly "mentalistic". The point at issue in this debate between naturalism and mentalism with respect to the nature of meaning turns on the question of whether an essentially private language is possible. The details of this debate need not concern us here as the parties to our particular dispute are all in agreement concerning the impossibility of such a language. However, it is important to recognise why semantic realists and anti-realists are in concert on this question because it is this agreement which provides the common conceptual framework in which the manifestation argument arises.

The principle that both semantic realists and anti-realists can accept, which is also the motivation behind the rejection of the possibility of an essentially private language, is clearly expressed in the opening paragraphs of Quine's essay "Ontological Relativity". There he quotes the words of Dewey: "Meaning... is not a psychic existence; it is primarily a property of behaviour" (1968, p. 27). Quine accepts this thesis as following from seemingly undeniable observations concerning the conditions governing the possible communication of meanings from one language user to another. The observations and reflections lead him to assert that "Language is a social art which we all acquire on the evidence solely of other people's behaviour under publicly recognisable circumstances" (ibid., p. 26). He goes on, "What the naturalist insists on is that, even in complex and obscure parts of language learning, the learner has no data to work with but the overt behaviour of other speakers" (ibid., p. 28).

The principal conclusion drawn from the recognition of the importance of overt behaviour to communication is that meanings must be "manifestible" in the overt linguistic and behavioural practices of language users. All meanings are gleaned from overt, public behaviour that embodies those meanings. This is the thinking behind the attack on the "pernicious" mentalistic schools of thought which situated meanings in the hidden recesses of each individual mind, or identified them with unobservable states of the soul. This mentalistic school allowed for the possibility that some aspect of meaning might not be amenable to manifestation in public behaviour and yet retain its status as a meaning. Such thinking opens the door to the theoretical possibility of an essentially private language, that is, a language that is not communicable to other members of one's community. This possibility is unequivocally rejected by modern semantic theorists who have unreservedly accepted the naturalist approach to semantics. This common attitude displayed by both semantic realists and anti-realists alike has been dubbed "semantic externalism", namely, the view that "no item which is epistemically private to the speaker – which no one other than he can know the nature of – can be essential to the meaning of any symbol, word or phrase he uses" (Appiah, 1986, p. 74).

Now the importance of semantic externalism, for the purposes of our debate, is that it places constraints on one's theory of what it is to understand a sentence, and additionally, what counts as manifestation of a speaker's grasp of a sentence. It is here that the debate between the semantic realist and anti-realist begins.

The manifestation argument

According to traditional realist semantics, to understand a sentence is to understand its truth conditions, that is, to understand what must be the case in order for the sentence to be true. The semantic anti-realist also thinks that knowledge of truth conditions is central to one's understanding of a sentence, but with an important difference. The truth conditions that one knows when one understands a sentence must be ones whose obtaining one is capable of recognising, and whose obtaining justifies the assertion of the sentence in question. In other words, for the semantic anti-realist, not just any truth conditions are acceptable; in particular, no truth conditions of a given sentence that are possibly verification-transcendent will be accepted in the account of the meaning of the sentence in question. The truth conditions of a given sentence that are acceptable by anti-realist standards are those that are epistemically constrained, ones that speakers are able to recognise as obtaining when they do obtain.

This difference in policy with respect to truth conditions has radical implications. By accepting possibly verification-transcendent truth conditions in his or her semantics, the realist remains at home with the intuitions of the metaphysical realist and common sense. Like the metaphysical realist, the semantic realist thinks that the mind-independent world is that in virtue of which a sentence has truth conditions, is that in virtue of which a sentence is true or false. Hence, it is a possible and indeed frequent occurrence that a sentence is true (or false) without our ever being able to know it to be true (or false). A sentence's truth conditions on this line of thinking are independent of the possibility of our knowing whether those conditions actually obtain. The semantic anti-realist by contrast says that that in virtue of which a sentence is true (or false) is a truth condition that we can recognise as obtaining. In other words, a sentence gets truth conditions when it is possible (at least in principle) to obtain a warrant to assert (or deny) it. A consequence of this position is that no sentence can be true or false if we do not have some sort of evidence available to hand (or reasonably available) that justifies the assertion (or denial) of the sentence. This is the thinking behind the rejection of the principle of bivalence and the law of excluded middle which characterises the Intuitionist logic associated with semantic anti-realists like Dummett.

The important matter at hand, however, is to understand the connection between the rejection of bivalence, the rejection of possibly verification-transcendent truth conditions and semantic externalism, for it is here that we find the heart of the manifestation argument. Why do semantic anti-realists reject verification-transcendent truth conditions? The thinking stems from reflections on the nature of language acquisition and the communication of meanings from one language user to another. What the semantic anti-realist is contending is that when we learn a sentence and come to understand what it means, we do not learn just any truth conditions; what we learn is when it is appropriate to assert or dissent from that sentence. For example, when we come to understand the sentence "Some apples are red", we do not learn what must be the case in order for this sentence to be true. What we learn is to recognise under what conditions one could assert this sentence, say, for example, some experience of red apples. An experience of red apples (or perhaps the testimony of a reliable witness) is the requisite condition for the assertion of the sentence "Some apples are red". What is more, one *manifests* one's grasp of the sentence by asserting or denying it as the circumstances dictate.

This is all very well, one might say, but it is unclear how this will justify the rejection of possibly verification-transcendent truth conditions in semantic theory. The crux of the matter is that semantic anti-realists claim that the semantic realist cannot manifest his grasp of sentences for which there is no warrant in some overt behaviour. The semantic realist claims that he understands sentences not currently known to be decidable by grasping their verification-transcendent truth conditions. But, says the anti-realist, he has no way of conveying this grasp in overt behaviour, which, as a naturalist, the realist must admit is necessary if the sentence is to have any meaning. Hence, it is not just that learning the meaning of a sentence means learning its epistemically constrained truth condition and not its verification-transcendent ones (the former being manifestible in observable behaviour when one asserts or denies a sentence), but that verification-transcendent truth conditions could never be learned at all because the grasp of such truth conditions is not manifestible in any overt behaviour of those from whom we learn our language. Consequently, if we agree that sentences not currently known to be decidable are understood by speakers of the language, the semantic realist seems forced to admit that verification-transcendent truth conditions are not those in virtue of which one understands such sentences. If the realist is forced to make this admission, he has for all intents and purposes abandoned semantic realism. Dummett expresses these key points as follows:

> Whenever the conditions for the truth of a sentence is one that we have no way of bringing ourselves to recognise as obtaining whenever it obtains, it seems plain that there is no content to an ascription of an implicit knowledge of what that condition is, since there is no practical ability by means of which such knowledge may be manifested.
>
> (Appiah, p. 74)

The denial of any "implicit" knowledge on the grounds that it is not manifestible is an application of semantic externalism, which denies that meanings can exist that defy manifestation in some overt behaviour. Hence, the semantic anti-realist accuses the semantic realist of being mistaken if the latter thinks that he understands sentences not currently known to be decidable by virtue of grasping their verification-transcendent truth conditions. The whole notion of truth as a possibly verification-transcendent property of sentences, which has been assumed by realists of all stripes, is therefore suspicious and must be rejected. But if this is accepted, it is then but a short step to the denial of the reality of a mind-independent past. As Dummett says, "this means there is no *one* past history of the world: every possible history compatible with what is now the case stands on an equal footing" (1992, p. 367). But this is *not* an epistemological claim. On Dummett's lips these words are used to say that the past itself is indeterminate and only becomes determinate when our recognitional capacities permit.

Tennant has presented this argument very clearly in his book *Anti-Realism and Logic*. There he shows that three separate commitments semantic realists are bound to accept are inconsistent. These commitments are referred to as "Manifestation", the claim that the meaning of a sentence "should be fully manifestible" in observable exercises of recognitional capacities concerning it; "Realism", the adherence to the principle of bivalence; and "Fact", the claim that currently undecidable sentences are nevertheless understood by competent speakers of the language. It is worth quoting an extended passage of Tennant:

> To Dummett belongs the credit for showing that Manifestation plus Realism plus Fact is inconsistent. In briefest outline, his argument is as follows: Accept Fact, so take any sentence S that is undecidable but understood by speaker X. That is, suppose that X grasps the meaning of S, but possesses no means by which he can recognise either that S is true or that S is false. By Realism, either the condition for the truth of S obtains, or the condition for its falsity obtains. If the former, X nevertheless, *ex hypothesi*, cannot show that he recognises the fact; if the latter, likewise. But now this contradicts Manifestation, which requires that X should be able to display his grasp of the meaning of the sentence X [sic] by the exercise of a recognitional capacity concerning it.
>
> (Tennant, 1987, p. 112)

Such then is the argument from manifestation which semantic anti-realists forward against the semantic realist. Such is the challenge to the coherence of all forms of realism, metaphysical, scientific and semantic, which rely on a verification-transcendent notion of truth. It should be noted that the force of the argument as presented by Tennant, if sound, would necessitate the dropping of any one of the three commitments. There is no particular reason why the commitment to the principle of bivalence in particular need be dropped. But given the realist's acceptance of "Fact", the pressure of the reductio is at least initially on the principle of bivalence. Let us now turn our attention to how the common sense philosopher might respond.

A common sense response

There are a number of ways in which a common sense philosopher might respond to the manifestation argument. But to begin with it is important to note that Dummett's semantic anti-realist challenge is pressing for the same kind of conclusions that we encountered in the case of Kantian constructivism. Ultimately, the claim in both cases is that the world does not exist independently of our representations of it, but is the way it is at least in part because of our activities. That this claim is radically at odds with common sense has already been illustrated. It is also important to remind ourselves that such a belief makes little sense when viewed through the lens of biology. Any animal that operated on the principle that the external world is constrained by his or her recognitional capacities would come to grief when navigating the treacherous seas of the predator/prey relationship. What makes sense from a biological view is an animal that errs on the side of caution. Rather than working on the principle, "If I can't see it, it's not there", it makes more sense for an animal to assume that absence of evidence is not evidence of absence (as noted in the better-safe-than-sorry argument). Consequently, we can safely say that the burden of proof in this case lies with Dummett and not with common sense.

But it is also important to note that, as was the case with neo-Kantian constructivism, Dummett's manifestation argument does not get a clean bill of health from the sciences. The driving force in research in linguistics since the mid 1960s has been Chomsky's Universal Grammar hypothesis, namely, the theory that human beings have a cognitive specialisation or module for learning language. Although this theory has gone through many developments and modifications since the publication of Chomsky's *Aspects of the Theory of Syntax* (1965), it still retains its commitment to *Mentalism* – the view that language is instantiated in the minds and brains of language users – and *Nativism* – the view that language learning and acquisition (while obviously triggered by exposure to one's environment, in particular, the linguistic behaviour of other language users) is made possible by a Language Acquisition Device, that is, an innate program for constructing a grammar on the basis of primary linguistic data. The point for present purposes is that the commitment to semantic externalism, a pre-condition of the manifestation argument getting off the ground, is not forced by the best available science. Consequently, one common sense response to the manifestation argument is simply to dismiss it since there is as yet no case to answer. Until linguists have reached a consensus in favour of semantic externalism, there is no need to take the basic assumptions of the reductio seriously.

But there is little to learn from such a dismissive attitude, although it is adequate in principle. In the hope that one can often learn from the interesting mistakes of philosophers, let us adopt, for the sake of argument, the shared assumptions and framework of the semantic realists and anti-realists and try to determine if the radical conclusions do indeed follow from these provisionally accepted premises. This is the approach I adopt in this chapter. What I intend to show is that the semantic anti-realist's conclusions in fact do not follow and that semantic realists can safely ignore Dummett's manifestation argument without having to wait for the outcome of the debate in linguistics. The reason for this conclusion is that the Dummettian reductio does *not* succeed in catching the realist in a commitment to an inconsistent triad of propositions. The appearance to the contrary is the result of semantic anti-realists illegitimately conflating the accepted challenge to square our conceptual equipment with recognised modes of language acquisition and manifestation, with Dummett's challenge to semantic realists as embodied in the manifestation argument. But Dummett's challenge, in whatever form it may be given, goes beyond that imposed by a commitment to semantic externalism by including the more exacting demand that one's understanding of a sentence be manifestable "as the exercise of a capacity to recognise whether the truth-condition of that sentence obtains".[1] Dummett's reductio is only as pressing as the need to accept this additional demand.

But there is no need for the realist to accept this additional demand. First, the demand is itself unworkable even for semantic anti-realists, for no notion of "recognition" has been formulated, nor is one in the offing, which renders Dummett's additional demand plausible for all areas of discourse while remaining true to anti-realist principles. Clearly, if no such notion is available, then no version of the manifestation argument can be taken to establish anything. What is more, I will show that semantic realism would not be threatened by any version of the manifestation argument *even if such a notion were to be formulated*. Semantic realists would be under no obligation to adopt this missing notion of recognition as a key element of their semantic theory since such a move cannot be forced by the commitment to semantic externalism. Let us consider these points in turn.

The missing notion of recognition

Without further ado, let us turn our attention to the infirmities of the manifestation argument's leading assumption, starting with the difficulties surrounding the notion of recognition. As Haldane has rightly noted in his sympathetic account of semantic anti-realism, the notion of recognition is "problematic", containing "pitfalls into which even the wary may unwittingly stumble" (Haldane, 1993, p. 25). The existence of these pitfalls should come as no surprise to anyone, since "recognition" now does duty for "verification".[2] Indeed, each formulation of Ayer's verification principle is more or less obviously connected to a corresponding notion of recognition. While the history of the verificationist's calamities is well documented, the present issue is whether the corresponding notions of recognition do any better.

The pitfalls surrounding the notion of recognition can reasonably be styled, the Scylla and Charybdis of semantic anti-realism. Since the anti-realist proposes to deny a truth-value to statements that cannot be given a warrant, interesting results will be produced only if the standard of warrant is kept high. So the first temptation is to impose high standards on the notion of recognition, standards analogous to Ayer's notion of conclusive verification here and now. It is not unusual to find "recognition" of p construed as the possession of a conclusive warrant for the assertion that p (Dummett, 1992, xxxviii). In such cases, recognition is taken to be an "all or nothing process" and "absolutely decisive" (Misak, 1995, p. 138). But while this notion of recognition arguably fits well with ordinary language use, it leads to what has been called the "severity objection". Appiah is right to insist that, while perhaps appropriate for the semantics of mathematical discourse, this notion is "hugely implausible and totally unmotivated" when applied to other areas (Appiah, 1986, p. 55).[3] There is simply no such thing as a conclusive warrant for empirical statements, let alone statements embedded in mature scientific theory, or statements about the remote past. Denying a truth-value to such statements on the grounds that they are not conclusively verified produces such intolerably counter-intuitive results that even those sympathetic to semantic anti-realism are soon searching for a more relaxed notion of recognition. It ought to be noted, however, that the search is no longer guided by purely semantic considerations since pre-existing metaphysical commitments have crept into the picture.

But if demanding a conclusive warrant is too sever a standard to place on the notion of recognition, the second temptation is to entertain more relaxed alternatives which lack the teeth to perform any interesting work. Ideally, the anti-realist wants a happy medium, a notion strong enough to produce results, but weak enough to avoid the severity objection. The problem is that this "Goldilocks" notion has not been easy to find. Two approaches have seemed most promising, each corresponding to a line taken by Ayer himself.

The first is to rely on counter-factual conditionals, and to grant a truth-value to a currently undecidable statement *p* if there is some possible dispensation in which one *could* have a conclusive warrant to assert *p*. This move corresponds to Ayer's notion of verification in principle. Possible formulation of this notion could be,

(a) *p* is recognisable in principle by A if A could identify a conclusive warrant for the assertion that *p* if presented with one;
(b) *p* is recognisable in principle by A if A would assert *p* if placed in epistemically ideal conditions;
(c) *p* is recognisable in principle by A if A would assert *p* if presented with all the evidence relevant to the truth or falsity of *p*.[4]

Despite the various nuances in these formulations, they all fall to two general considerations. The first, well known to verificationists, is that counter-factuals threaten to deprive semantic anti-realism of any bite whatsoever. One can imagine counter-factuals that involve the expansion of our cognitive capacities, by allowing one to live forever, travel in time, or develop entirely new perceptual systems and so on. Clearly, if such counter-factuals were permitted, very few statements could be deprived of a truth-value, and semantic anti-realism will have lost its teeth. So the anti-realist must insist that only certain counter-factuals are legitimate. But the trick, as yet unturned, is to provide a principle for distinguishing the legitimate from the illegitimate counter-factuals which begs no questions and relies on no more than the principle of semantic externalism. I have no suggestions on this score.

But the more serious problem with the notion of recognition in principle is that it will not satisfy the conditions laid down in the manifestation argument. All agree that competent language users do understand currently undecidable statements. And all agree that this understanding must be manifestable in some publicly accessible linguistic behaviour. Furthermore, Dummett states that a semantic theory is supposed to tell us what it is a speaker knows when he or she understands a sentence at the time he or she utters or encounters the sentence. If understanding is rightly construed as a kind of knowing, then one cannot have the understanding without the knowing. But if this is so, then it is no good telling us what speakers *will* know, or *would* know at some point in the future – if a language user understands a sentence now, then the corresponding knowledge must be currently manifestable in some overt linguistic behaviour (otherwise we revert to mentalism in semantics).[5] But in the counter-factual conditions sketched above, the language users are ex hypothesi unable to exercise their recognitional capacities at the time of understanding and manifest their understanding as anti-realist would have them do, despite the fact that the statements have been granted a truth-value (to avoid the severity objection, the idea was to grant a truth-value to statements as long as they are deemed recognisable in principle). So we are left with the following dilemma: Either language users do not understand statements recognisable in principle, which is admitted by no one; or they are understood, but that understanding is manifested in some manner which does not employ the exercise of recognitional capacities. Either way the result is not good for semantic anti-realists. Consequently, we must assume that these notions of recognition in principle will not do.[6]

If the notions of conclusive recognition and recognition in principle have been found wanting, another option is to develop a notion of "partial" recognition which makes use of only currently available evidence. This notion is the obvious analogy to Ayer's weak verification. Perhaps, one might say that A can partially recognise p if there is at least some evidence currently available that A accepts as counting in p's favour. In such cases, A could manifest his or her grasp of p since his or her recognitional capacities could be brought to bear on the available evidence. But ultimately this will not do either. Partial recognition re-opens the gap between truth and warranted assertibility, which must be kept firmly shut if semantic anti-realism is to fly. For if "partial" means anything it must mean "insufficient on its own to guarantee the truth of p", for if it could guarantee the truth of p it would be conclusive and not partial. Consequently, the notion of partial recognition must make room for the possibility that further evidence to be uncovered might count against the evidence currently available and not simply strengthen the original warrant. But defeasibility is intelligible only when one accepts that a warranted statement might not be true; but this is to re-open the gap between truth and warrant, which the semantic anti-realist cannot permit. Clearly, this notion of partial recognition will not serve either.

But there is one final set of notions concerning recognition due to Crispin Wright that needs to be considered. In the preceding paragraph, it was stated that the semantic anti-realist cannot allow for a gap between truth and warranted assertibility. This view is certainly favoured by some prominent anti-realists (e.g. Tennant, 1995b). But Wright's notion of superassertibility is offered as a conception of truth which is both acceptable to anti-realists and distinct from warranted assertibility. In addition, the notion of superassertibility supplies both a version of the notion of recognition in principle and a notion of partial recognition.

According to Wright, a statement is superassertible "if and only if it is, or can be, warranted and some warrant for it would survive arbitrarily extensive increments to or other forms of improvement to or information" (1992, p. 48). A simple warrant on the other hand need not survive improvements in our information. The distinction between warranted and superassertible statements is then one of defeasibility: Warrants are defeasible; superassertible statements are not. Now if superassertibility is identified with truth, then truth remains epistemically constrained, since superassertibility is defined in terms of warrants; but the extension of warranted statements is no longer identical to that of superassertible statements, so the distinction between warrant and truth has been established in a manner acceptable to (many) anti-realists.

With the notion of superassertibility in place, "partial" recognition can be redefined as the possession of a defeasible warrant, while "recognition in principle" is identified with superassertibility: p is recognisable in principle if it is superassertible. This version of "recognition in principle" does not fall to the arguments levelled at the other formulations of this notion discussed above. First, there is no appeal here to counterfactual conditionals concerning what we might come to recognise. If a statement is superassertible it is so *here and now*, despite the fact that we are not in a position to establish this conclusively. Second, there is no delay in the manifestation of one's grasp of superassertible statements because any warrant for p is a warrant for its superassertibility.[7] One can manifest one's grasp of a superassertible statement p by recognising that the present state of information warrants the assertion of p (even if that warrant proves to be defeasible).

Nevertheless, there is a serious challenge that must be met by anti-realists who wish to avail themselves of the notion of superassertibility. How is the distinction between defeasible warrants and indefeasible, superassertible statements to be maintained without appeal to the realist notion of truth that superassertibility was meant to replace? How does one explain why one warrant is defeasible while another is not without appealing to the way things are independent of our state of information? The realist has obvious answers to these questions. Some warrants are defeasible because there is a gap between warranted assertibility and truth, while some statements are superassertible because they correspond to ontologically independent states of affairs. No further investigations can overturn a superassertible statement *p* because investigations are not that in virtue of which *p* is true. The realist is owed an anti-realist response to this challenge since superassertibility looks to be parasitic upon the allegedly repudiated realist notion of truth.

I have now looked at the viability of a variety of notions of recognition: Conclusive recognition, which falls to the severity objection even by semantic anti-realist lights; recognition in principle, which fails the conditions laid down in the manifestation argument itself, or leads to the intractable problem of ruling on the legitimacy of counter-factuals; partial recognition, which is unable to keep the gap between truth and warrant firmly shut; and finally, we have seen that the anti-realist who wishes to use the notion of superassertibility suggested by Wright faces the challenge of establishing its independence from the realist notion of truth it was meant to replace. Now just as no acceptable version of the verification principle was ever formulated, no notion of recognition has been found that is both plausible for all areas of discourse and consistent with anti-realist principles. But until such a notion is available the manifestation argument cannot be taken to establish anything.[8]

The challenge of semantic externalism

The fact that no acceptable formulation of the notion of recognition has been found does not mean that one will never be developed. No doubt this fact is part of the explanation for why the search continues (at least in some quarters). I have tried to show that these obvious avenues are dead-ends. What I want to suggest now is that the search itself is misguided because there is no reason to believe that understanding cannot outstrip recognitional capacities. To establish this claim, I believe it is enough to show that the semantic realist's commitment to possibly verification-transcendent truth conditions is consistent with semantic externalism. All the realist must do is show that grasp of verification-transcendent truth conditions can be manifested in *some* overt linguistic behaviour. At issue is whether this challenge can be met. The answer, I think, is an unequivocal yes.

The first step in the defence of semantic realist is to accept something analogous to Quine's distinction between observation sentences and stimulus-analytic sentences.[9] The distinction need not be hard and fast. It is enough that these terms be allowed to mark extremes on a continuum. Observation sentences are those to which one can give assent under appropriate stimulus conditions (Quine's famous example being "It is raining") while stimulus-analytic sentences cannot be determined by appeals to empirical data. The point of the distinction is that one's grasp of different types of sentences will be manifested in different ways. If the sentence in question is an observation sentence, then it is to be expected that a language user will manifest his or her understanding of the sentence by assenting to (or dissenting from) it under the appropriate stimulus conditions. This use of assent and dissent to indicate one's grasp of a sentence will also be appropriate in the case of arithmetical sentences (the language user manifests his understanding by checking the calculation procedure offered in support of the statement) or in theoretical sentences in mathematics (the language user can check the proof offered in support of the given statement). However, if the sentence is stimulus-analytic, as are high-level theoretical sentences in the sciences or metaphysics, or observation sentences about a region of space–time beyond the limits of possible experience, then we must expect that one's grasp of these sentences will be manifested in some other fashion. The question is how. The obvious answer is that grasp of the meaning of such sentences will be manifested by the language user's identifying the relations that hold between such sentences and other sentences in the language. In other words, the realist must appeal to a form of moderate holism.

The realist who accepts this moderate holism will claim that he or she manifests his or her grasp of verification-transcendent truth conditions in part by his or her adherence to the rules of classical logic – in particular the introduction and elimination rules of "¬", the principle of bivalence and the law of excluded middle. But there is much more. Blackburn has offered the following list of abilities one can expect to find in those who understand a currently undecidable sentence:

> The ability to construct explanations dependent upon the truth or falsity of the putatively undecidable sentence, the ability to tell why attempts at verification are blocked, the ability to tell things of related sorts, even if not this one, the ability to work out what else would be so if the sentence were undetectably true, the ability to embed the sentences in complex contexts and so on.
>
> (Misak, 1995, p. 155)

Surely if a language user had at least some of these abilities it would be very hard to maintain that he or she did not understand the sentence in question. The ability to embed undecidable statements in a larger context is particularly significant since it leaves open the possibility that undecidable statements may be anchored in a context of decidable observation statements. For example, if the sentence in question were a highly theoretical statement in a mature, empirically adequate theory, it would be anchored in the empirical observations that give weight to the theory itself. By showing one's appreciation of the support the observations give to the theory, and by making predications concerning future observation sentences, one manifests one's grasp of the verification-transcendent truth conditions of the theoretical sentences in question.

If this is how the realist can deal with the twin tasks of satisfying the demands of semantic externalism while manifesting one's grasp of verification-transcendent truth conditions, then all that remains is to ask whether there is any principled objection to the reliance on moderate holism.

Moderate holism and the logical constants

Semantic anti-realists are in a tricky position when it comes to blocking the realist's reliance on moderate holism because, as Tennant and Dummett both admit, they are required to make use of holist manoeuvres themselves.[10] This significant concession aside, Tennant does try to restrict the use of holism to the explication of the meaning of "extra-logical primitives", while insisting the one remain a molecularist with respect to the logical constants. Since the debate between the semantic realist and anti-realist focuses primarily on the proper interpretation of the logical constants (in particular on the correct introduction and elimination rules of "¬") and not on extra-logical terms, the dispute remains alive. Consequently, the semantic realist who wishes to use holist principles to escape the manifestation argument must argue that holist principles can legitimately be employed to explain the meaning, not just of extra-logical primitives, but of the logical constants as well. So why does Tennant feel that the use of holist principles must be restricted to extra-logical terms? And are his reasons compelling? To answer these reasons we need to consider how logical constants get their meaning.

It is accepted by semantic realists and anti-realists alike that, although precise meanings cannot be assigned to all terms in a language (especially natural languages), precise meanings can be assigned to the logical constants. And again there is cross-party agreement that the meanings of the logical constants are determined by their introduction and elimination rules. But having said this, it is clear that we cannot assign just any rules to a logical constant and expect it to be a useful addition to a language. Ever since Prior's discussion of "Tonk", a hypothetical logical constant with the introduction rule of "v" and the elimination rule of "&", it has become clear that, if a logical constant is to be an acceptable addition to a language, it must lead to a conservative extension of the set of sentences in the language the language users believe to be true. The problem with "Tonk" is that its addition to a language would allow any sentence to be derived from any other sentence in the language, thereby doing away with the distinction between sentences in the language speakers hold to be true and those they hold to be false. With this in mind we can identify three criteria which any acceptable interpretation of a logical constant must meet: (a) the logical constant must be assigned a precise meaning (in terms of introduction and elimination rules) *which is learnable* (i.e. no radically holistic interpretation of the logical constants is permitted); (b) one's grasp of the assigned meaning must be *manifestible in use*; and (c) the logical constant must lead to a *conservative extention* of the set of sentences held to be true by the users of the language to which it is added.

With these criteria in mind we can now consider Tennant's claim that a moderate holist interpretation of the logical constants is not acceptable. When we compare the semantic realist's interpretation of the logical constant (an interpretation associated with the rules of Classical Logic) with that of semantic anti-realists (an interpretation associated with the rules of Intuitionist Logic), we find that *both* interpretations meet the three criteria mentioned above, albeit in different degrees. Both schools offer interpretations of the meanings of the logical constants which are learnable, manifestible in use (if adherence to the assigned rules is taken to be adequate manifestation of one's grasp of the assigned meanings – more of this anon) and conservative. However, there are significant differences between the two sets of rules. In particular, the rules of Intuitionist logic are conservative in a way the rules of Classical logic are not. The logical constants of Classical logic are said to be only "globally" conservative (i.e. the logical constants of Classical logic are conservative only when they are added to a language simultaneously), while the logical constants of Intuitionist logic are individually conservative (i.e. they are conservative even when added to a language one at a time). This entails that the meanings of the Classical logical constants are determined not by the introduction and elimination rules of each constant taken on its own (as is the case with the constants of Intuitionist logic), but by the introduction and elimination rules of all the constants taken together. In other words, the logical constants of Classical logic are interpreted in a holist fashion. But since there are only six logical constants and twelve rules to explain their use, the Classical logician can reasonably claim that this is a manageable holism in that the meanings of the logical constants are certainly learnable.

But if the interpretation of the logical constants offered by Classical logic meets the above-mentioned criteria, why should one opt for Intuitionist logic? More to the point, on what grounds does Tennant insist that holism should be restricted to the interpretation of non-logical terms? The Intuitionist interpretation of the logical constants has two features which recommend it. First, the logical constants of Intuitionist logic are more strongly conservative than those of Classical logic. But it is far from clear why this extra conservatism is necessary to avoid the problems associated with "Tonk". What is more, there are no principles in natural semantics acceptable to realists and anti-realists alike which would lead one to prefer an interpretation of a logical constant solely on the grounds that it is individually conservative. Second, the Intuitionist could claim to provide a theory of meaning in terms of recognitional capacities and canonical warrants rather than in terms of one's grasp of the possibility verification-transcendent truth conditions of a sentence (if they could find an acceptable notion of recognition). But the principle of semantic externalism places no restrictions on the *manner* in which one's grasp of the meaning of a sentence is to be manifested. If the grasp of the possibility verification-transcendent truth conditions of a sentence can be manifested in some overt linguistic behaviour, then the requirements of natural semantics have been met. And as yet no argument has been forthcoming to the effect that adherence to the rules of Classical logic does not constitute a genuine manifestation of one's grasp of a sentence in terms of its possibly verification-transcendent truth conditions.

But perhaps the following argument could be put forward on behalf of the anti-realist. The anti-realist might claim that one can replace the logical constants of Classical logic by those of Intuitionist logic without a corresponding loss of use or meaning within the language. If this substitution entails only a loss of "talk" it could be argued that the logical constants were not doing any real work in the language game, and that the apparent understanding of verification-transcendent truth conditions was illusory.

There are two responses the semantic realist can offer against this argument. The semantic realist can argue that there is no independently agreed criterion available by which to distinguish "real use" from empty or dispensable "talk". In fact it is not clear what empty talk might be if it is accepted that all well-formed sentences in the language can be understood by all competent speakers of the language. But until an explanation of what empty talk amounts to, and a mechanism to draw the distinction is available, any attempt to dictate which sentences in the language fall into which category will fail to be decisive. The anti-realist argument fails as a consequence since it depends on a distinction that cannot yet be drawn.

The anti-realist might try a softer line, however, and agree that while there is no hard and fast rule to distinguish real use from empty talk, there is a pre-theoretical intuition of what constitutes real use. But such a line plays into the hands of the realist because our intuitions inevitably support the view that the loss of the logical constants of Classical logic *does* incur a loss of real use. Adherence to the rules of Classical logic allows us to use sentences currently not known to be decidable (sentences about mass extinctions in the Ordovician, for example) in ways that seems to be a natural extension of belief systems and theories expressed within the language, and to avoid the counter-intuitive results stemming from the rejection of the principle of bivalence. If the rules of Classical logic allow such sentences to be used within the language in accordance with our intuitions, and such sentences cannot be shown to be empty or dispensable "talk", then it would seem that there is no reason not to assume that adherence to the rules of Classical logic is a genuine manifestation of one's grasp of verification-transcendent truth conditions.

Let us summarise our findings by way of conclusion. We have just seen that a commitment to semantic externalism does not force the semantic realist to opt for the Intuitionist interpretation of the logical constants. When this fact is coupled with the intractable difficulties associated with the notion of recognition, the inescapable conclusion is that the manifestation argument does not hold water. This is a result of some significance, given that the manifestation argument is generally agreed to be among the strongest arguments for anti-realism. But when this failure is seen against the background of the well-documented counter-intuitive results which flow from the rejection of bivalence, the unavoidable conclusion is that the case against semantic realism has well and truly collapsed.

7
Eliminating Eliminative Materialism

Introduction

In the last three chapters I have attempted to address specific challenges to specific common sense beliefs. I have sought to defuse the arguments supporting the view that it is irrational to believe the conclusions of well-constructed inductive arguments, that the world does not exist independently of our representations of it, and that truth is epistemically constrained. Now it is time to broach a challenge of an entirely different order.

The eliminative materialist claims that the notions of belief, desire, hope, fear, memories, intentions, recognition – all mental states, that is, with intentional content – must be rejected in the name of an as-yet-to-be completed neuroscience. According to the eliminative materialist, this completed neuroscience will not sanction such everyday statements as "The student missed the lecture today because she believed it had been rescheduled for Thursday", or "He went to the party because he wanted to confront his rival", or "I suddenly remembered that I had a dentist's appointment". This remarkable thesis is motivated by the prediction that this as-yet-to-be completed neuroscience will have no room for the archaic notions of what is derisively called "folk psychological theory", and that the fate which befell the notions of witches and wizards, phlogiston and caloric will be meted out to mental states describable by propositional attitude ascribing sentences. Now if this challenge holds good, it is not just the common sense philosopher who will be worsted; if eliminative materialism (EM) is true, *all* beliefs, revisionary and commonsensical alike, will be consigned to the dustbin of history.

Eliminative materialism will doubtless strike many as too outlandish even for philosophers, for it is not clear that its claims are even coherent, let alone worthy of serious consideration. What, after all, is one supposed to do upon reading the eliminative materialist's arguments? If I am persuaded by them, presumably, I ought to believe that EM is true, or at least that there are good grounds for thinking that it is a candidate for truth. But this is precisely what EM says I cannot do, for there are no such things as beliefs. In fact simply to state or to entertain the theory – to entertain the thought that folk psychology (FP) is false – seems to presuppose the falsity of EM, for this thought has intentional content.

One might reasonably expect a common sense philosopher to ignore EM on the grounds of incoherence, or at least to give it very short shrift indeed. But this would be to dismiss EM prematurely, a trap into which many have fallen. Despite its prima facie incoherence (which, as we shall see, Paul Churchland cheerfully admits), a rationale for EM does exist, a rationale grounded in the nature of the aporia at the heart of the philosophy of mind.[1] And while it is probably fair to say that most philosophers reject EM, it is not always clear that they do so for the right reasons. So, perhaps against expectations, I want to take EM seriously for the moment, to state the case for EM as well as I think it can be, and to explain the grounds on which a common sense philosopher ought to reject EM – for reject it we must. But in the interests of fairness, and in order to avoid a prematurely dismissive attitude to EM, it will also be useful at times to recall some of the other outlandish views in the philosophy of mind that have been discussed in all seriousness by serious thinkers, for eliminative materialists have been in good company in this regard.

The aporia

The principal challenge facing philosophers of the mind has been to accommodate and integrate seemingly well-established facts about human beings into a coherent philosophical psychology. But while the challenge is clear enough, overcoming it has proved uncannily difficult. A coherent account of human beings and their metaphysical location in the natural order continues to elude us despite our best efforts. The single most important explanation for our collective failure in this domain is to be found in the logic of the problem itself: The initial data on which the philosopher sets to work are both well grounded *and* seemingly irreconcilable. The unavoidable result, if we are not content simply to wallow in mystery or give way to quietism, is that some commonplace beliefs about ourselves must be sacrificed and some paradoxical thesis entertained. EM is simply a manifestation of the difficulty of this aporia. Let us begin then by quickly reviewing the lines of thought that lead to such disastrous conclusions. For starters, we can note that we all accept pre-theoretically that human beings, like all other animals, have bodies. We also accept that our bodies are composed roughly of the same sort of material stuff that other animal bodies are composed of. Our bodies, like animal bodies, are composed of organs and limbs, flesh and bones; these in turn are composed of cells of different sorts, which are themselves composed of various sub-parts composed of various large molecules, which are composed of proteins, amino acids and so on down to every more basic material units. Furthermore, our deaths and subsequent decomposition force upon us the realisation that, at a certain level of organisation at least, this material stuff out of which we are made is indistinguishable from that which makes up the bodies of inorganic and inanimate objects, objects, that is, with no life and no mental properties whatsoever. As the *Book of Common Prayer* unsentimentally has it, the body is ultimately nothing more than earth, ashes and dust. These views are backed up by the admittedly fragmentary but ever increasing information emanating from the neuro- and cognitive sciences regarding the internal organisation of our bodies, in particular our nervous system, and how these organisations or structures allow an organism to track states of affairs in the world. These so-called "wiring-and-connection facts" unearthed by biochemistry, neuroanatomy and physiology and the cognitive sciences all drive home the fully material nature of human beings.

But while we all accept that human beings are material organisms, no one really doubts that human beings also have a set of capacities normally associated with minds, and that human beings, while alive, have a set of properties found nowhere in the inanimate world. Unlike inanimate objects, we are capable of nutrition and growth, sensation and perception. We are conscious and capable of imagination, emotion and thought, knowledge and understanding. Moreover, human beings are self-moving agents whose actions are understood by reference to beliefs and desires, goals and intentions. Indeed, it is only common sense, seemingly, to distinguish between the minded and the unminded, the knowing and the unknowing, the rational and the arational, the self-moving and the immobile. And, again, these pre-theoretical views receive support from the sciences insofar as the social sciences incorporate and build upon the main elements of FP.

This common sense understanding of psychological phenomena is generally taken to have at least two elements. FP has an *ontology* which includes beliefs, hopes, fears, intentions, desires and other propositional attitudes and a set of *principles* or *explanatory laws* governing the behaviour of propositional attitudes. For example, we are told (Churchland, 1981, p. 71) that FP contains laws involving quantification over propositions, such as

(x) (p) [(x fears that p) → (x desires that ¬ p)]
(x) (p) [{(x hopes that p) & (x discovers that p)} → (x is pleased that p)]
(x) [(x is angry) → (x is impatient)]
(x) [(x suffers bodily damage) → (x is in pain)]

It is by appealing to beliefs and desires and laws of this sort that we are able to explain and predict the behaviour of human agents. These general laws can be added to perhaps indefinitely, but this ontology and laws of this sort form the bare bones of FP.

The conceptual apparatus of FP is sometimes enriched by the addition of personality traits or characteristics, traits which are then governed by a further set of laws or "trait implications". It is not just that we make inferences about the psychological causes of our behaviour and the behaviour of others in terms of beliefs and desires. According to this enriched FP, we also see ourselves and others as vain, boring, happy-go-lucky, modest, reliable, prudent, stupid, vapid, optimistic and so on for a myriad of other character traits. Moreover, we think that these traits tend to come in inter-connected groups rather than as discrete items. This clumping of traits in coherent groups allows for certain inferences to be drawn. For instance, if we think that so-and-so is a warm-hearted chap, we also tend to assume in advance of any further evidence that he will have other positive traits as well – he will be generous, kind, wise, happy and so on. Conversely, if we find someone to be a bit of a cold fish, we are likely to believe that he is also a bit tight with money, probably humourless, critical rather than supportive and so on.

Now if we put these two lines of thought together, combining an acceptance of the physical basis of human beings with FP, we quickly arrive at the view that human beings (and the higher animals, although not in exactly the same ways) are minded material entities – material things that can think. This is certainly a view that commends itself to the common sense philosopher. The problem is that philosophers of all stripes and historical eras have struggled to explain *how* apparently mindless matter – earth, ashes and dust – can display properties associated with minds, particularly consciousness and intentionality.[2] Furthermore, our inability to answer this how-question, indeed our inability even to conceive of the form the answer might take has led many among us to doubt what the endoxa seem to force upon us, namely, that human beings are material things that can think.[3] The result has been that philosophers have been tempted by two kinds of solutions: First, to claim that human beings are more than their material bodies; or second, to claim that human beings are less than fully minded, and perhaps not minded at all.

Let us not forget, for example, that not too long ago we were routinely told that human beings have the capacities to associate with minds because we are more than our bodies, and more than what supervenes upon our bodies. A range of supernatural, immaterial, extras have been canvassed to play this missing element of human beings, some going so far as to suggest that our thinking is not really done by us at all, but is carried out by a divine power, an "intellect from without", which somehow infuses us. This view was certainly widespread amongst the ancients and medievals. Augustine argued that a contingent and finite human mind could grasp eternal mathematical truths only because God "illuminated" our minds by slipping mathematical notions into our intellects. The later medievals, following the lead of Averroes, took the intellect by means of which we are able to entertain abstract thoughts to be one and the same for all individuals, and to be hardly distinguishable from God. It is worth noting that we have to wait until the arrival of Duns Scotus in the 1300s to get a theory of cognition from a major philosopher that does *not* require the intervention of a divine or other supernatural agent in our cognitive life. His discussion of cognition in *Ordinatio I, dist. 3, pt. 1, qu. 4* is the first fully naturalistic account of thought by a major figure in the West. Unfortunately, it did not prove as historically effective as one might have hoped. For although monopsychism eventually gave way under pressure from theologians keen to preserve the individuality of each human being's mind, Descartes, like Augustine and the majority of the Scholastics, still needed to appeal to God in order to sanction his reliance upon clear and distinct perceptions, and substance dualists still had to appeal to a divine power in the course of their philosophical psychology in order to account for the interaction obtaining between individual immaterial minds and their respective individual material bodies. Descartes could not explain this interaction, the pineal gland notwithstanding. But both the occasionalist and the pre-established harmony theorist eventually had recourse to God, with God either intervening in the natural order of things on each and every occasion of apparent interaction or at least setting up our minds and bodies on a synchronised dual track so that interaction at least appears to occur.

Perhaps inevitably there was an eventual backlash against these extravagant theories, and attempts have subsequently been made to explain how thinking and cognition in general is possible for a wholly material animal. For while few philosophers these days believe that the mind is a substance of any sort, let alone an immaterial substance somehow joined to a material human body, no one really doubts that human beings are conscious, have beliefs and desires, sensations and memories and the usual gamut of mental features. But while this ontological parsimony is to be welcomed, it remains the case that we still do not know how neurophysiological processes give rise to consciousness and intentionality. All the brave attempts of the twentieth century to account for consciousness in a physical world inevitably leave something of the mind out of the picture. If the ancients, medievals and early moderns were tempted to incorporate supernatural extras into their philosophical psychology, the current temptation has been to offer as a complete account of the mind theories which ignore inconvenient properties we all know we possess in virtue of being minded. For example, we have been told by some philosophers that the mind is *just* behaviour, or dispositions to behave (behaviourism); that there is *nothing more* to pain or love than certain neurons firing in the brain (identity theories); that the mind is essentially a *syntactic* engine like a computer with no capacity for semantic (intentional) properties, and that robots can have minds (functionalism, strong AI); or, most radical of all, that the world simply does not contain entities with beliefs, desires and the like at all (EM). My point here, to reiterate, is that *everyone*, the common sense philosopher included, has found it very difficult to say anything sensible on this issue, and EM is simply another manifestation of this difficulty.

Doubts that sense can be made of human beings as material things which can think have come to the fore again in recent times as philosophers and cognitive scientists have become increasingly concerned that the dominant and more-or-less straightforward solution to the problem canvassed for the last 30 years looks more and more likely to fail. Since Fodor's *The Language of Thought* (1975), philosophical psychology has been preoccupied with a particular hypothesis regarding the nature and structure of the human mind. The hypothesis has been (i) that FP constitutes or embodies a *theory* of the internal organisation and structure of the human mind. This would mean, at a minimum, that the human cognitive system at a neurophysiological level has at least two sub-systems, one for registering states of affairs in the world and how that world might be changed, and another, a preference system, which ranks those possibilities in a hierarchical order. Psychologists have been betting that neuroscientists will eventually discover structures and processes in our nervous tissue which embody our beliefs and desires, structures and processes in virtue of which we have beliefs and desires. Now if this hypothesis were correct, then one could assert (ii) that we are able to predict and explain the behaviour of human agents because we operated with this theory and can successfully deploy it when required (as required by common sense and the social sciences) and finally (iii) that we are successful at predicting and explaining the behaviour of human agents because this theory is at least roughly true. The hope then has been that the intuitions of FP are generally right because they provide at least a rough guide to how the human mind is organised at a neurophysiological level.

Many now believe that this straightforward coordination strategy has failed. For one, it has proved very difficult to find neurological correlates to the psychological notions of beliefs, desires, consciousness and intentionality. This has lead some, like Paul Churchland, to assert that

Our commonsense conception of psychological phenomena constitutes a radically false theory, a theory so fundamentally defective that both the principles and the ontology of that theory will eventually be displaced, rather than smoothly reduced by completed neuroscience.

(1981, p. 67)

In terms of the project outlined above, we can say that Churchland agrees that FP does include a theory of the wiring and connection facts of neurophysiology. But he categorically rejects (iii), namely, that FP is a true description of these facts. According to Churchland, FP constitutes a singularly bad, not to say false, theory of the wiring and connection facts, and it must be rejected along with the common sense notions of belief, desire, propositional attitudes and so on. This effectively solves the aporia by eliminating the problematic endoxa. Of course, this leaves the eliminative materialist radically at odds with common sense and the social sciences and without any obvious explanation as to how we are able to predict and explain the behaviour of human agents if our means of conceptualising human behaviour is entirely wrong. But whatever the ultimate explanation of this phenomena, beliefs and desires and the like will have at best an instrumentalist (as-if) role to play.

The current situation is thus far from satisfactory from a common sense point of view, for the alternatives on offer fall into three unhappy categories. In the first category we find those theories which claim that human beings are more than material bodies, containing, perhaps, something of the divine – a suggestion in open opposition to informed thinking about the brain. In a second category are those theories which claim that human beings are not minded in the ordinary sense at all. Such theories come in two subgroups, one more radical than the other, but both fly in the face of common sense and the social sciences. First, there are those theories which do allow that we have minds but minds very different from those we think we have. The second more radical group contains theories which "go the whole hog", denying the existence of mental states with propositional content which play a causal role in the production of action. In the third and final category, we can place those souls who claim that human beings do have the mental features which we normally take ourselves to have, but that we have them in some altogether mysterious fashion which makes us inexplicable to ourselves – a suggestion which, while at least conserving the endoxa, is an indication of philosophical failure.

No attempt will be made here to present a coherent philosophical psychology, to solve the mind/body problem or to explain how consciousness and intentionality are possible for wholly material entities. This is entirely beyond us at the moment. But I do expect, perhaps over-optimistically, that these difficulties will eventually succumb to the various neurosciences and psychology just as the difficulties we previously faced understanding the nature of life eventually succumbed to biochemistry. In the meantime, however, it is incumbent upon the common sense philosopher to keep common sense beliefs on these matters alive so that eventually these beliefs can be assigned their appropriate place in an as yet-to-be-developed philosophical psychology. It is to this end that I focus in this chapter on Churchland's EM, for it appears, at least at first sight, to be the most revisionary of the counter-intuitive theories currently on the market, since it recommends, on one reading at least, that we abandon all hope of saving the notions of beliefs and desires and other mental states with propositional content. Let us turn then to Churchland's argument for EM.

The "theory" argument for eliminative materialism

When in confident mood, the eliminative materialist maintains that when we have a completed neuroscience, we will find that it has no place for the likes of beliefs, desires and character traits. When this day dawns we will recognise that, like witches and wizards, phlogiston and caloric, the world contains nothing that answers to these concepts. That this is breathtakingly counter-intuitive is clear enough. And it is likely that anyone in their right mind (not just the common sense philosopher) would require extremely strong arguments before they would be willing to take such a thesis seriously. Nonetheless, it is worth taking the time to shift the burden of proof in the manner in which our methodology demands.

It is probably sufficient for this purpose simply to note that taking EM seriously in the ancestral environment would have done little for one's reproductive success. If a person did not operate with this aspect of our conceptual scheme, truly eschewing beliefs and desires and their connections with action (rather than simply adopting this point of view for the sake of argument in one's working hours as a philosopher), then it becomes difficult to see how such a person could have distinguished between inanimate objects and plants on the one hand, and animals and human beings on the other. Failing to make such a distinction could have serious consequences for one's reproductive success. Dawkins provides a vivid illustration of this point in the following extended passage concerning an animal's frequent need to manipulate objects in its environment:

A pigeon carries twigs to its nest. A cuttlefish blows sand from the sea bottom to expose prey. A beaver fells trees and, by means of its dams, manipulates the entire landscape for miles around its lodge. When the object an animal seeks to manipulate is non-living, or at least is not self-mobile, the animal has no choice but to shift it by brute force. A dung beetle can move a ball of dung only by forcibly shifting it. But sometimes an animal may benefit by moving an "object" which happens, itself, to be another living animal. The object has muscles and limbs of its own, controlled by a nervous system and sense organs. While it may still be possible to shift such an "object" by brute force, the goal may often be more economically engineered by subtler means. The object's internal chain of command – sense organs, nervous system, muscles – may be infiltrated and subverted. A male cricket does not physically roll a female along the ground and into his borrow. He sits and sings, and the female comes to him under her own power. From his point of view this *communication* is energetically more efficient than trying to take her by force.

(1999, p. 59)

Now in the case of human beings, we most commonly seek to "manipulate" other people, as opposed to non-living objects, by "infiltrating" and "subverting" their "internal chain of command" by means of *persuasion*. We get someone to do something for us by appealing to their beliefs, desires and other propositional attitudes. Dawkins uses advertising as a human analogue of a cricket's singing: "The advertiser uses his knowledge of human psychology, of the hopes, fears and secret motives of his targets, and he designs an advertisement which is effective in manipulating their behaviour" (ibid., p. 62). The point here is that it is not at all unreasonable to suggest that a person who was unable to avail himself or herself of this means of manipulation would not be as proficient at navigating his or her social environment as those who can. And of course, we do not need to rely solely on armchair speculation. We know that a form of "mind blindness" does exist in the form of autism, and that severely autistic people do face real challenges in their attempts to cope successfully with their social environments.

One could of course insist that this line of thought only justifies an instrumentalist reading of beliefs and desires. One can acknowledge the pragmatic need to operate with the conceptual apparatus of FP while insisting that this need is satisfied as long as one views other human beings "as if" they were minded. But on this line, there is no pragmatic requirement that one believes that other people *really are* minded. However, the difficulty with instrumentalist readings of successful theories (and FP is successful in its proper sphere) is the cosmic coincidence problem. The instrumentalist/anti-realist is always left struggling to explain why a false theory can be used so successfully to explain and predict events it fails to represent accurately. This is not a decisive response to instrumentalism, but it is enough to put it on the back foot. For the best (because the simplest) initial explanation for the success of FP is that it is at least roughly true. Consequently, we are well within our rights to demand a very good reason to depart from this initial position. Furthermore, until an alternative to FP is on offer, we are faced with the choice of adopting the only available theory (and one that happens to do pretty good job) or no theory at all. Since a plausible explanation is always preferable to a mystery, let us assume that we can safely shift the burden of proof in this case onto the shoulders of the eliminative materialist. What, then, is the argument for such a radical revision of common sense beliefs?

Paul Churchland's argument for EM begins by taking seriously the suggestion that FP is a theory. FP, he says, is an empirical theory which "brings a simple and unifying organisation to most of the topics in the philosophy of mind" (1981, p. 68). It constitutes a theoretical attempt to explain such diverse psychological phenomena as behaviour and action, the semantics of mental predicates, the other-minds problem, the intentionality of mental states, the nature of introspection and the mind/body problem (ibid., p. 68). FP's status as a theory is underlined elsewhere in a story he offers, borrowed from Sellars, of a visionary theorist living at a stage in human pre-history when *Homo sapiens* had acquired language but had not yet developed mentalistic vocabulary. This visionary, so we are told, hits upon the revolutionary idea that vocal utterances ought to be paired with "covert, utterance-like events called 'thoughts' " (1995, p. 308). This idea, so the story goes, was then expanded by our visionary to include the positing of a connection between these covert thoughts and the actions of other human beings. This theoretical breakthrough proved so useful and powerful a tool that it quickly caught on in the theorist's local band before eventually spreading to the rest of the species.

The next move in Churchland's argument is to suggest that our failure to realise that FP is a theory is the reason we have not long since rejected it. For, as he goes on to argue, FP is a particularly bad theory as theories go. He has three main criticisms. After admitting that FP does enjoy great success in some domains, he says (1) FP has nothing to say about such psychological phenomena as mental illness, sleep, creativity, memory, intelligence differences and the nature of the learning process (1981, p. 73). "A true theory should not have such yawning explanatory gaps," he insists (1995, p. 311). He also points out that (2) there has been little or no development of FP in the last 2500 years. No decent research programme can be as unfruitful as this and remain a going concern. Finally, (3) if FP is true, then we would expect it to be smoothly reducible to our other mature theories in the natural sciences. But no such reduction is in the offing; so FP is likely to be incompatible with mature science, which is good reason to think it is likely to be false.

A final move is needed before Churchland can draw his desired conclusion. For he wishes to assert not that FP is a false theory about beliefs and desires and the like (thus leaving it open that one might develop a better theory of the same phenomena) but that there are no such things as beliefs or desires or intentions to have a correct theory about. To reach this stronger conclusion Churchland needs to call upon a theory in the philosophy of language regarding the semantics of theoretical terms. He says,

This approach entails that the semantics of the terms in our familiar mentalistic vocabulary is to be understood in the same manner as the semantics of theoretical terms generally: the meaning of any theoretical term is fixed or constituted by the network of laws in which it figures.

(1981, p. 69)

The point for Churchland's purpose is that if one changes the network of laws in which terms for theoretical entities are embedded, then one changes the subject entirely in the sense that the entities mentioned in the altered laws are *not* the entities mentioned in the initial set of laws but entirely new creations altogether. Moreover, if one rejects these laws outright, then one can no longer speak meaningfully of the entities mentioned in those laws, for the terms for these entities have a meaning only in virtue of the now rejected network of laws. Reject the laws and you reject the entities themselves. With this semantic theory in place, Churchland can then draw his desired conclusion.

Initial responses

One could be forgiven for thinking, at least at first blush, that it would be very difficult indeed to find any other single argument which contained as many obvious mistakes as this offering from Churchland. For starters, the initial premise that FP is a theory strikes many as highly implausible. Far from being theoretical entities, beliefs and desires and the like appear rather to be among the *data* that theories have to accommodate. To describe thoughts as "theoretical" thus strikes many as a straightforward misuse of language, and to efface the distinction between theoretical and non-theoretical terms.[4] And while it is true that there are logical relations between psychological concepts, and that these concepts form something of a conceptual network, this is not enough to confer the status of theory upon them.[5] What is more, the story of the visionary theorist will strike many as incoherent, for no noise emitted by anything would count as an "utterance" in the first place if it were not already paired to a thought, so one could not have language without mentalistic concepts already in place. And why should we think that accepting FP commits us to being able to solve all the problems that Churchland mentions? Why should FP have a full-blown theory of mental illness and an explanation for intelligence differences? Did it ever claim to? And if FP is not a theory, let alone a research programme, why would we expect it to have been heuristically fruitful? On a more technical note, the theory of the semantics of theoretical terms on which Churchland relies is also widely recognised to be deeply problematic. Our theories of gravity, for example, have changed considerably over the centuries; but this is not generally taken to mean that we have changed the subject. The more sensible interpretation of these theoretical changes is that we are slowly groping our way towards an improvement in our understanding of the nature of gravity. In fact, one is likely to think that the only serious consideration Churchland offers is the already familiar one that beliefs, desires and the like have so far resisted integration with the neurosciences. But we knew that already, so Churchland has not offered us any further reasons to worry about beliefs and desires. What is more, the same argument can be run in the other direction. The common sense philosopher has no reason as yet to give priority to the natural sciences over the social sciences. Both sets of sciences are sources of endoxa. We need to recall that FP has a claim on the common sense philosopher because it embodies common sense, but also because it shares whatever authority we might wish to assign the social sciences. Thus, the logic of the situation is such that one could quite legitimately insist that our inability to reduce beliefs and desires to neurophysiological processes requires one to alter our understanding of those processes in order to accommodate the social sciences, rather than the other way round. Although this move goes against the general tendency to give lower level theories priority, nothing in Churchland's argument rules out the insistence that occasionally lower level theories might need to be altered to suit well established higher level theories. Finally, as noted earlier, the conclusion of Churchland's argument is itself prima facie self-defeating.

These initial reactions have much to recommend them. Nonetheless, Churchland's argument can be reformulated in such a way as to avoid the grosser of these errors. Since it serves no useful purpose to attack the weakest version of any given argument, let us see if an improved version can fair any better. First, we must find a sense in which FP is rightly said to be a theory. Second, we need to find some recalcitrant phenomena that really do fall within the remit of FP. Third, we need to be clear about precisely what it is that Churchland is claiming when he says that beliefs, desires and the like are to be rejected. Once this reconstructive work is accomplished, we are left with a far more respectable argument. But, as so often happens, this comes at something of a cost for EM. We shall see that a plausible version of the argument renders EM far less revisionary, and so far less interesting, than the unreconstructed original.

The argument reformulated

I begin then with the first of our efforts at reconstruction. In what sense can FP be called a theory? If FP does not stray beyond the boundaries of common sense, then FP *cannot* be characterised as a theory in the same sense in which Churchland insists that there are folk theories regarding the nature of "fire, of the sky, of matter, of heat, of light, of space, of life, of numbers of weather and climate, of birth, death and disease... " (Churchland, 1983, p. 7). It is true that "the folk" have entertained certain beliefs regarding these entities; but it is important to notice that these beliefs do not constitute an element of common sense in the sense in which that term is used in this chapter. In these cases, common sense would only insist that one can meet with fire, sky, material things, hot things, space, light and so on, in one's everyday dealings with the world. Common sense is *not* committed to any particular beliefs regarding the fundamental nature of these entities. Beliefs of this sort really are vulnerable to advances in the sciences; but these advances do not touch common sense unless they lead to the denial that one can meet with what we commonly take to be fire, sky, space and the like. Similarly, common sense is committed only to the existence of beliefs and desires and the like but has no view on the ultimate nature of these entities.[6] That, presumably, is the domain and prerogative of the neuro- and cognitive sciences. Of course, if FP does stray beyond the boundaries of common sense into the domain of theorising, then it would be vulnerable to advances in the sciences. But while some might want to say that this is precisely what FP does, I think it would be more accurate to say that this is what Fodor and co-workers have done rather than something that can be attributed to the folk. If I am right about this then FP is not a "theory" in this particular sense of "theory" at all.

It is also obvious to most that FP does not deal in unobservable entities, another hallmark of theories. While no one these days would want to endorse the view that we have infallible first person knowledge of the workings of our own minds via introspection, there is nonetheless a clear sense in which my thoughts are not "covert" to me. In most cases, I do not have to "discover" what I think and feel, for our thoughts and desires are in most cases immediately obvious to us.[7] There is no inference procedure I engage in when I notice, for example, that I desire a beer. It would be a very strange experience indeed if I were to find myself moving in the direction of the kitchen, say, and then having to postulate that I must have certain appropriate beliefs and desires (a desire for a beer, say, and a belief that there is beer in my fridge). And even the thoughts of others are often only too obvious to any observer.[8] For the pseudo-problem of other minds to emerge, one has to adopt Cartesian assumptions about when it is permissible for one to accept a belief. Of course, it is logically possible that other people really are automata; but if I accept the general principle that similar causes have similar effects, and I believe that my body is constituted along the same lines as those of other human beings, then I need an argument to maintain that others do *not* have minds, not that they do.[9]

This is all eminently sensible, and it all turns on a reasonable expectation of what constitutes as theory. But theories do not always need to postulate unobservable entities and processes to count as a theory. If the principal objective of a theory is to provide explanations of phenomena by referring to their causes, and if we assume that beliefs, desires and the like are among the immediate causes of our behaviour (as the folk would have it), then there is a perfectly good sense in which FP *is* a theory after all. And as Crispin Wright has pointed out (1993), if FP is *not* a theory in this sense, if, that is, beliefs, desires and the like are *not* deemed to be among the real causal antecedents of human behaviour, then talk of beliefs and desires can no longer be seen as describing what is real, which is tantamount to conceding that EM is correct after all.[10] So if we are to remain realists about beliefs and desires, as common sense requires, we need to concede that FP *is* a theory in at least one important sense of that term.[11]

Of course, whether FP is a theory that is likely to be wholly false is quite another matter. Certainly the concerns raises by Churchland do little to strike fear into the hearts of the folk once the sphere of FP is restricted to its proper domain of application. But the defender of FP should concede that there are familiar phenomena that do fall within the remit of FP, phenomena which do pose something of a puzzle to the folk. We might be right to say that FP is not required to offer insights into the nature of sleep or the learning process. But as Sterelny (1993, p. 311) reminds us, it does seem reasonable to expect FP to have something to say about the nature of self-deception and akrasia. How can one deceive oneself? I can lie to others easily enough, but how do I hide from myself my intention to deceive myself? How do I come to accept as true (or false) what I know to be false (or true)? And if human behaviour is to be explained in terms of an agent's beliefs and desires, then why is it that agents frequently act in ways their beliefs and desires ought to preclude? These age-old phenomena do present a challenge to FP and suggest that there is more to human psychology than meets the folk's eye. But again, it is not clear to me that these phenomena give rise to anything more than the analogues of the puzzles of normal science.

Let us accept, nonetheless, that there is a sense in which FP is a theory, and that there are phenomena which are genuinely puzzling from a FP perspective. Let us turn then to the final question regarding precisely what it is the eliminative materialist wishes to eliminate on the strength of these two premises. This is not entirely straightforward, for there are at least three distinct readings of EM to be extracted from Churchland's writings. On the strongest possible reading, EM is the claim that

EM1: There are no mental states that can be described by propositional attitude ascribing sentences.

On this reading one cannot say that an agent performed an action because he or she believed x, y and z, and had desires a, b and c. And the reason for this claim is that there are no representational states of mind, states of mind with intentional content. On this reading of EM, the suggestion is that one cannot have beliefs or desires because beliefs and desires have conditions of satisfaction and such conditions are entirely absent from neurophysiological processes.

This is the "catastrophic" reading of EM, the reading that has no doubt won it so much attention. But it is not clear that this version of EM is even coherent. Indeed, as Baker (1987) and Boghossian (1990) have stressed, it looks as though merely stating, let alone accepting, EM presupposes acceptance of precisely what the eliminative materialist wants to eliminate. Now there is some doubt as to whether Baker and Boghossian have succeeded in establishing that EM is in fact incoherent. But we can set these doubts aside because Churchland himself openly admits the incoherence of EM. He simply denies that this tells against EM. In fact, he asserts that the charge of incoherence itself begs the question. According to Churchland the prima facie incoherence of EM

signal[s] only the depth and far-reaching nature of the conceptual change being proposed. Insofar, [it is] only to be expected, and [does] nothing to mark FP as unreplaceable. Even if current FP were to permit no coherent denial of itself within its own theoretical vocabulary, a new psychological framework need have no such limitation where the denial of FP is concerned. So long as a coherent, comprehensive alternative to FP can be articulated and explored, then no argument a priori can rightly single out FP as uniquely true of cognitive creatures.... In short, the incoherence argument covertly begs the question in favour of current FP, the very framework being called into question.

(1995, p. 311)

The problem with this response to the charge of incoherence is that the counter-charge of begging the question reveals that Churchland misunderstands the dialectical situation in which he finds himself, at least vis-à-vis the common sense philosopher. It might in fact be the case that one day EM will receive a formulation that is not incoherent. But while this response might impress Baker and Boghossian, who wanted to establish that EM is false on a priori grounds, the common sense philosopher will remain unmoved. The reason for this is that FP is not on all fours with EM, despite Churchland having called FP into question. The burden of proof in this case lies with Churchland, not the defenders of FP. So it is not enough to claim that it is theoretically possible that one day EM might be expressible in a coherent fashion in the vocabulary of some as yet to be developed neuroscience. As far as the common sense philosopher is concerned, until that day has arrived EM1 will not have been as much as coherently articulated. The common sense philosopher can thus quite rightly ignore EM1 until Churchland and the new neuroscience make good on their promissory note.

The charge of incoherence brought against EM1 stems from the fact that it denies the existence of mental states with representational content. This reading is certainly encouraged by certain passages to be found in Churchland's writings. But there are other passages in Churchland's works where he positively advocates a representationalist theory of mind. In fact, at times, he appears to grant everything that a common sense philosopher could possibly want. Consider these lines:

> [T]he naturalist [Churchland] suggests we view ourselves as epistemic engines. Call an epistemic engine any device that exploits a flow of environmental energy, and the information it already contains, to produce more information, and to guide movement. So far as natural (wild) epistemic engines are concerned, survival depends on a fit between information contained and the world it inhabits... the naturalist suggests we dethrone language as the model for the structure and dynamics of representational activity generally. Representations – information-bearing structures – did not emerge of a sudden with the evolution of verbally competent animals.... Whatever information-bearing structures human enjoy, such structures have evolved from simpler structures, and such structures are part of a system of information-bearing structures and structure-manipulating processes.
>
> (1983, pp. 12–13)

There is nothing here the common sense philosopher need object to. Quite the reverse. These are precisely the sorts of views I have urged at various times myself in this chapter. So what then is the eliminative materialist eliminating? It would appear that the principal target of this version of EM is not so much FP, but rather Fodor's Language of Thought hypothesis. On this reading, Churchland's complaint is not with representational states per se, but with a particular view of how those states "hook up" with the world. In particular, he is suggesting that we abandon Fodor's view that information-bearing or representational states are "sentence-like" (ibid., p. 13). More precisely, he is attacking Fodor's view that mental processing occurs in a language different from one's natural language, the so-called "Language of Thought". On this reading of EM, all that is to be eliminated is Fodor's Language of Thought hypothesis. This gives us:

EM2: Contrary to EM1, there are representational (information-bearing) states; but there are no quasi-sentential tokenings in a quasi-linguistic inner code.

But this is entirely consistent with common sense. Common sense requires only that there are information-bearing mental states which are causally efficacious in the production of human behaviour. It is not committed to any particular theory of the fundamental nature of those states and how they hook up with the world. As far as common sense is concerned, these states might be as Fodor describes them, but then again they might not. This is a matter for the cognitive sciences to determine; it is not a matter for the folk. So EM2 poses no threat at all to our common sense view of the world. At best, it suggests that beliefs are not quite what Fodor and co-workers thought they were.

There is a final version of EM one might claim to find in Churchland's writings. If EM1 advocates the rejection of representational states, and EM2 Fodor's Language of Thought hypothesis, there are other times when Churchland appears to be arguing for the following much weaker position:

EM3: The eliminative materialist is willing to entertain the possibility of rejecting FP (i.e., he or she is willing to entertain either EM1 or EM2).

Because FP is an empirical theory, he says, we must admit that it is theoretically open to revision. He says, for example, that a "theory that meets this description must be allowed a serious candidate for outright elimination" (1981, p. 76). And he continues,

We can of course insist on no stronger conclusion at this stage. Nor is it my concern to do so. We are here exploring a possibility, and the facts demand no more, and no less, that it be taken seriously. The *distinguishing feature of the eliminative materialist is that he takes it very seriously indeed.*

(Ibid., p. 76)

We are now at some significant distance from the original thesis proposal.[12] Originally we were told that EM is the thesis that FP *is* false and will eventually be displaced, and Churchland's arguments were intended to establish precisely this (1981, p. 67). But now all that Churchland is claiming is that the falsity of FP is a possibility to be explored. This is a significantly different thesis; but, though plausible, it is entirely without interest. For this thesis could be asserted by the common sense philosopher of *any* set of beliefs whatsoever. Since no beliefs are sacrosanct, all beliefs are in principle up for revision; thus any belief might someday be replaced. So to claim that FP might one day be replaced is to assert nothing about FP that the common sense philosopher would not have accepted prior to the commencement of the argument. So if this is what EM really amounts to, then again there is no threat to common sense, and EM is in fact entirely innocuous.

Summary

I have tried to show that Churchland's argument for EM can be reformulated in such a way as to avoid the more obvious errors which crippled the original. There is a sense in which FP can rightly be called a theory, and there is a range of phenomena which do give rise to genuine puzzles that the common sense philosopher ought to attend to in due course. I have suggested, however, that these puzzles are not particularly threatening and certainly not sufficient on their own to warrant the conclusion that FP is false. But I have not pressed this point as hard as I might have done. For things go from bad to worse for Churchland once we focus on precisely what it is that he hopes to eliminate from our theorising about the mind on the basis of these two premises. I suggest that there is no reading of EM which is *both* incompatible with common sense *and* an established threat. EM1 is certainly incompatible with common sense; but it has yet to be coherently expressed, and so does not constitute an established threat. Meanwhile, EM2 and EM3, while perhaps receiving some support from the two premises, are entirely consistent with common sense. I conclude then that while serious and difficult problems remain unsolved in the philosophy of mind in general, and that there are some puzzles which ought to occupy the common sense philosopher in the fullness of time, there is no good reason at this point to countenance the wholesale rejection of FP. The common sense philosopher can therefore continue confidently to trade in the currency of FP at least until such time as the prophesied completed neuroscience has seen the light of day. And this is just as well, for we shall be assuming that FP is largely correct in the chapters to follow.

8
Freedom and Responsibility

Introduction

Perhaps the hoariest old chestnut in the philosophy playbook is the question regarding the so-called "freedom of the will". It is asked, Are human beings ever really responsible for their actions? Are human beings really fit subjects of praise and blame, resentment and gratitude, guilt and forgiveness and the other reactive attitudes? Or is it rather the case that there is only one action ever open to us, that alternatives are just an illusion, and, consequently, that entreaties, rewards, punishments and the like are entirely out of place? As in so many other cases, we find a good number of philosophers parting company with common sense on these issues. For while most of the educated classes are now familiar with the thesis that we are simply the products of our genes and socio-cultural environment, and while it is true that we often pay lip service to these ideas, in our pre-theoretical moments, we never so much as raise these questions. Nonetheless, it seems that philosophers are never short of reasons for suspecting that one of our most cherished beliefs – that we are indeed the authors of our own biographies and not automata or puppets on strings – might be an illusion.

Of course philosophers no longer believe in Fate, or Destiny, or the occult powers of astrological bodies. And philosophers no longer take seriously the concerns raised by God's foreknowledge of our future actions. But there are still plenty of other forces beyond our control that can be called upon to fill the shoes of these now departed ghosts: logic, the laws of nature, past events, the unconscious, genes, the environment, socialisation – all have been used either alone or in various combinations to lend credibility to the worry that our actions are not really ours at all, at least not in the sense in which it is reasonable to say that we are responsible for them. But it would be inaccurate to suggest that philosophical worries about determinism arise solely from the belief that the external world contains various forces that move us to act as we do. An important contributory factor is that the concepts at the heart of the free will debate, the concepts of action, freedom and responsibility, are very difficult indeed, and our intuitions regarding them often pull in seemingly contradictory directions. In short, our conceptual house is not entirely in order in this domain; this disorder no doubt contributes substantially to the worry that our actions might indeed be beyond our control.

I will begin this discussion of the free will debate as one might expect, with initial considerations designed to show that the belief in human free agency should be accorded the status of default position. The burden of proof thus shifted onto the shoulders of determinists, attention is then focussed on the arguments used to undermine belief in human free agency. Of course, it is impossible to consider all such arguments, but we can examine those considered to be the strongest, and those which have attracted most attention in recent years. It is with these considerations in mind that I have chosen to examine the so-called "consequence argument" of Peter van Inwagen and Galen Strawson's "basic argument". Having shown that neither establishes its intended conclusion, and that the opposition's burden of proof has yet to be discharged, I conclude that when working on the set of issues found at the intersection of the philosophy of action, mind, ethics and law, the common sense philosopher can confidently set about his or her task assuming that human beings are, at least on occasion, responsible agents. More precisely, he or she can assume that in the normal course of events, human beings are usually responsible for their actions in a way that is consistent with our normal practices of praising and condemning, of rewarding and punishing.

Responsibility as default position: shifting the burden of proof

That in our pre-theoretical moments we believe and act as though human beings are usually responsible for their actions is clear from the fact that the so-called "reactive attitudes" come so naturally to us. Indeed, one might well wonder if human life as we know it would be recognisable if we were no longer able to adopt the attitudes of, say, admiration, resentment, gratitude or indignation vis-à-vis other people, or if we could never feel guilt, shame or pride when reflecting on our own behaviour. Of course, the fact that terms for these attitudes exist in most languages, and that humans beings the world over are able to use them so naturally, is insufficient to establish that human beings are in fact responsible agents. But these considerations sit easily alongside the observation that one is not likely to question the belief in human free agency in the ordinary course of events unless specific doubts about it are raised.

What is also clear is that the major philosophers in the common sense tradition have also assumed that the belief in free agency is an element of the common sense view of the world. Aristotle provided a detailed and sophisticated account of the concept of responsibility in the *Nicomachean Ethics*, an account to which I will return below. He also dealt with a challenge from a form of fatalism in his famous discussion of future contingents[1] and responded to the challenge of determinism stemming from the view that there are causal laws of nature.[2] In the twentieth century, Moore offered an Ordinary Language defence of free agency by going to great lengths to show that there are perfectly good senses of "could" and "can" in which it is possible to say that one often "can" do what in fact one does not do, and that this means that one could have acted otherwise.[3] And Reid used the occasion of his discussion of the free will problem to illustrate the distinctive feature of the meta-philosophy of common sense. He wrote,

> This natural conviction of our acting freely, which is acknowledged by many who hold the doctrine of necessity, ought to throw *the whole burden of proof* upon that side; for, by this, the side of liberty has what lawyers call a *jus quaesitum*, or a right of ancient possession, which ought to stand good till it be overturned. If it cannot be proved that we always act from necessity, there is no need of arguments on the other side to convince us that we are free agents.[4]

But more is required before the burden of proof can be justly shifted onto the opposition. I have suggested that a belief ought be counted as a common sense belief and treated as a default position if that belief has ecological and social fitness value.

What, then, is the fitness value of the belief in human free agency? To answer this question, we need to imagine an empirically plausible scenario in which the belief in human free agency would have been advantageous during the relevant period of human evolution. Such a scenario is in fact quite easily envisaged.

Not surprisingly, it is in the social sphere that the advantages of this belief are most clearly visible. All recognise that *H. sapiens* is a social animal, and that individual human beings, if they are to be reproductively successful, must be able to cope with specifically social demands. It is also recognised that in addition to living in small groups comprised of immediate family members, human beings often congregate in larger groups which include members more distantly related. The necessity of group life stems from the fact that individual human beings are not self-sufficient, while its desirability is explained by the fact that the quality of life achievable in moderately large groups is far higher than that achievable on one's own or even with one's nuclear family. This higher standard of living is in no small part due to social cooperation, to our agreeing to work together to our mutual benefit. However, it is also a commonplace that social cooperation is a double-edged sword. For all its undoubted benefits, cooperation at all levels comes at the price of leaving oneself open to various unavoidable dangers. In the first place, cooperating involves letting down one's guard at least for some period of time, which inevitably leaves one vulnerable to attack by those taken to be friends. And there is also the less immediately obvious threat of free-riders, defectors, or cheats, that is, those who take advantage of the benefits of social cooperation without making their own contribution and incurring any costs. These dangers make cooperation with other humans beyond one's immediate family a risky venture. Nonetheless, the benefits of cooperation are significant enough to make it worthwhile to run these risks as long as they are not intolerably high. What is needed, then, is a general rule of engagement that minimises the dangers of cooperation without jeopardising its benefits.

Such a rule has been identified by game theorists. The rule – brought to public attention by Axelrod and Hamilton (1981), and further developed by Axelrod in his book length study (1984) – is simplicity itself. It also has the virtue of being immediately recognisable because it is exemplified everyday in households, schoolyards, boardrooms and battlefields the world over. Axelrod showed that if the individuals living in a group follow the "tit-for-tat" rule, returning a good turn for a good turn and harm for harm, then an evolutionarily stable environment for cooperation and reciprocal altruism emerges. The rule allows one to begin by offering to cooperate, which, if responded to in kind, leads to further efforts at cooperation from the initiator. If these too are met with similarly helpful responses, then a virtuous cycle of reinforced and reinforcing cooperation is underway. But if harm if offered first, or is ever offered in return for a kindness, then cooperation with the offending individual is brought to an abrupt end, protecting the would-be co-operator from further harm or loss. What Axelrod established is that individuals and groups that follow this simple rule of engagement do significantly better than those who cooperate unconditionally in spite of free-riders and cheats and better also than those who constantly defect.

So much by way of preliminary background and scene-setting. Now what is interesting about Axelrod's work on the emergence of cooperation for present purposes are the pre-conditions for the successful employment of the tit-for-tat rule in human societies. If, other things being equal, it is in one's interest to keep cooperating with fellow co-operators, and if we recognise, as we surely must, that people often make mistakes, acting out of ignorance or inattention or carelessness, then we can begin to appreciate why it would be a great advantage to an individual if he or she were able to distinguish between those actions of his or her fellows performed intentionally and deliberately, and those performed through, for instance, ignorance, carelessness or duress. If a fellow group member performs an action which harms me or my interests, then a crude reading of the tit-for-tat rule demands that I immediately break off cooperation with the offending individual. This allows me to protect myself, but it also entails forgoing the benefits to be accrued through future cooperation. But if I am able to see that the offending individual, while indeed harming me, did so *involuntarily*, and that, despite appearances, bears me no ill will, then the tit-for-tat rule dictates that I continue to cooperate (although perhaps more cautiously than previously) and thereby avoid an *unnecessary* loss of benefits. By contrast, if I am sure that someone has harmed me intentionally, then I can very happily cease cooperating with that individual knowing that the future benefits forgone were never likely to materialise in any case.

The point here is that to follow the tit-for-tat rule to one's best advantage one needs a nuanced conception of the "tit" one is "tating", and this means knowing something about the way the action was performed, in particular whether it was performed *intentionally, deliberately* and *on purpose*, or *unintentionally, inadvertently, by mistake* or *under duress*. An individual unable to make these distinctions, an individual, that is, who is unable to distinguish between *voluntary* and *involuntary* actions, is at a marked social disadvantage vis-à-vis those individuals who are able to operate with these concepts. The upshot of this discussion then is that there is a scenario in which one can appreciate that the belief in what is loosely called "the freedom of the will" does have a social fitness value.

Two philosophical challenges

Let us take the burden of proof in this case to have been duly shifted. What might induce us to give up our firmly rooted pre-theoretical conviction in the appropriateness of reactive attitudes? There have been many arguments forwarded by philosophers to this end, but space considerations allow consideration of only two. I will present both arguments in turn before offering any critical comments upon them.

Peter van Inwagen (1983) has presented a challenge to our default position in the form of his "consequence argument". The key idea is that we human beings cannot be held responsible for our actions because what we do is not "up to us". Our actions, it is claimed, are the direct result of past events along with the laws of nature, neither of which was within our control. Van Inwagen's argument can be presented in five premises and a conclusion as follows:

1. There is nothing one can now do to change the past.
2. There is nothing one can now do to change the laws of nature.
3. There is nothing one can now do to change the past or the laws of nature.
4. If determinism is true, one's actions are the necessary consequence of the past and the laws of nature.
5. There is nothing one can now do to change the fact that our actions are the necessary consequence of the past and the laws of nature.

6. There is nothing one can now do to change the fact that our present actions occur. (Our present actions are not "up to us".)

Strictly speaking van Inwagen's argument is designed only to show that belief in human free agency is incompatible with an acceptance of determinism. It is for this reason that van Inwagen can quite rightly help himself to premise 4. But since few are attracted to the prospects of developing an account of freedom that eschews determinism,[5] this argument for the incompatibility of freedom and determinism can quickly be turned into an argument against human free agency itself.

Our second argument, due to Galen Strawson (1986), can be presented as follows:

1. You do what you do because of your nature and character.
2. To be truly responsible for what you do, you must be responsible for your nature and character.

3. But to be responsible for your nature and character, you would have to have done something in the past for which you were responsible which led to your nature and character being what they are.
4. But if that were to be possible, you would have had to have been responsible for your nature and character at that earlier point.
5. But to have been responsible at that earlier point, you would have had to have done something prior to that earlier point for which you were responsible which led to your nature and character being what they are at that earlier point, and so on ad infinitum.
6. One is never responsible for one's nature or character.
7. One is never responsible for what one does.

Initial comments

These two arguments have been amongst the most widely discussed in the literature in recent years. What ought the common sense philosopher to make of them? I will argue that the conclusions of both arguments are entirely avoidable, because the premises of both arguments rest on faulty, dubious or at least unforced analyses of the concepts of action, freedom and responsibility. If the common sense philosopher can offer alternative and acceptable analyses of these notions, analyses that do not entail the denial of human free agency, then the errors of our two arguments will become apparent. That is the strategy I will adopt here. In particular, I will revisit Aristotle's analysis of the concept of responsibility, argue that it is acceptable as it stands, and use it to undermine the premises of our two target arguments.

But it is worth pointing out that it is not just the common sense philosopher or the Aristotelian who takes issue with the conceptual analyses of the notions of action, freedom and responsibility at work in van Inwagen and Strawson's arguments. Both of these arguments depend on at least two contentious points: (a) That responsibility and freedom are identical, so that if one is ruled out so is the other and (b) that freedom demands that one be able to act otherwise than one actually does. Both of these points have been contested in the recent literature.

In *Responsibility and Control*, Fischer and Ravizza argue that while freedom does require the existence of alternative courses of action (the forking-paths-into-the-future view of freedom), responsibility does not, and so the two cannot be identical. The key feature of the concept of responsibility, say Fischer and Ravizza, is control. They distinguish between *regulative control*, which requires freedom in the above sense, and *guidance control* which does not, and argue that guidance control is sufficient for responsibility. The details of this work need not detain us unduly. I call attention to it only to show that more work needs to be done to establish that our two arguments do not rest on a faulty analysis of the concept of responsibility. For if Fischer and Ravizza are right about the nature of responsibility, then our two arguments, while possibly right about freedom, would leave responsibility unscathed.

But many argue that a Fischer/Ravizza inspired approach to these arguments concedes far too much. At issue here is the analysis of the notion of freedom itself, and whether to be free one really does need to have genuine alternatives as both arguments assume. Frankfurt (1969), for example, famously denies that alternatives are a necessary condition of freedom, so van Inwagen's argument is entirely beside the point. Frankfurt (2003) argues that the significant contrast to be drawn in this domain is not between uncaused, free actions and fully caused, determined actions, but between the actions of "wantons" and the actions of "persons". A person has free will and is responsible for their actions, says Frankfurt, if those actions are in conformity with and caused by their second-order desires, whereas a "wanton" acts impulsively on the basis of their first-order desires. But, says Frankfurt, since the actions of both persons and wantons are fully determined, van Inwagen's argument simply fails to hit the mark.

Others have followed Frankfurt's lead while suggesting modifications to this general position. Watson (2003), setting aside Frankfurt's discussion of a hierarchy of desires, has suggested that a person is free if their actions flow from their values and reasons as opposed to their desires and passions. And Wolf (2002), finding both Frankfurt and Watson's "deep-self" theories inadequate as they stand, insists that free agents must also be sane, that is, capable of acting on the basis of reasons and in conformity with agreed moral rules and standards. Again the details of these claims need not detain us. I draw attention to them only to underline the point that serious thinkers have taken issue with van Inwagen and Strawson's basic conceptions of the crucial notions involved in this debate, and graphically to illustrate that our conceptual house is not in order in this domain. For this, brief survey of the literature has already presented us with at least six different positions. We have been told that

a. An agent is free and responsible for his or her actions if he or she has genuine alternatives at the time of acting (van Inwagen).
b. An agent is responsible for his or her actions if his or her actions flow from his or her nature and character, and he or she is the source of his or her nature and character (Strawson).

c. An agent is free if he or she has genuine alternatives, but responsible for his or her actions if he or she has guidance control (Fischer and Ravizza).

d. An agent is free and responsible for his or her actions if he or she is a person, that is, an agent whose actions are determined by his or her second-order desires (Frankfurt).

e. An agent is free and responsible for his or her actions if his or her actions flow from his or her reasons and values (Watson).

f. An agent is free and responsible for his or her actions if his or her actions flow from his or her reasons and values, and he or she is sane (Wolf).

To begin to see our way clear I suggest we focus primarily on the notion of responsibility. Responsibility is the crucial notion in this domain inasmuch as if it can be established that we are, at least on occasion, responsible for our actions, then we can let the portentous notion of freedom fall where it may. For it seems that the only interest that freedom (in the forking-paths-into-the-future sense) might have for us is that we think it would deliver responsibility into our hands.

It is with these thoughts in mind that I want to revisit an old, and, to my mind, oddly neglected account of responsibility first developed by Aristotle and later refined by Aquinas. At the core of this account is the suggestion that our capacity for responsible action is grounded in our ability as humans to perform actions knowingly and for a reason. On this view, having "a will" is not to have a distinct mental faculty on a par with the intellect, memory, or imagination, but simply to have rational appetites or desires.[6] Space considerations make it impossible to deal with this line of thought here with the thoroughness it deserves, but we shall be returning to it in subsequent discussions. Fortunately, a complete study will not be necessary for our purposes since the point of this section is merely to show that the arguments of Inwagen and Strawson rest on faulty, or at least unforced, analyses of responsibility.

Aristotle on responsibility

In the first chapter of the third book of the *Nicomachean Ethics*, Aristotle sets out a classic analysis of the concept of responsibility.[7] The leading intuition is that an agent is rightly held responsible for an action if the agent is the principal cause of the action. But an agent is deemed to be the cause of the action in the requisite sense only if he or she performed the act voluntarily. The rationale for this claim is not far to seek: If the act is not voluntary, then some other cause distinct from the agent is the true cause of the action. This shifts the focus of attention to the notion of a voluntary action. And, according to Aristotle, an agent acts voluntarily only if (1) the source or origin of the action is within the agent (specifically, in his or her decision or choice), *and* (2) he or she *knows* what he or she is doing in the performance of that action. It is worth noting that Aristotle thinks these conditions are usually met in the ordinary run of things. In fact, it is simply assumed that an agent is responsible for his or her actions unless it can be shown that he or she was coerced by some external force or acting in ignorance. Agent responsibility is here taken to be the norm rather than the exception.

The claim that external coercion is incompatible with voluntary action is perfectly familiar as it is shared with classic compatibilism. What is less familiar is the insistence on the centrality of knowledge and ignorance to the notions of voluntary action and responsibility, and so it is worth pausing for a moment to consider this condition in some detail.

That knowledge and ignorance are relevant to questions of responsibility is easily appreciated when particular examples are considered. Consider the following unhappy scene: While hunting in deep woods I spy what I take to be a magnificent stag in the middle distance, and shoot it dead. Elated by my success, I rush to claim my prize, but find to my horror that the stag is in fact my now dead father who, unbeknownst to me, had donned druidic garb for the purposes of conducting some quaint New Age ceremony. Am I a parricide? Most certainly not. For while it is true that the principal cause of my father's death was my decision to fire my weapon, it would be wrong to call me a parricide because I did not realise that I was shooting my father, and since I did not know that I was shooting my father I could not have consented to shoot him, and so could not have shot him intentionally or voluntarily. As Aquinas would put it, the will does not enter the equation until the intellect has been appropriately engaged, and it is precisely this lack of intellectual engagement which is at work in the case of agents acting in ignorance. This intuition is backed by Anscombe's observation that an action cannot be attributed to an agent unless the action is described in a manner which the agent himself or herself would accept at the time of acting.[8] If asked what I was doing at the time of the shooting I would have said something like: "I am trying to bring down that stag", not "I'm trying to kill my father."

However, it is important to recognise that not all forms of ignorance are relevant to questions of responsibility. Aristotle provides a list of features of an action non-culpable ignorance of any of which would preclude the agent being held responsible for the action. These include (i) who is acting, (ii) what the agent is doing, (iii) to whom or to what, (iv) with what, (v) to what end and (vi) the manner in which the action is performed.[9] This list is best seen as illustrative rather than exhaustive, but the important point is that there are many features of an action of which the agent will be ignorant but which have no bearing on the question of responsibility. If I knowingly shoot a man, I am held responsible for the shooting of the man despite the fact that I might not know the year my gun was made or the particular factory it was made in, or the exact height and weight of the man I shot, and myriad other similar details. These sorts of features of the action are simply not relevant to the question of responsibility because knowledge of them would presumably have made no difference to my carrying out the action.

On the other hand, I may be ignorant of a particularly relevant feature of an action and still be held responsible if that ignorance is culpable. There are indeed cases where an agent acts without relevant and important knowledge which one could reasonably expect the agent to have had. In such cases, we use condemnatory phrases like "You should have known better" or "You should have made an attempt to find out" when someone presents their ignorance as an excuse. In short, there are some cases of relevant ignorance for which we can be held responsible, and others in which we cannot, and it is only the latter that provide the basis for an excuse and a discharging of responsibility.

Now, on this analysis, an agent is held to be responsible for an action, and so an appropriate subject of the for-reactive attitudes, if the agent is the cause of the action in the sense just outlined. This analysis of responsibility might be called a version of new compatibilism since it goes beyond classic compatibilism by including the second condition regarding knowledge and ignorance; but, for reasons that will emerge later, it is significantly different from the compatibilisms of, say, Frankfurt, Watson or Wolf, although all of these new compatibilists make some use of the notion of reason. But its immediate interest for us is that it contains no explicit mention of freedom, or alternative possibilities, or uncaused acts of the will. This suggests that the notion of responsibility need *not* be linked conceptually to the forking-paths-into-the-future sense of freedom, as Inwagen assumes. So even if we were to accept that van Inwagen's argument rules out the possibility of freedom in this sense, we could still insist that it does nothing to suggest that agents cannot still be responsible for their actions in the Aristotelian sense. Moreover, the Aristotelian analysis of responsibility contains nothing to suggest that one must be responsible for one's nature or character in order to be responsible for one's actions, as premise (2) of Strawson's argument claims. Consequently, ready responses to the arguments of van Inwagen and Strawson are at hand if the Aristotelian analysis can withstand critical scrutiny.

So what might one say against this analysis of responsibility? Some have argued that Aristotle's analysis seems "somewhat insensitive" because we are inclined nowadays to accept that there can be forms of compulsion that are internal as well as external. The stock example is the case of the kleptomaniac who "cannot help" but steal because of an "internal disorder in the psyche".[10] The kleptomaniac seems to satisfy the Aristotelian conditions for responsible action since the source of the action is within the agent (there is no external compulsion) and kleptomaniacs presumably know what they are doing (there is no relevant ignorance). But, it is asked, can we really say that kleptomaniacs are responsible for their characteristic behaviour?

The Aristotelian has two sorts of possible response. On the one hand, he or she could simply bite the bullet and insist that insensitivity is not an overriding consideration. For even if one accepts that kleptomaniacs do suffer a form of compulsion, because this compulsion is internal rather than external, it is reasonable to think that it falls to the kleptomaniac to address this issue since they know, or certainly ought to know, that they are stealing and that stealing is generally frowned upon. On this line, the suggestion would be that if one suffers from coercive internal impulses, then it behoves one to take steps to cope with them. If I fail to take such steps, then I am responsible for my behaviour despite its being compulsive. So even if one is right to view theft induced by kleptomania as significantly different from garden-variety theft, this does not mean that one should see it as entirely excusable. And as a matter of fact, it seems pretty clear that we do *not* view it as completely excusable. Now if this type of response is reasonable in the case of kleptomania, then there is nothing to stop the Aristotelian from generalising it to cover all forms of behaviour that stem from coercive internal impulses.

While this line of response seems adequate on the face of it, it will no doubt strike some as harsh. However, a kinder and gentler response is open to the Aristotelian. He or she could accept that uncontrollable internal impulses do exist and agree that agents suffering from such impulses are not properly seen as responsible for actions caused by these impulses. Modern sensibilities can then be accommodated by modifying the Aristotelian analysis of responsibility by adding the qualification that an agent is responsible for his or her action only if he or she knows what he or she is doing, and he or she is free from *both* external compulsion and internal compulsion *due to psychic disorders*. Indeed, this line of thought is already present in Susan Wolf's view that an agent must be deemed sane if they are to be held responsible for their actions.[11] And it has been suggested that this qualification is in fact implicit in Aristotle's own discussion of responsibility.[12] As we have seen, on this analysis, it is a necessary condition of an agent being responsible for an action that the action has its source in the agent. And, at least in paradigm cases of responsible action, the source of the action lies in the *decisions* of the agent. But decisions usually follow the *deliberations* of the agent, and genuine deliberation requires rationality on the part of the deliberator. But if the agent is suffering from a psychic disorder sufficient to preclude the possibility of adequate deliberation, as might be the case with kleptomaniacs, then the conditions of responsible action are simply not met.

If we now combine the two lines of response sketched here, the defender of the Aristotelian analysis of responsibility can present the following response to the objector impressed by the counter-examples raised by coercive impulses: An agent's coercive internal impulses are either sufficient to preclude adequate deliberation or they are not. If the impulses do not constitute a serious psychic disorder, then it is incumbent upon the agent to deal effectively with these impulses; if he or she fails to do so, then he or she remains responsible for his or her compulsive behaviour. If, on the other hand, the impulses are sufficient to disrupt the agent's deliberations, then the conditions of responsibility are not met. Either way the Aristotelian has effective means of coping with the challenge posed by cases of internal compulsion.

Now if the case of the kleptomaniac suggests to some that Aristotle's analysis of responsibility might be too wide, others have claimed that it is too narrow as well. It has been suggested that there are legitimate cases of responsible action that this analysis cannot account for. For example, there are cases of actions due to forgetfulness, carelessness, inattention or negligence which involve no intentional action on the part of the agent but for which we hold the agent responsible.[13] Behind this question is the threat that an agent might be genuinely blameworthy on account of his or her actions despite the fact that, on the Aristotelian account of voluntary action, the action was not performed voluntarily. But, it is asked, was it not the case that the class of voluntary actions was supposed to include all actions for which reactive attitudes are appropriate?

At issue here is whether one can ever forget something knowingly, and whether one can be wittingly inattentive, or careless or negligent. The case of negligence is perhaps the easiest to accommodate. Part of the notion of negligence is that one knowingly fails to acquaint oneself with certain facts or to perform some required action. For example, if a building contractor neglects to ensure that safety standards are maintained on the building site, it is impossible to say that he acted, or failed to act, because he was ignorant of the relevant facts because all building contractors as a matter of routine are made aware of the existence of these requirements. So all cases of negligence are culpable in a manner consistent with Aristotle's analysis.

But what about forgetting? Say one forgets an important piece of information and that this forgetting had serious implications for others. One does not knowingly forget, so how can forgetting ever be culpable according to Aristotle's analysis? The way to deal with this kind of case is to recognise that there are actions prior to the forgetting which lead directly to the forgetting for which the agent is responsible according to the Aristotelian analysis. If I am given an important piece of information, and I recognise that the information is important prior to forgetting it, then the culpable action is the failure to take appropriate measures or safeguards against a possible forgetting. One ought to have made notes in a diary, or tied a piece of string around a finger, or asked someone reliable to remind one of the information and so on. No forgetting is intentional, but failing to take reasonable precautions against this eventuality is. There is an analogy here with Aristotle's treatment of behaviour performed while drunk. One is responsible for one's drunken behaviour even if one was in no fit state at the time to understand what one was doing. The reason for this is that the initial act of drinking was itself performed in full knowledge of the likely consequences of inebriation, and so the responsibility for this initial act carries over to actions performed while under the influence.

What about ignorance due to carelessness or inattention? I believe these can be treated along the same lines as those employed to cope with cases of forgetting. While one does not act carelessly, or inattentively intentionally (one cannot knowingly act carelessly – to do so is to pretend to act carelessly, taking care to appear careless and the same for inattentive actions), again, there are actions which precede these careless or inattentive acts which confer their status as voluntary acts onto the careless and inattentive acts. These are best seen as instances of failing to pay due attention where one might have been expected to know that such instances are cases where due attention is required.

Consider the unhappy event of my behaving carelessly in a museum, and consequently breaking a priceless Ming vase. Unless I can reasonably claim that I did not and could not have known that I was in a museum (can one walk inadvertently into a museum?) then no excuse of carelessness is possible. For it is common knowledge that museums are the sort of place where paying due attention to one's surroundings is important and required. Failure to pay attention resulted in my carelessness and the breaking of the Ming vase; but since this initial failure was voluntary since I knew I was in a museum, and so aware that due care was required, my carelessness was itself voluntary, and so I am rightly held to be responsible.

There is, however, a more radical objection that many will no doubt wish to press against the Aristotelian analysis of responsibility. Whatever the merits of the lines of response to the two objections already canvassed, some will feel that what has been offered so far amounts to little more than a defence of what we might call *legal* responsibility, and that this falls far short of what defenders of free agency think is required.[14] Some will want to say that *moral*, as opposed to merely *legal*, responsibility requires "radical" or "ultimate" responsibility. On this line, an agent is morally responsible for an action only if (a) there are genuine alternatives from which the agent can choose (responsibility requires metaphysical freedom, as van Inwagen assumes) and (b) the agent is responsible for anything that is a sufficient reason, cause or motive for an action. On this view, it is not enough that the agent be the source of the action. To be held morally responsible, the agent must also be the source of the source of the action (as Strawson maintains). In short, the analysis of responsibility offered so far, however adequate, is not an analysis of the required concept but is an analysis of something else.

One can begin to respond to this objection by asking why there is any need for a notion of responsibility stronger than that of Aristotelian legal responsibility. If the primary task in this domain is to provide an analysis of responsibility strong enough to establish the appropriateness of our reactive attitudes vis-à-vis other human beings, have we not already done enough by showing that the Aristotelian analysis of responsibility is, on the face of it at least, a tenable position? Why demand more?

To appreciate that Aristotelian legal responsibility is in fact sufficient for present purposes, it is enough to consider the conditions under which our reactive attitudes may differ. By way of illustration, consider two prison guards in a Nazi concentration camp required to carry out their ghastly orders on pain of immediate execution. One does so willingly (in the Aristotelian sense) and with sadistic relish, while the other does so only under duress. I would submit that there is a significant moral difference between the actions of the two guards, and that our reactive attitudes to them will (quite rightly) be significantly different as a consequence, and this despite the fact that neither had realistic alternatives to carrying out their orders and neither, presumably, was the source of their own nature and character. We are likely to feel unalloyed disgust, contempt and outrage at the actions of the first guard, while we are likely to have mixed emotions about the second, emotions that will very likely include a measure of pity. But if neither guard was radically or ultimately responsible for their actions, and if we assume, as common sense would have it, that it *is* appropriate to have different attitudes vis-à-vis the two guards, then it would appear that something less than ultimate responsibility is in fact sufficient to bring about and justify differences in reactive attitudes. The differences in our reactive attitudes are explained by the fact that the first guard willingly performed his deplorable actions (in the Aristotelian sense) while the second did not. Consequently, it is natural to think that first guard "owns" his actions (they *are*, in fact, his actions) in a way that the second does not. The points here are essentially Frankfurt's, that is, that I can quite willingly perform the only action open to me, and that it is my willingness to perform an action that counts from a moral point of view, not the number of options available to me.[15]

However, another line of response to this third objection is worth exploring, for it is highly probable that many will still feel the instinctive pull of the idea that "real" responsibility requires genuine alternatives. In fact, I think this intuition is on the right track, but that the nature of the connection between freedom and responsibility has been misunderstood. As we have seen, it is often assumed either that freedom and responsibility are identical in that to have the one is to have the other, or, at the very least, that freedom is a necessary condition of responsibility. Neither of these views is correct. Nonetheless, I hope to show that it is *usually* the case, indeed perhaps almost always the case, that if an agent has acted voluntarily, and so is rightly held responsible in the Aristotelian legal sense, then that agent will as a matter of fact have had genuine alternatives from which to choose and could have acted otherwise if he or she had so chosen. It is because this is almost always the case that there is a feeling that responsibility and freedom are inextricably linked.

In order to make this case we need to begin by focusing rather on the second element of the notion of ultimate responsibility. Why is it thought that one needs to be responsible for the source of the source of one's action in order to be responsible for that action? The answer to this question appears to be the claim that one's actions are determined by one's nature or character, and if one is not in control of one's nature or character then one is not really in control of one's actions either. This, after all, is the basic thrust of Strawson's argument. But I would submit that this is to misconstrue the nature of our explanations of action in a very important way, and by exposing this error, one can begin to see how the Aristotelian analysis of responsibility might just be able to account for the mistaken intuition that responsibility requires genuine alternatives.

The first premise of Strawson's argument is that one does what one does because of one's nature and character. This amounts to saying that one's actions can be *fully explained* by one's nature or character. But this runs directly counter to the most widely held theory in this domain, namely, the Humean belief/desire theory of motivation. We will have occasion to discuss this theory in some detail in the next chapter in another context, but for present purposes, it is enough to note two points. The first is that an agent's *beliefs* play an ineliminable role in the explanation of the agent's actions.[16] An agent's desires, which are presumably determined or shaped by one's nature or character, are not enough on their own to explain why the agent does what he or she does. Consequently, if the Humean theory of motivation is correct, then premise (1) of Strawson's argument is false, or at least seriously incomplete. The second point is far less obvious but crucial to my thesis regarding the true relationship between Aristotelian responsibility and freedom.

The truth about the connection between responsibility and freedom is that they have the same roots or pre-conditions, and this explains why the two are so often thought to be inextricably linked. The point I wish to bring out and insist upon is that beliefs are *both* a necessary condition of Aristotelian responsibility *and* the ground of the possibility of alternative courses of action, and hence freedom. It is this second point I wish to focus on now. For if it can be seen to be credible then we will be able to argue as follows:

1. Human agents have beliefs.
2. If an agent has beliefs, then, other things being equal, the agent has genuine alternatives.
3. If an agent has genuine alternatives, then the agent is free (in the forked-paths-into-the-future sense).
4. In the normal course of things, human agents are free.

This argument is formally valid. Premise (1) is crucial to the Humean belief/desire theory of motivation (and established on independent grounds in Chapter 9) while I take (3) to be a conceptual truth. It remains then to establish premise (2).

As we have seen, knowledge is a necessary condition of Aristotelian responsibility because one is not held responsible for acts committed unwittingly – one must know what one is doing in order to be the principal cause of an action. Our new claim, however, is that as a matter of metaphysical fact, knowledge, belief and reasons are *also* the ground of our freedom because these mental states, regardless of their particular content, afford an agent greater independence of his or her environment than is otherwise possible. It is important to see why this is the case. This claim rests on two features of beliefs: the first is that beliefs are "decoupled mental representations"; the second is that having beliefs allows an agent to track states of affairs in the world *as it actually is* while permitting the agent to conceive of the world being *other than it is*. Let us take these points in turn.

Recall the distinction first encountered in Chapter 2 between cognitive systems which operate merely as detection systems and those cognitive systems able to produce beliefs (here understood as decoupled representations). It was noticed that some animals function with detection systems alone, while others, humans in particular, also have beliefs or decoupled representations. The distinction between these two sorts of cognitive state of interest to us here concerns the manner in which these states mediate an adaptive response to signals from the environment. Animals relying on detection systems alone produce mental representations which are rigidly connected to specific behavioural responses. For instance, cockroaches are able to evade capture by toads by detecting gusts of wind of the appropriate speed, gusts caused by the toad's quickly advancing head.[17] Once an appropriate gust has been detected, one, and only one, behavioural response is triggered. Similar stories can be told about frogs and the detection of fly-shaped shadows, rabbits and the detection of eagle-shaped shadows, herring gull chicks and the detection of moving red dots on medium sized bodies. In all such cases, the mental representations produced by the detection systems trigger a specific response. Things are very different with beliefs. Beliefs, being decoupled representations, are "accurate tracking states *potentially relevant to many acts*" (Sterelny, 2003, p. 31). Beliefs are "decoupled" from specific behavioural responses, trigger no specific action and allow the agent a degree of *behavioural flexibility* unavailable to cockroaches, frogs, rabbits, herring gull chicks and the like. It is precisely this flexibility that confers fitness value on beliefs in the first place, for they allow a move from animals which act strictly and rigidly in response to sensations and drives to those who can act on account of their assessment of their situation, assessments based on decoupled representations of how the world is and preferences concerning how the agent would like it to be. It was suggested that beliefs have fitness value particularly in complex environments where "pre-programmed" behaviours are less likely to be successful.

It is interesting to note that this particular feature of beliefs, that of being at the disposal of a variety of courses of action, was not lost on Aristotle or Aquinas, although it was framed in different language. Aquinas too was keen to insist that the lower animals act strictly in response to sensation. But humans, he insisted, can also act in virtue of their deliberations. Deliberation, meanwhile, proceeds by means of comparison. In particular, human agents compare alternative courses of action, and choose the one that best suits us. The ground of this possibility, according to Aquinas, is our intellect. We are free in the sense that there are genuine alternatives available to us to compare, says Aquinas, precisely because we are rational (*Summa Theologiae*, q. 83, a. 1, *Quaestiones disputatae de veritate*, 24.2). The reason for this is that to know or to conclude that p necessarily involves the belief that p. But to believe that p (as opposed to merely detecting that p), one must be able to understand the statement that p in order to know what one is assenting to. And, as we have already seen in Chapter 6, to understand the statement that p is to know its truth conditions. This means knowing the conditions under which p is true and the conditions under which p is false. But this means that to understand p, one must also understand its negation, which in turn implies the ability to conceive of p's possibly being false. Consequently, to have the belief that p is to view the world as being in one particular state while being able to conceive of other ways in which the world might be. The upshot of this is that an intellect furnished with beliefs is at least implicitly aware of alternative ways the world might be, something entirely beyond the ken of animals with mere detection systems. When a rabbit detects the presence of an eagle, for example, it is not also in a position to entertain alternative ways the world might be. The rabbit simply responds immediately and instinctively to the detection of the eagle with a fixed behavioural pattern. But if one understands or knows how to heal a sick person, say, because one knows what medicines or treatments to administer in this particular case, then one is at least implicitly aware of two courses of action. There is nothing to stop one from choosing to heal by administering the required treatment (because one can entertain this possibility), or from choosing to withhold treatment (because one can entertain this possibility as well).

It is important that this point not be lost. Others have maintained that reasons are important in the context of the free will debate because they are taken to represent the agent's true self, or deepest self, or the agent's second-order desires. I believe Frankfurt and Watson are simply wrong on this score, having conflated responsibility and freedom with the related but distinct concepts of self-control and self-discipline. What is important about beliefs in this context is that beliefs are the kind of mental representation they are, that is, representations decoupled from any specific responses which allow the agent to conceive of alternative courses of action. In fact we can go so far as to say that to be an animal with beliefs just is to be an animal with behavioural possibilities because this is precisely the biological point or function of beliefs in the first place.

What these reflections suggest is that human free agency is possible not because our actions are uncaused or because we can be the source of the source of our actions, but because, in virtue of the cognitive apparatus we are equipped with, we have the ability to conceive of possibilities that the lower animals are unable to entertain. While we too act on the basis of our desires and preferences, nature and character, what distinguishes human agents from the lower animals is that we can choose how to act on the basis of our desires and preferences after having deliberated, that is, after having compared alternative courses of action. This is what Aquinas means when he says that human beings can have rational appetites and desires. The severest restriction on our freedom comes then not from our nature or character, or past events and the laws of nature, but from our ignorance and poverty of imagination. Conversely, our freedom, our control over our own lives, is a matter of degree, increasing as our knowledge and awareness of possibilities increases.

If this account of human free agency is on the right track, then the fact that we have alternatives, and the fact that we can be, at least on occasion, responsible agents, is no longer mysterious, and the arguments of van Inwagen and Strawson will no longer be tempting. We do not need to be able to change the past or the laws of nature in order to be free. Nor do we need to be the source of the source of our actions in order to be responsible. It is rather the case that both human freedom and responsibility are made possible by the very nature of our biologically based cognitive apparatus. Our evolutionary history, our biology, far from being the bogies of determinism so many have held it to be, are the very grounds of these distinctly human characteristics.

9
On the Existence of Moral Facts

Introduction

In the last four chapters I have tried to offer a defence of the following beliefs: That the world available through sense perception exists independently of our representations of it, and that, contra Kant and other constructivists, we can know something of this world within the limits of our evolutionarily endowed capacities; that truth is a verification-transcendent property of sentences, and so, contra Dummett and the semantic anti-realists, the principle of bivalence ought to be maintained for beliefs about regions of space and time that lie beyond our verificational capacities; that human beings and other animals have representational states like beliefs, desires, hopes, expectations and so on, and that these states can be adverted to in order to explain behaviour, contra the Churchland and other eliminativists in the philosophy of mind; and finally that we human beings can be, and often are, responsible for our actions in a manner which makes us appropriate subjects of reactive attitudes, contra van Inwagen and Strawson. The pattern of these defences has been uniform throughout. I begin by shifting the burden of proof onto the opposition by establishing that the target conclusion is rightly granted the status of default position, and then, by identifying the errors in the arguments of the opposition, show that this burden has yet to be discharged. The leading idea has been that the target conclusion wins by default once these errors have been identified and so requires no further independent proof.

Now, in this final study, I want to consider one further topic in much the same manner as the preceding four. At issue is a cluster of related meta-ethical questions regarding the nature of moral judgements and the existence or otherwise of moral facts. I intend to show that there is as yet no good reason not to believe that there are moral facts, and that these facts, like any facts, are independent of our representations of them. After a few preliminary remarks, I proceed as usual to the sorts of considerations the reader will now have come to expect, considerations which invite the conclusion that moral realism and moral cognitivism ought to be taken as default positions. I then turn to what in recent years has become perhaps the most widely discussed of the perceived threats to moral realism, a threat stemming from considerations concerning the relationship between moral judgement and motivation. This challenge has been returned to prominence by the meta-ethicist Michael Smith in his book *The Moral Problem*. But as we shall soon see, the roots of the problem lie in Hume.

Preliminary remarks

Meta-ethics used to be a much simpler affair. For the first third of the twentieth century, there was one basic meta-ethical question, namely, does the world contain a realm of mind-independent moral facts in virtue of which moral judgements are true or false? And there were only two general answers with clear-blue water between them. On the one hand, there were those who answered the question in affirmative, and, following Moore's example, backed a metaphysically and epistemologically extravagant version of non-naturalistic, intuitionist, moral realism. This school maintained that moral facts do indeed exist, although these were not the sort of facts that could find a home in a scientifically respectable worldview. According to this school, moral facts are not discovered by empirical studies of a scientific nature but were to be "intuited" in a fashion never fully articulated. Meanwhile, the camp of naysayers housed those inclined to metaphysical and epistemological austerity. Moral anti-realists denied outright that the world contained anything, non-natural or otherwise, that could serve as the truth makers of moral judgements, thus sparing themselves the metaphysical and epistemological tasks of locating moral facts in a physical world and explaining how one might come to be acquainted with them.

Now armed with this leading question and these general answers, the happy observer could quite readily identify a moral realist or anti-realist when presented with one. Subsequently, the task of identification became even easier following the defeat of intuitionism in the 1930s after which time moral realists became increasingly thin on the ground. That rarest of creatures – a philosophical consensus – had emerged. For much of the remainder of the century, philosophical orthodoxy espoused some form of moral anti-realism or non-cognitivism, namely, the view that moral judgements are not truth-apt, and do not express beliefs that are made true or false by some realm of moral facts, but are rather expressions of sentiment or attempts at persuasion or the offering of advice, all of which were thought to lie beyond strictly rational appraisal.

Times have changed. Moral anti-realism and non-cognitivism now have as many detractors as supporters. But this has not meant a return to the heady days of the Bloomsbury group. Rather, the last third of the twentieth century witnessed the gradual convergence of these hitherto polarised camps on a subtlety-nuanced but still uncertain middle ground. Gone are the days of the ontologically extravagant neo-Platonic realist. But the naïve and somewhat crass Emotivism of A. J. Ayer has also been banished as a relic of bygone times. In their stead, the observer is now faced with a proliferation of competing positions on both sides of the divide. There has also been a blurring of the distinctions between the two great camps as a range of interrelated but distinct questions have pushed themselves forward for consideration.[1] Indeed, the formerly clear-blue water that used to separate the two camps has now become so murky that at times it is far from obvious just what the outstanding issues of the realist dispute in meta-ethics are.[2] Some have even suggested that the differences in meta-ethical positions ought no longer to be framed in terms of their commitment to or denial of the existence of a mind-independent realm of moral facts.[3] And the impression that the centre of meta-ethical gravity has shifted to other issues is strengthened by the observation that meta-ethicists can apparently agree on the ontological status of moral properties but disagree as to whether this status is consistent with moral realism or anti-realism.[4]

There is no doubt that the stark differences between moral realists and anti-realists have given way to a more sophisticated appreciation of the meta-ethical terrain. And there is no doubt that a degree of convergence on a shared middle ground does represent something of a philosophical advance. But there are limits to the accommodation the moral realist can offer the anti-realist if he or she is to remain consistent with common sense. For while common sense does not have a view on the precise metaphysical nature of the moral realm (it does not, for example, have a view on whether the moral facts are natural or non-natural, and if natural whether they are reducible to non-moral facts or not), the intuitions of common sense nonetheless favour the view that there is a realm of moral facts which exists independently of our representations of them. Consequently, it is incumbent upon the common sense philosopher with an interest in meta-ethics to sketch a position which is at least consistent with this fundamental assumption, and to defend it from the threats and challenges posed by moral anti-realists and non-cognitivists. It is for this reason that the following discussion is focussed on what may appear to some meta-ethicists as the slightly old fashioned question – Are there moral facts? – and will as often as not pass over in silence many of the important differences between the varieties of moral realism currently on offer.

That said, for present purposes I shall take common sense moral realism to be the combination of two claims: (i) the ontological claim that the world contains moral facts which exist independently of our representations of them and (ii) the epistemological claim that we can, at least on occasion, know what those facts are. A natural companion to moral realism is moral cognitivism, namely, the psychological claim that moral judgements express beliefs that are in the market for truth, and are not simply expressions of attitudes. Together, moral realism and cognitivism amount to the claim that moral judgements are expressions of beliefs which are truth-apt in virtue of the mind-independent moral facts these beliefs accurately or inaccurately track. I would suggest that these are the essential claims of any meta-ethical position that could reasonably call itself consistent with common sense, and they are likely to be included in any version of moral realism. However, the argument to follow will at times go beyond this bare-bones account of moral realism. It will be suggested, for example, that moral facts supervene on facts relating to *non*-moral value, and that what is of non-moral value is largely a function of human nature and our ecological and social environment. On this construal of moral realism, moral facts would not continue to exist if all human beings were to perish. That is, the moral realist is not committed to the quasi-Platonic view that moral facts exist prior to and independently of us, or that the moral facts "owe nothing to our nature". To say that the moral facts exist "independently of our representations of them" is simply to say that the moral facts are not determined by our perspectives, decisions, conventions, likes or dislikes, but by a realm of facts which owe nothing to these.[5]

Shifting the burden of proof

Why should we consider common sense moral realism and moral cognitivism to be default positions? Perhaps the best reason we have for this assumption is that all parties to the dispute seem to grant this as a matter of course. For instance, of his own error theory, which denies moral realism while accepting moral cognitivism, Mackie writes,

> since it goes against assumptions ingrained in our thought and built into some of the ways in which language is used, since it conflicts with what is sometimes called *common sense*, it needs very solid support. It is not something we can accept lightly or casually and then quietly pass on. If we are to adopt this view, we must argue explicitly for it.
>
> (1977, p. 35, emphasis added)

The implication of this passage appears to be that Mackie has accepted that there is a basic asymmetry in this debate in that it is incumbent upon the anti-realist to make his case, to provide it with "very solid support", while, presumably, the moral realist need not argue explicitly for his or her position. But it is also the case that moral realists often go about their business as though they are free to assume that moral realism is a default position, designing their arguments not so much to establish moral realism directly but rather to defend it from attack. For example, in his account of moral realism, McNaughton employs now familiar metaphors to describe the general strategy of the moral realist. He writes, "Just as, in a criminal trial, the presumption that the defendant is innocent until he is proved guilty places the burden of proof on the prosecution, so, the realist claims, the burden of proof in this debate rests with the non-cognitivist" (1988, pp. 39–41).

But the practice of philosophers notwithstanding, it is best to review the arguments that can be put forward for the claim that moral realism ought to be treated as a default position. A particularly strong argument for this view is that our pre-theoretical ethical beliefs, practices and experiences presuppose the existence of moral facts. For example, everyone is familiar with the experience of struggling with serious moral dilemmas. On these occasions it is not at all unusual for one to hesitate and agonise over what one ought to do in the given circumstances. This hesitancy, this agonising over the possibility of making a mistake, the very stuff of life and literature, suggests that in our pre-theoretical moments we assume that there are right and wrong answers to moral questions, and that the rightness or wrongness of these answers, in no way, depends upon our subjective likes and dislikes. Indeed, if we believed that all answers to moral questions were on a par, and that from an objective point of view it makes no moral difference what course of action one chooses, then a very significant element of the phenomenology of our moral life would be quite inexplicable.

Another widely acknowledged fact among meta-ethicists of all parties is that the assumption that moral judgements are truth-apt is reflected in the very grammar of ordinary language and the meaning of moral terms.[6] It is widely recognised, for instance, that moral judgements expressed in sentences like "Murder is wrong", or "Honesty is the best policy" have the same subject-copula-predicate form as obviously descriptive statements like "Water is H_2O" and "Heat is the mean kinetic energy of molecules". A further complication is that moral judgements can appear as premises of prima facie valid arguments, in both embedded and non-embedded contexts. Non-cognitivists have struggled manfully to cope in various ways with these uncomfortable facts. But the attempts to explain away the apparent truth-aptness of moral judgements, even if initially plausible in the case of expressions in non-embedded contexts, have failed to win widespread support.[7]

To these linguistic facts we can also add authority of the three leading figures of the common sense tradition. Aristotle and Reid were both naturalistically inclined moral realists,[8] while Moore defended a version of non-natural moral realism. Moore's contribution to meta-ethics, however, is somewhat ironic. For if modern meta-ethics begins with Moore's *Principia Ethica*, and his forceful statement of a version of moral realism, he is also responsible for the one argument which perhaps more than any other led to the rise of non-cognitivism. Moreover, Moore's argument contains the fatal error I have associated with the principle of separability and the Condemnations of 1277. It is worthwhile then for purposes of illustration to digress, if only briefly, to consider Moore's Open-Question argument.

[Moore's Open-Question argument was designed to refute all versions of naturalistic moral realism, and it struck most of Moore's early readers as successful.[9] But many balked at Moore's alternative, intuitionism or non-naturalistic realism, because it forced one to entertain entities and properties that could not be reconciled with a naturalistic metaphysics and epistemology. Given the alleged refutation of naturalistic realism and the distastefulness of Moore's non-naturalistic realism, it is not surprising that many abandoned all hope of finding any acceptable version of moral realism. But a little reflection shows that Moore and his early readers all made a similar mistake.

Moore's argument is designed to show that moral properties referred to with terms like "good" or "bad" cannot be reduced to or identified with non-moral properties (as naturalistically inclined moral realists had hoped). The Open-Question argument was taken to show that this kind of reduction is impossible because for any alleged definition of "good", say, it was always possible to ask of the definiens, say "desirable", whether it was itself good. If this question seemed to betray no conceptual confusion, as it inevitably did not, it was then concluded that the definition could not possibly be correct because the two terms were obviously not synonymous, and so the proposed reduction could not go through. But the assumption underlying this move is that if there is no conceptual connection between "good" and "desirable", say, then the extra-linguistic entities or properties picked out by these terms could not themselves be identical either but had to be ontologically distinct. The reasoning behind this conclusion, if explicitly drawn out, would go something like this:

1. If the referent of "good" is identical/reducible to the referent of "desirable", then it is necessarily the case that these referents are identical.[10]
2. But if (1), and the only necessity is logical necessity, then "good" ought to be conceptually analysable by "desirable".
3. "Good" is not analysable by "desirable" (or by any other non-moral term), as is *shown by the Open-Question Argument*.
4. The referents of "good" and "desirable" (or any other non-moral term) are not identical.

In effect, we have the principle of separability at work yet again and having no small impact on the course of western philosophical thinking.

Of course, armed with the sense/reference distinction and the rehabilitated notion of natural or physical necessity, it is now widely appreciated that Moore's version of the Open-Question argument poses a threat only to analytical reductionism, a version of moral realism few are attracted to today. It is also worth noting, if only in passing, that it is for these same reasons that moral realists of a naturalistic bent are no longer concerned about the notorious is/ought distinction, and the charge that it is impossible to derive an ought from an is. Since one can claim that moral properties are identical to, or supervene upon natural properties without there being a deductive or semantic or conceptual connection between these properties, it is no longer incumbent upon naturalistic moral realists to show that there is a conceptual, semantic or deductive relationship between propositions about natural states of affairs and propositions containing moral or normative language.]

Finally we ought to ask what light evolutionary biology throws on this particular dispute in meta-ethics. Are there good biological reasons for assuming that moral realism ought to be taken as a default position?

A quick review of the literature on this point is enough to establish that this question remains highly controversial despite the fact that enormous efforts have been made in recent times to view ethics through the lens of evolutionary biology and other empirical sciences. The relationship between biology and ethics in particular remains highly contentious. Even amongst those biologists who believe that the sciences do have something to say on ethical matters, there is often little agreement as to what that say might be. For example, Williams (1988, 1989) argues that the ends of evolutionary processes are morally dubious, and so any adaptive moral characteristics we might have, be they dispositions or beliefs, are painted with the same black brush. The moral of the story, on this line anyway, is that we need to look critically at, and perhaps radically re-evaluate, our deeply ingrained moral intuitions. Others, like Richard Alexander (1979, 1985, 1987), see evolutionary ends as morally neutral, and are consequently more sanguine about the need to revisit current moral attitudes with a suspicious eye; while still others, like E. O. Wilson (1978), argue that biology provides the very foundations of morality itself. But whatever the virtues of "biologicizing" ethics, no clear and unambiguous message has so far emerged from this endeavour as far as our present debate is concerned. This is due in no small part to the fact that the primary interest of many biologists with an interest in ethics, and ethicists with an interest in biology, has been to identify the evolutionary processes behind the emergence of moral sensibilities and capacities in general (and altruism in particular) rather than the niceties of the meta-ethical debate as I have presented it here.[11] The pressing issue for this group of researchers has not been the proper understanding of the nature of moral judgements, but rather how creatures with moral sensibilities could have arisen in the first place given that they are products of evolution by natural selection, and so prey to "selfish" evolutionary incentives that seem to militate against those very sensibilities. Contestants in this dispute generally divide up into two groups, those favouring a reciprocity-based account on the one hand and those favouring a punishment-based account on the other. But as fascinating as this debate is, it has little or no direct light to shed on our present meta-ethical concerns.[12]

What is also becoming clear is that the nature of one's understanding of the meta-ethical debate inevitably influences the kind of empirical facts one hopes to turn up in the course of one's empirical research, as well as one's interpretation of those facts. For instance, some cognitive neuroscientists with an interest in meta-ethics have recently argued in favour of what they call "sentimentalism" – a form of non-cognitivism – on the empirical grounds that moral judgements are cognitively impenetrable in much the same sense in which Pylyshsyn first introduced the term in the context of vision.[13] On the other hand, others have tried to support what they call "rationalism" – a form of moral realism and cognitivism – on the empirical grounds that moral judgements are, *pace* the sentimentalists, cognitively penetrable.[14] Battle has then been joined over the empirical question concerning the impenetrability or otherwise of moral judgements.

Unfortunately, as interesting as this debate is, it does not touch the essentials of ours. Our debate concerns the existence or otherwise of moral facts, and whether moral judgements express beliefs which are truth-apt or merely expressions of sentiments or attitudes of approval or disapproval, and it is far from the clear that the cognitive processes involved in the fixing of these moral judgements are at all relevant. Cognitive neuroscientists have been asking whether moral judgements are innate or the products of innate dispositions – and so cognitively impenetrable – or whether they are the products of rational engagement with the available evidence – and so cognitively penetrable. But the answers to these questions, I suggest, tell us little about the metaphysics of ethics. For concept nativists do *not* hold that a belief loses the property of being truth-apt for being the result of the triggering of an innate concept or disposition. So even if the entire process of belief formation for a particular belief were cognitively impenetrable, that belief – simply in virtue of being a belief – remains truth-apt nonetheless. Cognitive impenetrability is therefore no sure marker of a non-cognitive attitude or sentiment. Similarly, whether moral judgements can be influenced subsequently in a rational manner following an alteration in one's non-moral beliefs tells us nothing about whether moral judgements are in the market for truth or not. Certainly we all recognise that many people can hold on to a belief in spite of the fact that they accept, at some level at least, that all the available evidence counts against it. But, again, these beliefs remain truth-apt despite being held on insufficient grounds, or in the face of all the available evidence. Irrationality, therefore, is not a sure marker of a non-cognitive attitude or sentiment either. And as we shall see, the paradigm examples of non-cognitive mental states, our desires, are themselves open to revision following changes in our non-moral beliefs. So rational revisability is no sure marker of a cognitive mental state either. Consequently, we must set aside the empirical work on the cognitive impenetrability or otherwise of moral judgements as irrelevant to our present concerns.

Nonetheless, it is not difficult to see how moral realism and moral cognitivism could be advantageous from a biological point of view. For if moral facts supervene on facts concerning *non*-moral value, as I would contend, then tracking these facts, and taking them to be facts (as opposed to conventions, say) would be advantageous for precisely the same reason that tracking facts and having true beliefs in general is advantageous, only more so. For if we accept that certain objects, actions, character traits and practices have non-moral value insofar as they are necessary to, or tend to promote, the health and general well-being of human beings given the sorts of creatures we are, then we can reasonably suggest that an action or character trait, say, has moral value insofar as it encourages or promotes the distribution of items with non-moral value among as many people as possible. If something like this account of the nature of moral facts is accepted, and we assume that human nature is not a product of our representations, then the mind-independence of these facts in the sense outlined above is secure, as well as their biological and social utility. Indeed tracking these facts is crucial to the over-all well-being of both individuals and the groups to which they belong since these facts pertain directly to the physical, emotional and psychological health of the individual and the health of the body politic.

To sum up the discussion so far: I have suggested that there is good reason to assume that moral realism is rightly taken as a default position. Not only has this assumption won widespread acceptance among all parties to our dispute, significant phenomenological and linguistic facts also point in this direction. Moreover, the three leading figures of the common sense tradition themselves all defend some version of moral realism. And finally, if moral facts supervene on facts relating to non-moral value, and if these facts are significant from an ecological and social point of view, then evolutionary biology appears to favour moral realism as a default position as well. Let this suffice to shift the burden of proof onto the shoulders of the non-cognitivist and let us now turn our attention to their efforts to discharge that burden.

The Moral Problem

Again it is impossible to discuss all the arguments non-cognitivists might appeal to in an attempt to justify their characteristic conclusions but we can at least discuss those perceived to be the strongest on offer. It is with this in mind that I have chosen to discuss issues recently brought back into focus by Michael Smith's *The Moral Problem*. But the challenge outlined by Smith is also attractive because it epitomises perfectly the general nature of philosophical problems as set out in the opening chapter of this book.

In his widely discussed work *The Moral Problem* Smith argues that to make sense of the current state of play in meta-ethics one has to recognise that meta-ethicists are pulled in two seemingly contradictory directions at once by two equally plausible intuitions. As we have seen above, there is on the one hand the feeling or sense that moral judgements do in fact express beliefs, that these beliefs are truth-apt, and that through deliberation and discussion we can know that particular moral judgements are true or false (or at least begin to converge on a consensus regarding the rights and wrongs of a particular action). It is this intuition, or set of intuitions, that pulls in the direction of moral realism and its psychological counterpart cognitivism. For ease of exposition we can follow Smith and call this cluster of intuitions the "objectivity claim".

On the other hand, there is the equally strong intuition that moral judgements are intimately connected with action in a way that non-moral judgements are not. For example, if I make the non-moral judgement that my fridge contains all the necessary ingredients for spaghetti alla carbonara, I will not be motivated to act on this judgement unless I happen to want to make this dish. Moreover, my not proceeding to make the dish provides no grounds for doubting that I sincerely believed that my fridge contained all the necessary ingredients. Things are otherwise with moral judgements. We tend to think that moral judgements have a particular kind of authority which makes it impossible not to be motivated to act in accordance with them. If someone is *not* motivated by their moral judgement as expected, then an onlooker would quite naturally be inclined to believe either that the judgement was not sincerely held, or that the person was suffering from some form of irrationality. For example, we would find it rather odd if someone agreed that it is morally right to donate one's kidney to save an ailing sibling and yet failed to be motivated to do so when the occasion arose.[15] Following Smith, we can call this intuition the "practicality claim".

The "moral problem", says Smith, echoing Hume, Mackie, Hare, Blackburn and others, is that the "objectivity" and "practicality" claims regarding moral judgement are, under certain interpretations at least, in tension *if* one also assumes that the Humean belief/desire theory of motivation is correct.[16] Although the nature of the problem is now widely familiar, it is worth while rehearsing the details to see precisely how the tension is supposed to emerge. The claim is that meta-ethicists are faced with a prima facie inconsistent triad of plausible propositions, and the task has been either to show that the inconsistency is merely apparent, or to determine which of the triad is to be abandoned. Since it is widely thought that the tensions are indeed genuine, most efforts have been devoted to arguing in favour of the rejection of one or other of the three propositions.

The propositions of the inconsistent triad can be expressed more sharply as follows:

1. Moral judgements express a subject's beliefs about matters of fact, in particular a fact about what it is right for him or her to do.
2. If someone judges that a certain act in a given set of circumstances is the right act to perform, then he or she is *ipso facto* motivated to perform that act.
3. Someone is motivated to perform a particular act if they have the appropriate desire and mean/ends belief, where beliefs and desires are "distinct existences".

Point (1) is an expression of cognitivism and the objectivity claim. Point (2) is a version of the practicality claim known as "internalism". Internalism is the claim that the motivation to perform the act in question is "internal" to the moral judgement in the sense that the judgement requires nothing in addition to itself to produce the motivation. The point is often expressed by saying that there is a *conceptual connection* between the moral judgement and the corresponding motivation.[17] Internalists posit this particularly strong connection between moral judgement and motivation in order to account for the practical or categorical nature of moral judgements which so clearly distinguishes them from non-moral judgements. Point (3) is an (incomplete) expression of the Humean theory of motivation.

Now the non-cognitivist challenge is that the tension between these propositions, combined with the perceived merits of (2) and (3), is sufficient to warrant the rejection of (1), that is, the rejection of moral realism. This challenge is the focus of our attention here, and it will serve to guide our interpretations of (2) and (3), for there are numerous formulations of these principles only some of which produce a tension which threatens (1). Since I am here concerned with the fate of moral realism, I will ignore those interpretations under which (2) and (3) do not threaten (1).[18]

Essentially the non-cognitivist claim is that moral judgements cannot be both cognitive and intrinsically motivating (as demanded by (1) and (2), respectively) if (3), the Humean theory of motivation, is true.

Since (3) is widely regarded as orthodox philosophical psychology at its finest, the situation quickly becomes uncomfortable for the moral realist, particularly if the moral realist is taken to be committed to both (1) *and* (2).[19] But even if the moral realist is formally committed only to (1), as I would contend, the pressure is still on the moral realist because (2) coheres with (3) while (1) does not.

The pressure on (1) is said to arise in the following manner: If (1) is right, then moral judgements are expressions of beliefs. But if Hume's belief/desire theory of motivation is true, then it becomes unclear just how moral judgements could be instrinsically motivating, as demanded by (2). For Hume's belief/desire theory of motivation states that beliefs and desires play different roles in the production or emergence of a motivation.[20] The crucial point for present purposes is that, according to Hume, all beliefs, in virtue of being beliefs, are motivationally inert. Beliefs on their own, says Hume, never lead one to perform any action at all.[21] It is desires, a completely distinct non-cognitive mental state, which contain the motivational "umph" that beliefs lack in and of themselves but which is thought to be conspicuously present in moral judgements. It is only when accompanied by the relevant desire that a belief is able to generate the motivation to perform a particular act.[22] This is enough to threaten the moral realist who accepts internalism. For moral realists committed to internalism maintain that moral judgements *on their own* are sufficient to produce a motivation. This runs directly contrary to Hume's belief/desire theory of motivation if moral judgements are taken to be beliefs.

But the moral realist is not finished yet. He or she might think that the practicality claim does not require a commitment to there being a conceptual connection between moral judgements and motivation, as maintained by internalists. If the cognitivist were to grant that moral judgements need the external support of a desire in order to motivate, but maintain nonetheless that there is a reliable but non-conceptual connection between beliefs and desires, the cognitivist could claim that this is all he or she needs to square his or her position with the practicality claim. For he or she could then claim that a moral judgement in tandem with a desire to which it is reliably connected results in the generation of the expected motivation, with the moral judgement playing the leading role in the production of that motivation. But again Hume's theory frustrates the cognitivist's hopes. For beliefs and desires, says Hume, are separate and distinct mental states.[23] This entails, in accordance with the principle of separability discussed in Chapter 4, that there can be no reliable connection between beliefs and desires because there are no conceptual or logical connections between them. So externalist moral realism is blocked by Hume's theory of motivation as well. This leaves the moral realist and cognitivist without any apparent means of squaring their position with the practicality claim. By contrast, the non-cognitivist claim that moral judgements are expressions of sentiment rather than expressions of beliefs coheres perfectly with internalism and the Humean belief/desire theory of motivation.

We can sum up the moral realist's problem then as follows: If the Humean theory of motivation is true in all respects, then, as a matter of conceptual necessity, moral judgements cannot be both expressions of belief *and* prescriptive, directional or action-guiding. For on this theory beliefs are not motivational in and of themselves but neither are they reliably connected to any desires. But if a putative moral judgement is not motivational, then, according to the practicality claim, it is not a moral judgement at all. The upshot is that acceptance of (2) and (3) seems to force the rejection of (1).

A common sense response to The Moral Problem

The standard solutions to the moral problem canvassed by moral realists are forced by the logic of the situation. If the tensions are genuine, and all agree that they are, then the moral realist must reject either (2) or (3) or both. The rejection of internalism is the course taken by externalist moral realists such as Brink and Railton, while others, for instance Nagel, McDowell and McNaughton, think it better to reject the Humean belief/desire theory of motivation and to develop a cognitive theory of desire that is thought to apply at least in the case of moral judgements. Neither of these courses of action, in all their details, is the option to be defended here. Like McDowell, I agree that the Humean theory of motivation must be rejected as it stands but for different reasons. Nor I do not think the prospects are at all good for a purely cognitive theory of desire. This route has been extensively explored;[24] but all such theories suffer from the fact that they postulate very peculiar mental states indeed, namely, mental states with contradictory directions of fit.[25] But it is not obvious that a cognitive theory of desire is needed. In fact, I contend that McDowell and others have been attacking the wrong aspect of Hume's theory and suggest rather that there is an eminently plausible version of the belief/desire theory of motivation which is consistent with moral realism, cognitivism and the practicality claim. However, I also agree with Brink and other externalists that the version of internalism used to generate the threat to moral realism is also untenable as it stands.

Nonetheless, the practicality claim cannot be rejected out of hand. I will suggest that there is a version of externalism that can be defended from Hume's attack and still do justice to the practicality claim. In short, I reject both (2) and (3) as they stand, but offer versions of both which do justice to our original intuitions while remaining consistent both with each other and with (1). This will suffice to defend moral realism from this particular anti-realist threat.

The principle of separability and the importance of distinctions

The moral problem as outlined above is best defused by first examining and rejecting the Humean theory of motivation as it currently stands. For as we shall see, the grounds for rejecting (3) also provide the grounds for rejecting (2) in its current form and for substituting a weaker but more plausible version of the practicality claim.

To anticipate, I will argue that Hume's version of the belief/desire theory is simply not an accurate account human motivation. But I will not attempt to argue for this by trying to show that beliefs, even special beliefs like moral judgements, can be motivational on their own. Rather I grant that Hume is right to insist that motivation requires both beliefs and desires (as Aristotle himself insisted), and that beliefs construed as decoupled representations are motivationally inert in and of themselves. What I deny is that there are no reliable connections between these two types of mental state, at least within psychologically healthy human beings. But without this element of Hume's theory in place, the threat to cognitivism dissolves. For the non-cognitivist challenge as outlined above emerges only on the assumption that Hume's theory of motivation is correct in all its details. In particular, it was seen to be a crucial ingredient of the theory that there can be no reliable connections between beliefs and desires because there are no logical or conceptual connections between these two distinct types of existences. This assumption was important because it was taken to undermine any hope the externalist moral realist might have had that there might be a reliable but non-conceptual connection between beliefs and desires that could account for the motive force of moral judgements when construed as beliefs.

But it is precisely this aspect of Hume's theory which incorporates two serious mistakes. First, although it is true that there are no logical connections between beliefs and desires, it simply does not follow that there are no other reliable connections between these two types of mental states. This is the same error which Hume made in the context of the problem of induction, and there is no need to review it again here. But if Hume had not compounded this error with a second, namely the failure to recognise the import of the distinction between two types of passions, he might well have noticed that there are, even by his own admission, reliable connections of a sort between beliefs and certain passions. It is this second mistake that will occupy us here.

Hume's argument that beliefs and desires are radically distinct existences relies on the assumption that there are only two distinct kinds of mental states relevant to motivation: beliefs, which are motivationally inert, but representational and so fit objects of rational critique, and desires or "passions" which are motivational, but not representational and so not fit objects of rational critique. Hume proceeds as though all mental states relevant to the production of action fall neatly into one or other of these two categories, and that there are no mental states which combine properties of both beliefs and desires. But Hume's neat dichotomy fails to do justice to the range of mental phenomena that even he acknowledges.

If one is even to begin to arrive at a complete list of mental states relevant to the production of action, one would have to include beliefs as decoupled representations (Hume's beliefs) but also representational states which are functionally tied to the triggering of a distinct behavioural response (e.g. the frog's detection of a fly-shaped object triggers the firing of the tongue, the herring gull chick's detection of a small red spot on a moving object triggers the pecking of the mother's bill). Contra Hume, this second type of representational mental state is "motivational", at least in the sense that it is able to produce an action seemingly without the addition of a desire. So there is at least one kind of mental state connected to action that does not fit into Hume's clear-cut dichotomy.

In defence of Hume, one might insist that humans do not have representational states which trigger behavioural responses in this fashion, or, if they do, that the question of motivation proper does not arise in these contexts, or that such behaviour does not constitute action in the requisite sense. I have some sympathy with this collection of reposts. But whatever their merits in this instance, they will not suffice to undermine the import of the distinctions we undoubtedly need to draw on the desire/passion side of Hume's dichotomy. For even Hume implicitly recognises a clear distinction between two kinds of "passions", namely, the distinction between the emotions and physiologically based appetites. For as Hume himself admits, emotions like anger, love, hope and fear are linked to beliefs in a way that appetites like hunger and thirst are not. Thirst, for example, is purely physiological and arational. It does not arise in response to beliefs of any sort, nor will it "yield" to reason under any circumstances.

Things are otherwise with emotions. First, the emotions have an intentional or directional quality which the appetites do not have. One gets angry *about* something or *with* someone, falls in love *with* someone, is hoping *for* something, is fearful *about* something and so on with the rest of the emotions. Moreover, and most importantly, the emotions arise in response to our cognitive appreciation of our situation. To use just one example from Aristotle, it appears to be a fact about psychologically healthy human beings that we cannot feel anger unless we have certain beliefs, in particular the belief that someone has intentionally and deliberately harmed or slighted us or our friends.[26] What is more, it would appear that in psychologically healthy adults such beliefs are usually not only necessary but also sufficient for the production of the anger, although this is not universally the case.[27] Similar accounts can be provided for all the other emotions.[28] Indeed, awareness of the relationships between beliefs and the emotions forms the stock and trade of the successful politician or advertiser. After all, the rhetor and the salesman are in the business of persuading and motivating an audience to pursue a certain course of political action or to buy a certain product, and they achieve this end principally by inducing in their audience appropriately positive sentiments about the proposed action or product. The desired attitudes are in turn secured by getting the audience to *believe* what the rhetor or salesman wants the audience to believe about the action or product (i.e. whatever beliefs typically generate the desired attitudes).

The general point here that the emotions depend upon beliefs, albeit psychologically if not logically, is granted by Hume himself. He notes, "The moment we perceive the falsehood of any supposition, or the insufficiency of any means, *our passions yield to our reason* without any opposition." (*Treatise*, p. 416, emphasis added). But this has an important implication. Hume also admits, as he surely must, that anger and the other emotions *are* in fact subject to rational critique insofar as the emotions, unlike hunger and thirst, arise in response to certain beliefs. If, for example, my anger towards a particular person were "founded on a false supposition" and did not evaporate upon my discovery of the error, then my anger would rightly be deemed irrational. What is more, if my anger suddenly arose in my breast of itself, unbidden by any beliefs at all, or in response to beliefs having nothing to do with harm suffered at the hands of others, then again my anger would rightly be deemed inappropriate and irrational. Similarly, my failure to get angry when the appropriate beliefs are in place is a good indication that not all is well with me.[29]

The admission that certain passions are connected to beliefs in the fashion outlined above, and consequently that certain passions can be subjected to rational critique, constitute highly significant concessions on Hume's part[30] because they point to the very different nature of emotions and physiologically based appetites. The emotions, like the appetites, are motivational, but unlike the appetites, they are at least quasi-intentional because they are directed at something in the world and quasi-rational because subject to rational critique. So it must be recognised that certain mental states related to motivation and action are mixed, having the properties associated with both beliefs and desires. And yet in spite of his acknowledgement of the fact that the emotions are modifiable by modifications of belief, a feature which in no way belongs to states like hunger and thirst, Hume still insists on lumping emotions and appetites together as undifferentiated "passions". He writes,

> A passion is an original existence, or, if you will, modification of existence, and contains not any representative quality, which renders it a copy of any other existence or modification. When I am angry, I am actually possest with the passion, and in that emotion have no more reference to any other object, than when I am thirsty, or sick, or more than five foot high.
>
> (*Treatise*, p. 415)

This conflation of emotions and appetites is simply false to the facts. The emotions are *not* simply physiological states to be understood in purely physiological terms. The emotions cannot be understood without reference to the agent's beliefs about the object or situation upon which the emotion is directed. And it is precisely this close connection between belief and emotion that accounts for the fact that one's emotions can be modified by modifications of one's beliefs, as Hume goes on to admit in his very next paragraph.

The upshot of this discussion is that a catalogue of human mental states relevant to human motivation has to include as least three distinct kinds of states: *beliefs,* or decoupled representations, which are much as Hume described them; *arational appetites* like hunger and thirst; and *emotions* or *desires,* which seem to be appropriately described as *rational appetites.* We can define "rational appetites" as intrinsically motivational states whose existence in psychologically healthy people depends upon the presence of certain relevant beliefs.

Hume's failure to do justice to the distinct nature of the emotions renders his version of the belief/desire theory of motivation untenable. For while it remains highly plausible that motivation requires both beliefs and "passions" of some kind, it is simply *not* the case that there are no reliable connections between beliefs and the emotions, at least in psychologically healthy people. Despite the fact that there are no logical connections between beliefs and desires it is simply *not* the case, as Hume's official theory requires, that one can have *any* set of desires whatsoever regardless of one's beliefs without being subject to rational criticism.[31] The rational appetites, the emotions, simply do not float free of beliefs in the way Hume suggests. Rather, desires appear to be reliably connected to beliefs, at least in psychologically healthy adult human beings. This is significant because the moral realist can now accept a modified but highly plausible version of the belief/desire theory of motivation and still satisfy the practicality claim. Moral judgements are indeed motivational, but not because moral judgements are themselves conceptually connected to motivation, but rather because in psychologically healthy adult human beings moral judgements are reliably connected to emotions which, when taken together, provide the motivational "umph" which moral judgements themselves lack.

Externalism and the charge of rule fetishism

So far I believe that I have shown that moral realism and cognitivism is in fact consistent with plausible versions of (2) and (3) and is under no pressure to accept those versions from which a threat emerges. However, the externalist account of moral motivation just sketched faces a further objection that can be pressed by internalists of all stripes. The objection is that any account of moral motivation consistent with the practicality claim must be able to explain in a satisfactory fashion why a change in motivation reliably follows a change in moral judgement. The charge is that internalists can meet this challenge while externalists cannot. I close this chapter with a discussion of this final point.

There is no denying that any acceptable account of moral motivation needs to be able to explain why our motivations change in accordance with changes in our moral judgements. And there is no doubt that if internalism were acceptable on other grounds, it would provide such an explanation. The internalist would say that changes in motivation reliably follow changes in moral judgement because there is a conceptual connection between judgements and motivation. But, says the internalist, this explanation is not available to the externalist since he or she denies there are conceptual connections between moral judgements and motivation, *and no other kind of explanation will do*. The argument for this last claim needs spelling out. I will follow Smith's (1994, pp. 71–76) account of the argument here.

Smith claims that if one denies the existence of a conceptual connection between moral judgements and motivation, then one is committed to maintaining that the connection between moral judgement and motivation is "wholly contingent", and that any motivation associated with a particular moral judgement is a "rationally optional extra" (1994, p. 75). And, says Smith, if there is no conceptual connection between judgement and motivation, the only remaining possible explanation for the fact that changes in motivation reliably follow changes in moral judgement must run through the nature of the "good and strong-willed person". In particular, the externalist must advert to "the content of the motivational dispositions possessed by the good and strong-willed person" (ibid., p. 72). But, asks Smith, what is the content of this disposition if it is not simply "to do the right thing, where this is now read *de dicto* and not *de re*"? (ibid., p. 74). The allegation appears to be that on this externalist account a good person is not motivated by, for example, honesty, justice, or equality per se, but rather by an abstract desire simply to do the right thing in general. It is as if someone were to think along the following sorts of lines: "This particular action, because it is just, is the right course of action in these circumstances; and since I have a standing moral disposition to do whatever is right, I will take this particular course of action." The internalist complaint is that form of moral reflection is vicious "rule-fetishism" and false to the phenomenological facts. The good person, says the internalist, is motivated simply by the fact that the action is just, and there is no need for the self-conscious "extra thought" that the act also happens to be the right thing to do.

If the externalist account of moral motivation sketched in the preceding section were committed to such a position, then it would indeed be unacceptable. But it is not. Smith's challenge to the externalist assumes the Humean view of the relationship between beliefs and the emotions which we have already rejected. Consequently, we simply have no reason to believe that the connection between moral judgement and motivation is "wholly contingent" if this is taken to imply that the connection is purely accidental or co-incidental. Nor can we accept that motivations are "rationally optional extras" which may nor may not follow upon the acceptance of certain judgements. In psychologically well-ordered adult human beings, the emotions are reliably connected to beliefs in such a fashion that a change in beliefs will reliably bring about a change in emotional state. So there is no difficulty explaining why changes in motivation reliably follow changes in moral judgement despite there being no conceptual connections between them.

As for the charge of rule fetishism and the need for the unacceptable "extra thought", again the externalist has a ready response. In psychologically well-ordered adults, no such extra though exists and so the charge of rule fetishism misses the mark. If the moral education an individual receives in childhood is appropriate, then, barring any cognitive disorders, the adult's responses to honesty, justice and equality, say, will be automatic, habitual, second-nature responses, with no self-conscious extra thoughts entering the equation. The need for extra thoughts might arise in the early stages of one's moral development, when one is still learning what is *de re* right and wrong, acceptable and unacceptable, honourable and dishonourable and so on, and prior to one's having habituated oneself to respond in certain ways to the morally salient features of one's circumstances (before, that is, one has fixed and stable dispositions). But this is not the situation with morally competent adults. In fact, it is precisely this complete lack of extra thoughts which lends prima facie plausibility to internalism. It is not unreasonable to think that the internal lives of many psychologically healthy adult human beings are ordered in such a way that it appears that moral judgements on their own are sufficient to produce the motivation to act as those judgements demand. Phenomenologically, this is precisely how it does feel, for the emotional life of the psychologically healthy individual just is well-ordered in the sense that such individuals automatically feel appropriately given their appreciation of their situation on account of their now habitual dispositions.

The upshot of this is that the externalist *does* have a perfectly adequate explanation of the fact that changes in motivation reliably follow changes in moral judgement after all. Thus, the intuitions that pull in the direction of internalism are equally consistent with externalism. And since the externalist is not hampered with the problem of queer mental states with contradictory directions of fit, externalism is by far the preferable of the two theories of moral motivation. And since it is strong enough to secure the practicality claim, the cognitivist has all he or she needs to answer the non-cognitivist challenge to moral realism.

Afterword

My intention at the outset of this book was to provide an account and defence of the metaphilosophy of common sense and to illustrate this approach to philosophy by applying it in practice. The primary motivation for such an undertaking was to develop a plausible conception of the proper business of philosophy were it finally to renounce its love of paradox and rediscover its roots in the prosaic beliefs of the philosophical layperson. The extent to which I have succeeded in this admittedly rather ambitious endeavour is a judgement best left to others. Nonetheless, it would be well to bring this study to a close by pointing out where the weaknesses of my efforts are likely to be found (if they are not obvious enough already) and to draw attention to the issues which require much further work.

I do believe that some progress on the common sense project has been made on a number of fronts. Much work remains to be done, and many lines of thought are likely to require significant redrawing, but I think that on the first and second points some progress has been made. An enduring weakness of common sense philosophies in the past has been that no account of what constitutes a common sense belief has been forwarded which meets two basic requirements: First, that the putative common sense beliefs are at least reasonable approximations to commonplaces found among the uncorrupted philosophical laity; and second, that these same beliefs have a reasonable claim to the status of default position. It is not good enough, for example, to suggest that common sense beliefs are beliefs that most people find "obvious", because being obvious to many or most people is not in and of itself a good reason to give such beliefs the benefit of the doubt if they conflict with sophisticated philosophical theories. Similar objections can be raised against the other main contenders. A strength of the present effort is that an account of what constitutes a common sense belief has been floated which meets both desiderata. If we stipulate that common sense beliefs are those beliefs which tended to increase one's reproductive fitness in the ancestral environment, and if the revised evolutionary argument sketched in Chapter 2 is on the right lines, then we have every reason to place a good deal more confidence in these beliefs than in the paradoxical conclusions of philosophical theories and arguments. It is also reasonable to assume, although certain caveats are required, that beliefs with this evolutionary pedigree are likely to remain commonplaces among the uncorrupted philosophical laity despite the vast cultural and intellectual changes that have occurred since the Pleistocene.

However, there is an obvious weakness in this strategy, a weakness shared with evolutionary biology in general. The problem I have in mind is *not* that many will continue to find reasons to reject evolutionary biology in general, or that many will want to resist the application of evolutionary thinking to philosophical topics. The pressing concern is rather that the strategy, while sound in principle, will be difficult to apply in practice. The reason for this worry is that it is often extremely difficult to establish that a particular trait is genuinely an adaptation. The techniques most commonly employed by evolutionary biologists to make these determinations are at their least effective in the case of human beings.

Consider the techniques of comparative biology, for example. If trait x is found in species A but is absent in closely related species B (say both species belong to the same clade); and if trait x is not found in their most recent common ancestor, then it is likely that trait x is a recent adaptation in species A to a new selective environment. This method of comparative biology is quite powerful when we are dealing with clades with many closely related species that are available for such comparative studies to be carried out. However, the hominid clade has never been well populated, and, to make matters worse, all the other species of the clade are now extinct. This means the techniques of comparative biology, while not useless, are not particularly powerful when applied to the evolutionary history of human cognition. We are forced to drawn comparisons between ourselves and the great apes, and between ourselves and reconstructions of our extinct cousins, neither of which can be entirely satisfactory in all cases.

A similar story can be told for the other standard method of determining whether a trait is an adaptation. If one works on the general assumption that a genuinely adaptive trait will be optimal, then one can set about constructing quantitative models of the selective environment of the organism at the relevant time, and on the basis of these models generate a view regarding which values of the trait x are optimal and which are sub-optimal. One can then compare this result with that found in the real world. If the value of the trait found in the real world matches that predicted by means of the quantitative model, then there is good reason to believe the trait is an adaptation; if not, then not.

The problem with this method in our particular case is that the results are only as safe as the information used to generate the qualitative model of the selective environment, and this information is precisely what we often lack. Moreover, things are made more difficult in the case of human beings once we recognise the need to distinguish between an organism's physical environment and its selective environment. Because we human beings have for some time now been able to alter our physical environment in important ways, our selective environment is not identical with our physical environment. Our selective environment is to a large extent determined by culture, for culture can mitigate the selection effects of the purely physical environment. But our knowledge regarding the culture of our ancestors living during the Pleistocene is far less sure than our information regarding the physical environment of the time. The result, again, is that a standard method of determining whether a trait is an adaptation is less than entirely effective when it comes to reconstructing our cognitive history.

In the face of these difficulties, I have had to adopt the method of evolutionary psychologists Cosmides and Tooby. That is, I have had to consider a task our ancestors would most likely have been faced with on a regular basis, and then to imagine what beliefs would have been required in order for them to cope successfully with those tasks. I have been at pains to avoid unwarranted armchair speculation on these matters and to draw where possible on the work of those whose expertise in the relevant fields is sufficiently well regarded to inspire some confidence. I have also focused quite consciously on beliefs for which a plausible case is most easily made. Nonetheless, it remains the case that one will often be working in something of an information vacuum, a vacuum which can easily tempt one to invent plausible but self-serving "just-so" stories. Thus, one of the key outstanding challenges remaining to this metaphilosophy of common sense is to address the epistemological problems regarding our knowledge of the remote past, particularly our early cognitive history. This is necessary if the dialectical strategy employed here is to be applicable to more than a few select cases. Thus, despite my disparaging remarks about the Cartesian obsession with epistemology, in fact, there are *some* epistemological issues that really do merit the attention of the common sense philosopher.[1]

Of the third task, namely, dealing in a piece-meal fashion with the seemingly endless supply of philosophical paradoxes, I have little to add at this point. I chose the examples discussed in this book with a view to the currency of the paradoxes themselves; but the main concern in these distinct studies was to illustrate the metaphilosophy of common sense at work in a number of areas. Of course, I would like to believe that these efforts have succeeded in disarming the philosophical paradox in question; but if they have failed this regard – and this would hardly be surprising given the near impossible task of mastering an array of topics each with its own massive and growing literature – hopefully they do at least illustrate a methodology that might be employed more successfully by others.

My attempt to address the fourth task is very much a work in progress. New types of philosophical errors are likely to present themselves once one begins consciously to look for them, and it is very likely that familiar errors can be reclassified in a more heuristically useful fashion. However, I remain convinced that a fuller knowledge of the medieval origins of the spirit of modernity will only enhance the credentials of my own contribution presented in Chapter 4.

It is with respect to the fifth and final task that this book has been least successful. In fact, little or no attempt has been made to present a metaphysical account of what is implicit in our common sense beliefs. There are a number of reasons why this task has not been broached here. First, there is only so much one can do within the confines of a single readable book. More importantly, the common sense philosopher cannot profitably begin to construct the desired metaphysics until he or she is reasonably confident that at least some of the initial data to be accounted for has itself been secured. This book can thus be seen as a necessary preliminary step that must be taken before work on the fifth task can begin. Finally, there is a sense in which this task has already been addressed, and addressed with such astonishing success that any attempt to duplicate the effort would be redundant. Because Aristotle has already developed one of the most sophisticated metaphysical systems ever produced, there is a sense in which, with respect to the fifth and final task, I can do no better than to commend the *Metaphysics* to the reader.

But of course there is, in fact, much more to be done. Aristotle's metaphysics is indeed the closest thing we currently have to a complete metaphysics of common sense, and as such it must be the point of departure for any contemporary attempt to address our fifth and final task. But no informed student of Aristotle thinks his metaphysical system is free of difficulties. Moreover, as common sense philosophers, we must recognise that there are other sources of endoxa besides Aristotle. Anyone persuaded by the main lines of this book will have to accept that the neo-Darwinian synthesis in particular is an authority to be reckoned with. A final reason then for leaving the fifth task to a later date is that it will involve, among other things, a comprehensive study of the compatibility or otherwise of Aristotelian metaphysics and evolutionary biology. I have every confidence that the two are indeed compatible, and I am not alone in this respect. But establishing this thesis is undoubtedly work for another day.

Notes

Introduction: Two Tribes

1. There is something suspicious about Plato's story which does lend credibility to this interpretation because Thales was also renowned for having turned his studies to practical use. In Aristotle we read, "For when they reproached him [Thales] because of his poverty, as though philosophy were of no use, it is said that, having observed through his study of the heavenly bodies that there would be a large olive-crop, he raised a little capital while it was still winter, and paid deposits on all the olive presses in Miletus and Chios, hiring them cheaply because no one bid against him. When the appropriate time came there was a sudden rush of requests for the presses; he then hired them out on his own terms and so made a large profit, thus demonstrating that it is easy for philosophers to be rich, if they wish, but that it is not in this that they are interested" (*Politics*, A11, 1259a9).
2. See also the *Republic*, 517a for similar views.
3. Heraclitus, the weeping philosopher, was particularly scathing about the intellectual abilities of the average human being: "Of the Logos which is as I describe it men always prove to be uncomprehending, both before they have heard it and when once they have heard it...men are like people of no experience...men fail to notice what they do after they wake up just as they forget what they do when asleep" (Kirk, Raven and Schofield, p. 187).
4. Ariew, Cottingham and Sorell, pp. 53–55.

1 The metaphilosophy of common sense

1. (1962) "Philosophy and the Scientific Image of Man", in *Frontiers of Science and Philosophy*. Ed. Robert Colodny. Pittsburgh: University of Pittsburgh Press.
2. He writes, "The strange thing is that philosophers should have been able to hold sincerely, as part of their philosophical creed, propositions inconsistent with what they themselves *knew* to be true; and yet, so far as I can make out, this has really frequently happened" (1963, p. 41).
3. Moore perhaps came the closest to giving an extended discussion of philosophy in general in the first lecture of *Some Main Problems of Philosophy*. As will become evident, the account of philosophy I offer here owes something to the account offered by Moore, but it includes further important details to which he may or may not have wished to commit himself.
4. Graham Priest. (2003) "Where is Philosophy at the Start of the 21st century?", *Proceedings of the Aristotelian Society*, Vol. CII, Part I, pp. 94–95.
5. The birth of chemistry from the ashes of alchemy is perhaps the best example of such a mutation.

6. Not all great philosophers fall into this camp, but it is clear that Plato, Aristotle, the late Hellenistic thinkers, Aquinas and the Scholastics, Descartes, Spinoza, Hume and Kant, not insignificant figures, do. All these figures made contributions to all the core sub-disciplines of philosophy, and all were concerned not just with the theoretical aspects of the discipline, but with its practical consequences as well. Of course such a task is seldom undertaken by any one individual today given the need to specialise to a greater degree in one particular area if one hopes to make any significant contribution at all to the discipline.

7. This paragraph owes much to Sellar's description of what he calls "The Philosophical Quest". He writes, "The aim of philosophy, abstractly formulated, is to understand how things in the broadest possible sense of the term hang together in the broadest possible sense of the term. Under 'things in the broadest sense' I include such radically different items as not only 'cabbages and kings', but numbers and duties, possibilities and finger snaps, aesthetic experiences and death. To achieve success in philosophy would be, to use a contemporary turn of phrase, to 'know one's way around' with respect to all these things, not in the unreflective way in which the centipede of the story knew its way around before it faced the question, 'how do I walk?' but in that reflective way which means that no intellectual holds are barred." (Philosophy and the Scientific Image of Man).

8. One could try to mask the grandiose nature of philosophy by describing it in more homely language. Sellars's phrases, "finding our way around", and showing us how things "hang together", are attempts to do just this. But once these phrases are fleshed out one finds philosophy's grandiose nature returning to view.

9. Again, as my methodology demands, this view is hardly original. The standard view that philosophy is not a first order discipline is again nicely expressed by Sellars, who writes, "Philosophy in an important sense has no special subject-matter which stands to it as other subject-matters stand to other special disciplines... What is characteristic of philosophy is not a special subject-matter, but the aim of knowing one's way around with respect to the subject-matters of all the special disciplines." (Philosophy and the Scientific Image of Man).

10. A relatively recent and perhaps novel example of philosophical excursions into the sciences is presented by so-called "Experimental Philosophy". Those working in this vein often attempt to support or discredit the "arm chair intuitions" of philosophers by conducting experiments and surveys on ordinary people in order to ascertain precisely what the philosophical layperson thinks about various topics of philosophical import. What is interesting about such work, however, is that its practitioners are fully aware of the extra-philosophical nature of these experiments, despite the fact that the results may have philosophical import. See Kauppinen (forthcoming) and Sosa (forthcoming) for discussion of this movement.

11. This view of the nature of what I am calling co-ordination problems is found in Ryle's *Dilemmas*. In Chapter 1 of this work, he writes, "Certain sorts of theoretical disputes, such as those we are to consider, are to be settled not by any internal corroboration of those positions, but by an arbitration of

quite a different kind – not, for example, to put my cards on the table, by additional scientific researches, but by philosophical inquiry" (p. 5).

12. These points draw heavily on the following extended passage from Aristotle's *Metaphysics*: "We must, with a view to the science [metaphysics] which we are seeking, first recount the subjects that should be first discussed. [The 'subjects' being a set of aporia.] ... For those who wish to get clear of difficulties [i.e. aporia] it is advantageous to discuss the difficulties well; for the subsequent free play of thought implies the solution of the previous difficulties, and it is not possible to untie a knot of which one does not know. But the difficulty of our thinking points to a 'knot' in the object: for in so far as our thought is in difficulties, it is in like case with those who are bound; for in either case it is impossible to move forward. Hence one should have surveyed all the difficulties beforehand, both for the purposes we have stated and because people who inquire without first stating the difficulties are like those who do not know where they have to go; besides, a man does not otherwise know even whether he has at any given time found what he is looking for or not; for the end in not clear to such a man, while to him who has first discussed the difficulties it is clear" (995a23–995b4).

13. It should be noted of course that this is a somewhat idealised account of philosophical activity. The routine efforts of most academic philosophers are largely devoted to the discussion of the views of other philosophers who themselves took a crack at solving a co-ordination problem. These second level efforts take on a life of their own, generating a veritable cottage industry of seemingly endless discussions, commentaries and critiques emanating from second-order aporia (i.e., tensions involving attractive *philosophical* lines of thought) during the course of which the original problem is often lost sight of entirely.

14. I infer this from Descartes' putting free will on a par with the Incarnation and creation *ex nihilo*. In a journal begun on the 1st of January 1619, he wrote, "The Lord has made three marvels: things out of nothingness; free will; and the Man who is God" (1990, p. 5).

15. Although a modern day Pyrrhonian sceptic might be envisaged here.

16. Further examples will be presented in Part II.

17. *Discourse on Method*, p. 18. Descartes' first rule is "never to accept anything for true which I did not clearly know to be such; that is to say, carefully to avoid precipitancy and prejudice, and to comprise nothing more in my judgment than what was presented to my mind so clearly and distinctly as to exclude all grounds of doubt" (ibid., p. 21).

18. *Critique of Pure Reason*, p. 11.

19. When considering how and when to make revisions in one's set of beliefs, Quine mentions favourably our "natural tendency to disturb the total system as little as possible", and espouses what one might call a "pragmatic conservatism". (See "Two Dogmas of Empiricism" in *From a Logical Point of View*, pp. 44, 46.)

20. It is probably fair to say that Moore did not have much to offer in the way of systematic treatment of the first two tasks, although it could be said that he anticipated the answers to be defended in the next chapter at the close of his *The Elements of Ethics*, p. 193.

21. cf. Langford's "The Notion of Analysis in Moore's Philosophy", in *The Philosophy of G.E. Moore*. Ed. Schlipp. Open Court, 1942.
22. It is for this reason that I will not concern myself with conducting surveys in the manner of the so-called "experimental philosophers".

2   The "evolutionary argument" and the metaphilosophy of common sense

1. This argument is found in Chapter 6 of Moore's (1965).
2. This is precisely the attitude taken by Searle (1987), regarding Quine's indeterminacy of translation thesis in the philosophy of language. If Quine's thesis entails that there is no difference between my meaning "rabbit" as opposed to "undetached rabbit parts" or "rabbit stages", then, says Searle, so much the worse for Quine. The only interesting philosophical issue is determining precisely where Quine's argument went wrong.
3. See *Philosophical Investigations*, Sections 89–133, 194–196, 254–255, 309, 464, 599.
4. He writes, "all three propositions ['I know that the pencil exists', 'the pencil exists', or 'the sense data which I directly apprehend are a sign that it exists'] are much more certain than any premise which could prove them false" (2002, pp. 125–126).
5. Hume takes this to be the mark of the arguments of the sceptics (1985, p. 155).
6. Reid attempted to break the stalemate in favour of common sense by insisting (a) that common sense beliefs are simply "obvious", (b) that one cannot help but assent to common sense beliefs, (c) that common sense beliefs appear early in childhood without any explicit instruction, (d) that common sense beliefs are held by the vast majority of people, as is seen from the structure of all known languages. It has also been suggested (e) that Reid provides the rudiments of an Alstonian type "track record" argument (De Bary, pp. 152–160). But none of these claims would or should move a committed revisionist since they assume what is at issue, namely that our natural faculties are not "fallacious". Of course, Reid also claimed that (f) such faculties and beliefs have a divine provenance, (g) has not been a popular move for some time, and it ought not to have satisfied Reid either. For Reid trusts his senses, for example, because they are the work of his maker. But the maker is equally responsible for the cognitive capacities employed in our philosophical researches. No obviously acceptable theological explanation as to why God would give us reliable senses but untrustworthy philosophical intuitions and abilities was offered.
7. Austin's memorable line.
8. Frank Jackson (2000) makes frequent appeals to what he calls "the folk", and the assumption that the folk are not badly confused. E. J. Lowe also takes common sense intuitions seriously when evaluating philosophical arguments and positions (2002, cf., pp. 48, 52). But it is clear that he is not entirely sure about this. For example, regarding essentialism he writes "... at least [it] has common sense on its side, for what that is worth" (ibid., p. 114). In his work (1997) Michael Devitt assumes that common sense is philosophically respectable and ought to be treated as a default position.

Lawrence Bonjour's (1991) also contains as clear an example of arguments exemplified by A2 and B2 as one could wish. Peter Railton in his work (1996) quite consciously and explicitly, and also without explanation, insists that philosophical theorising cannot stray too far from what common sense will accept, and that revisionism is to be looked upon with suspicion.

9. It is certainly the case that the debate between "particularists" and "methodists" in Chisholm's sense has never been satisfactorily resolved.

10. See, for example, Stewart-Williams (2005).

11. See also Ruse (1986), Sober (1981), Fodor (1981), Millikan (1984, 1987), Goldman (1986), Lycan (1988) Sorenson (1992), Nozick (1993) Papineau (1993, 2000) and Searle (1992).

12. Oddly enough, some have dismissed the argument with little more than a reference to Stich and a note to the effect that Darwin doubted the trustworthiness of "the convictions of man's mind, which has been developed from the mind of the lower animals" (De Bary, p. 87). This approach is decidedly odd in the case of De Bary, who realises, along with Lehrer that by substituting the principle of natural selection for Reid's principle of divine benevolence one updates Reid's metaphilosophy of common sense into a "thoroughly modern doctrine" (ibid., p. 66).

13. The literature on this point is extensive, but readers might wish to begin with Evans (1989); Solnick (1980); Tversky and Kahneman (1982); Kahneman and Tversky (1984); see also the commentary to John Anderson's (1991) in *Behavioral and Brain Sciences*.

14. This assumption concerning the link between perception and action is taken as central to a number of research projects. It is central to Godfrey-Smith (1991) and Sterelny's (2003) views on the evolution of human cognition in general. It is also a guiding assumption of Anderson's cognitive psychology (1991). It is central also to a number of projects in the science of vision. The assumption that perception and action evolved together is found in Gibson's ecological approach to vision (1979); in the biological approach of Maturana and Varela (1980, 1987); in the enactive approach to vision of Thompson, Palacios and Varela (1992); and Freeman's view of brain processes (1975; Freeman and Skarda, 1985; Skarda and Freeman, 1987).

15. Point (7) has to be qualified somewhat depending on the relative importance of the trait in question. Some biological functions are more important than others, which means an organism can often "get by" even if some of its elements are failing to perform their functions (particularly if the organism is able to secure aid from other con-specifics).

16. That natural selection does not guarantee perfection is now a common place amongst evolutionary biologists. See Chapter 3 of Dawkins (1999). But the point is easily overlooked.

17. Stich is, of course, a famous proponent of the view that beliefs, at least as understood by folk psychology, do not exist. But as far as I can make out, this is not a premise on which he relies in his attack on evolutionary psychology and epistemology.

18. One does not need the help of evolutionary biology to appreciate this point, as Descartes' comment shows, "... it was always my most earnest desire to learn to distinguish the true from the false in order to see clearly into my own actions and proceed with confidence in this life" (1990, p. 115).

19. I am reminded here of a passage from Descartes' *Discourse on Method*: "It appeared to me that I could find much more truth in such reasonings as every man makes about the affairs that concern himself, and whose issue will very soon make him suffer if he has made a miscalculation, than in the reasonings of a man of letters in his study, about speculations that produce no effect and have no importance to him – except that perhaps he will feel the more conceited about them, the more remote they are from common sense, since he will have had to use the greater amount of ingenuity and skill in order to make them plausible" (1975, p. 13).

20. As Mayr (2000, p. 588) points out, "[some philosophers] have had great difficulty in understanding that selection is statistical rather than an all-or-none phenomenon".

21. For a more recent discussion, see Dedrick's (2005).

22. Unless, of course, one is living in a Woody Allen picture.

23. See Pascal Boyer's (1994) for extended discussion.

24. This is the view defended by Z. D. Phillips. According to Phillips, religious beliefs are not statements, although they have the surface grammar of statements. As he says, "Talk of God's existence or reality cannot be considered as talk about the existence of an object" (1976, p. 174). " 'There is a God', although it appears to be in the indicative mood, is an expression of faith" (ibid., p. 181).

25. See Atran's (2002). It is interesting to note that Ian Hacking (2004), in his review of Atran's book, takes issue with Atran's account of the emergence of religious beliefs, but not with the problem Atran sets himself. There has been the suggestion recently that there might be a "God gene" selected for on account of the advantage conferred on groups with a moral sense, a sense thought to derive from the belief in an all-seeing judge who punishes misdemeanours one's fellows have failed to detect. But this does not sit well with the known history of religious thought. Connecting religion and morality, and the idea that the Gods might be moral, was a very late arrival.

26. However, he does try to argue that "it may not be necessary to reject [the argument] outright" despite the charge of circularity (ibid., p. 796).

3   Towards a taxonomy of philosophical error

1. My operating assumption is that such a list may prove useful because there is, alas, no general principle to which one can appeal in order to eliminate all philosophical paradoxes independently of consideration of the arguments used to support them. That such a principle might be identified was one of the great hopes of the Ordinary Language philosophers; but their efforts proved to be in vain.

2. For example, Wittgenstein observed that philosophers are prone to hasty generalisations (*Philosophical Investigations*, 593), while more than one philosopher has been accused of begging the question. I will treat these errors, and others like them, as not specifically or especially philosophical mistakes, although philosophers do make them. There is a certain arbitrariness about this distinction; but when in doubt, I have tended to leave an error out of

my considerations if it is the kind of error that generally receives coverage in introductory textbooks on critical reasoning.

3. For example, Peter Millican (2004) outlines nine different objections discussed in the literature before going on to present a tenth.

4. Moore used the term "analysis" in at least four different senses. "Analysis" could be used to mean (a) drawing out the concrete implications of abstract philosophical claims – analysis as "translation into the concrete"; (b) distinguishing between different senses of expressions; (c) breaking down a complex whole (either a proposition or a concept) into its constituent parts; or (d) translating or paraphrasing propositions of one type into propositions of another – the so-called "reductive" analysis. For more on Moore's use of the term "analysis" see Klemke (1969, pp. 64–87) and White (1958, pp. 66–68).

5. See Langford's "The Notion of Analysis in Moore's Philosophy" in *The Philosophy of G.E. Moore*, Ed. Schilpp. Open Court Publishing Company, 1942.

6. This is not the place for such a discussion, but interested readers might consider the second chapter of O'Connor's (1982).

7. It was partly this insight which led Grice to develop his theory of conversational implicatures. See the Prolegomena to *Studies in the Way of Words*. Cambridge, Mass.: Harvard University Press, 1989.

8. There is also the related failure to distinguish among the various senses in which a question can be taken, a failure which leads to philosophers offering competing and contradictory answers to what appears to be the same question, when in fact they are talking at cross purposes. Again it is Moore who insists upon this in his *Principia Ethica*: "It appears to me that in Ethics, as in all other philosophical studies, the difficulties and disagreements, of which its history are full, are mainly due to a very simple cause: namely to attempt to answer questions, without first discovering precisely *what* question it is which you desire to answer" (1993, p. 33). His claim in the ethical context is that standard ethical questions like "What ought I to do in this circumstance?", "Is this course of action morally acceptable?" or "Is loyalty a virtue?" all depend on answers to two further questions which are often not clearly distinguished, namely "What is good in itself?" and "What is good as a means?" He says, "these are the only questions which any ethical discussion can have to settle, and that to settle the one is not the same thing as to settle the other – these two facts have in general escaped the notice of ethical philosophers" (ibid., pp. 75–76).

9. *Essays on the Intellectual Powers of Man*, Essay IV, Chapter 2, in *The Works of Thomas Reid*.

10. See Section 2 of Chapter 1 of *The Concept of Mind*.

11. See Section 5 of Chapter 7 of *The Concept of Mind*.

12. Of course, as the Quine/Duhem thesis shows, there is no absolutely coercive evidence even in the sciences. Nonetheless, there is still room to suggest that evidence comes in degrees of coercive power, and that empirical observations are at the hard end of the sliding scale, with philosophical intuitions at the other.

13. See his *Critique of Pure Reason*, preface to the first edition, A vii.

14. Kant's account of this error is worth quoting in full: "The perplexity into which it thus falls is not due to any fault of its own. It begins with

principles which it has no option save to employ in the course of experience, and which this experience at the same time abundantly justifies it in
using. Rising with their aid... to ever higher, ever more remote, conditions,
it soon becomes aware that in this way – the questions never ceasing – its
work must always remain incomplete; and it therefore finds itself compelled
to resort to principles which overstep all possible empirical employment,
and which yet seem so unobjectionable that even ordinary consciousness
readily accepts them. But by this procedure human reason precipitates itself
into darkness and contradictions; and while it may indeed conjecture that
these must be in some way due to concealed errors, it is not in a position
to be able to detect them. For since the principles of which it is making
use transcend the limits of experience, they are no longer subject to any
empirical test. The battle-field of these endless controversies is called metaphysics." *Critique of Pure Reason.* Translated by Norman Kemp Smith. New
York: St Martin's Press. 1965, p. 7.

15. "Perhaps... the cause of the present difficulty is not in the facts but in us.
For as the eyes of bats are to the blaze of the day, so is the reason in our soul
to the things which are by nature most evident of all" (*Metaphysics*, 993b,
pp. 8–11).

16. Descartes announced four rules in his *Discourse on Method*, the first of
which was "never to accept anything for true which I did not clearly know
to be such... and to comprise nothing in my judgement than what was
presented to my mind clearly and distinctly as to exclude all ground of
doubt" (*Discourse on Method*, translation by Vietch. London: Everyman's
Library, 1975, p. 15). He goes on to explain: "The long chains of simple and
easy reasonings by means of which geometers are accustomed to reach the
conclusions of their most difficult demonstrations, had led me to imagine
that *all* things, to the knowledge of which man is competent, are mutually
connected in the same way, and that there is nothing so far removed from
us as to be beyond our reach... provided only we abstain from accepting
the false for the true, and *always preserve in our thoughts the order necessary
for the deduction of one truth from another.*" (Ibid., p. 16) Emphasis added.

17. *Essays on the Intellectual Powers of Man*, I. Chapter 2, p. 152.

18. See *Nicomachean Ethics*, Chapter 3 Book 1, and *Metaphysics*, Chapter 6 of
Gamma.

19. See his "Systematically Misleading Expressions", *Proceedings of the Aristotelian
Society*, Vol. 32, 1931–1932, pp. 139–170.

20. It is interesting to note that the corruptive influence of argument was a
concern for both Plato and Aristotle. In the *Republic*, Plato went so far as to
ban the teaching of dialectic. He writes, "must you not take every precaution
when you introduce them [i.e. the young] to the study of dialectic? and not
suffer them to taste of it while young? For I fancy you have not failed to
observe that lads, when they first get a taste of disputation, misuse it as a
form of sport, always employing it contentiously, and, imitating confuters,
they themselves confute others. They delight like puppies in pulling about
and tearing with words all who approach them. And when they have themselves confuted many and have been confuted by many, they quickly fall
into violent distrust of all that they formerly held true, and the outcome is
that they themselves and the whole business of philosophy are discredited

with other men" (539a–c). It has also been suggested that Aristotle's decision to teach ethics only to those with a sound moral education is motivated by his concern that argumentation and reasoning might lead some of his students to abandon moral beliefs when they ought not to. See Kraut (2001, p. 287).

21. Wittgenstein makes this point in *On Certainty* (19). He writes, "The statement 'I know that here is a hand' may then be continued: 'for it's *my* hand that I'm looking at'. Then a reasonable man will not doubt that I know. ____Nor will the idealist; rather he will say that he was not dealing with the practical doubt which is being dismissed, but that there is a further doubt *behind* that one.____That this is an illusion must be shown in a different way."

22. William James, it will be recalled, argued that one could legitimately hold a belief in the absence of relevant evidence if the choice to believe were "live, forced and momentous". (See his "The Will to Believe" in *The Writings of William James: A Comprehensive Edition*. Ed. McDermott. Chicago: University of Chicago Press, 1977.) But the point often overlooked is that this is acceptable, if it is acceptable, only when the available evidence is insufficient to tip the scales one way or the other. The problem with many post-modern thinkers is that the available evidence seems to play no role at all in the fixation of their beliefs.

23. My thanks to Mark Cain for drawing this to my attention.

4 Theology's Trojan Horse

1. Russell writes, "Hume's scepticism rests entirely upon his rejection of the principle of induction.... It is therefore important to discover whether there is an answer to Hume within the framework of a philosophy that is wholly or mainly empirical. If not, there is no intellectual difference between sanity and insanity. The lunatic who believes that he is a poached egg is to be condemned solely on the ground that he is in a minority..." (*History of Western Philosophy*, p. 646).

2. Popper admits as much himself when he recognises that a theory is not falsified by a single recalcitrant observation but only by a "falsifying law" (*Objective Knowledge*, p. 14).

3. As Lipton says, "We have a psychological compulsion to favor our own inductive principles, but, if Hume is right, we should see that we cannot even provide a cogent rationalization of our behaviour" (1991, p. 12).

4. There have been many attempts to circumvent the problem of induction in the twentieth century. Notable among these has been Russell (1912, Chapter 6), Reichenbach (1938, 1949), Ayer (1960), Popper (1972), Strawson (1952), Skyrm (1975) and BonJour (1986).

5. This point is recognised by BonJour who includes in his account of the problem of induction the supposition that "there is no collateral information available...concerning causal or nomological connections between instances of A and instances of B" (1994, p. 391). Without this additional assumption the problem has no legs.

6. This is not the place for a proper historical study of these factors. I hope to provide such a study elsewhere in due course.

7. For ease of exposition, I will not distinguish between physical, natural, causal or nomological necessity since all entail some form of non-logical necessity.

8. My own suspicion on this score is that Stalnaker is right to claim that the significance of Kripke's work on the nature of reference is that it removes obstacles to the acceptance of essentialism rather than serving as a positive argument for this metaphysical thesis. See Stalnaker (1999, p. 537).

9. See Hale's "Modality", Forbes' "Essentialism", Stalnaker's "Reference and Necessity" and Stanley's "Names and Rigid Designation" for the current state of the debate. All collected in *A Companion to the Philosophy of Language*.

10. See *A Treatise of Human Nature*, Book I, Part III, Section XIV.

11. It is difficult not to think that he is both. He writes, "Upon the whole, necessity is something, that exists in the mind, not in objects; nor is it possible for us ever to form the most distant idea of it, consider'd as a quality of bodies" (*Treatise*, pp. 165–166).

12. It is interesting to note that, despite rejecting "the principle of causality" as so much metaphysics, Popper still insists that the scientist must accept a "methodological rule" which "corresponds so closely to the principle of causality that [it] might be regarded as its metaphysical version". The rule is "that we are not to abandon the search for universal laws and for a coherent theoretical system, nor ever give up our attempts to explain causally any kind of event we describe. This rule guides the scientific investigator in his work" (*The Logic of Scientific Discovery*, p. 61). In fact, Popper wants to have intelligibility on the cheap: He wants to join the empiricists in their anti-necessitarianism, and yet keep all the benefits just the same. In this regard, it is interesting to note a remark by John Maynard Smith concerning the difference between science and "myth". He says, "Scientific theories tell us what is *possible*; myths tell us what is desirable." Emphasis added (p. 382).

13. Or we are forced to accept some form of Kantian idealism, itself in no small part a reaction to Humean scepticism.

14. Berkeley also connects conceivability with logical possibility. He writes, "It is, I think, a received axiom that an impossibility cannot be conceived." He also connects it with physical possibility: "My conceiving power does not extend beyond the possibility of real existence." See *Principles of Human Knowledge*, Section 5, Part I.

15. In *Modalities*, p. 175.

16. One might also ask why it took so long before the possibility of a posteriori necessities became visible.

17. God is said to be the "first" cause of everything that exists. But insofar as creatures themselves have causal powers, they are said to be "secondary" causes.

18. As a matter of historical interest, the same charge cannot be laid against the Islamic theologian Al-Ghazali (d. 1111) who, relying on the principle of separability, produced arguments remarkably similar to Hume's against the existence of a necessary connection between cause and effect. See selections from Averroes' *The Incoherence of the Incoherence* in Bosley and Tweedale, Section 1.4.

19. See Section V of "Essential Attribution", in *Modalities*, pp. 67–70.

20. Moore's Open Question Argument against naturalism in ethics is an important case in point to which we shall return in Chapter 9.

5 Metaphysical realism as a pre-condition of visual perception

1. By calling these positions "Aristotelian" and "Kantian", I am not suggesting that either Aristotle or Kant would recognise these theories as their own in all important details. Nonetheless, the views presented here under their names do have something of the flavour of both philosophers. Since I am not presently concerned with textual exegesis, there are few references to the works of either philosophers.

2. Kant writes, "while the matter of all appearance is given to us a posteriori only, its form must lie ready for the sensations a priori in the mind" (1965, p. 66). Whorf provides an updated version of precisely the same point: "pure intuition" is "a kaleidoscopic flux of impressions which has to be organised by our mind [and which we] organise into concepts, and significances as we do, largely because we are parties to an agreement to organise it this way" (1956, p. 213).

3. Devitt nicely sums up Kant's key step in his response to scepticism to be the move from (1) Certain conditions must hold if we are to know objects, to (2) Objects known must be constituted, at least in part, by these conditions (1997, p. 72).

4. See Austin's *Sense and Sensibilia* and Armstrong's *Perception and the Physical World* for extended discussion of these arguments.

5. Putnam has since abandoned the views associated with his internal realism. See also Part I of his book (1994) entitled *The Return of Aristotle*.

6. Here I am following Vision, who writes, "On the Aristotelian view being proposed what we see is already characterised by general features and principles of individuation and identity. *These* aspects need not be contributed by our constitution" (1998, p. 407). These features include "divisions into persisting solids, together with a range of their traditional sensory qualities" (ibid., p. 406). I will only be interested in establishing the existence of a featured or pre-structured world here, leaving the claim about persisting middle-sized objects to another occasion. For the purpose of this paper, I will also set aside the realist dispute concerning colour perception.

7. This effort seeks to build upon and extend the work already carried out in the defence of metaphysical realism by Armstrong (1961), Austin (1964), Dretske (1969, 1999, 2002) and Vision (1998) by adding empirical support to their analyses of perception.

8. For those interested in the metaphysical commitments of two-factor theories of perception, see Hatfield and Epstein's "The Sensory Core and the Medieval Foundations of Early Modern Perceptual Theory" (1979) and Metzger (1974, pp. 62–65).

9. See my work (1997) for further discussion of this distinction.

10. See Aquinas (1963) Part I, q. 84, a. 1.

11. Searle has given powerful reasons to be suspicious of the armoury of conceptual tools employed by the cognitive sciences (1994).

12. In "Thought and Talk", for example, Davidson argues that "*x* believes that S" is equivalent to "*x* holds a certain sentence true", the assumption being that one cannot hold a sentence true if one does not understand the concepts embedded within it. In Guttenplan (1975).

13. McDowell is helpfully explicit on this matter. He writes, "To avoid making it unintelligible how the deliverances of sensibility can stand in grounding relations to paradigmatic exercises of the understanding such as judgments and beliefs, we must conceive this cooperation in a quite particular way: we must insist that the understanding is already inextricably implicated in the deliverances of sensibility themselves. Experiences are impressions made by the world on our senses, products of receptivity; but those impressions themselves already have conceptual content" (1994a, p. 46).

14. In fact, the one concept on its own will not do since it is commonly assumed that concepts do not exist in isolation, but always as part of a conceptual scheme. If this is so, one cannot perceive an *X* unless one has at least the rudiments of a conceptual scheme in place. Again McDowell's views on the perception of colour are a case in point. He writes, "No subject could be recognised as having experiences of colour except against a background understanding that makes it possible for judgements endorsing such experiences to fit into her view of the world. She must be equipped with such things as the concept of visible surfaces of objects, and the concepts of suitable conditions for telling what something's colour is by looking at it" (1994a, p. 30).

15. Here I follow Dretske who insists that seeing is not believing, but that believing is something that usually accompanies seeing in human beings as a consequence of seeing. See Part II of *Seeing and Knowing*.

16. "Ignorance of *X* does not impair one's vision of *X*; if it did, total ignorance would be largely irreparable" (Dretske, 1969, p. 8).

17. See Chapter 2 of *Seeing and Knowing*.

18. *Seeing and Knowing*, p. 20. The subscripted 'n' marks the fact that Dretske is after the non-epistemic sense of seeing in this analysis.

19. The bonobo Kanzi, perhaps the best non-human animal candidate for the possession of language, has failed to convince all experts in animal cognition that he has demonstrated anything more than a "protolanguage" (Roitblat, 1999, pp. 114–120). Deacon writes that "Language training in other species have demonstrated that it is possible under certain circumstances for them to acquire limited symbolic activities, though these are far more limited than at first suspected" (Deacon and Feyerabend, 1999, p. 220).

20. Marcus proposes an "object-centred" account of belief which avoids this problem. According to her analysis "*x* believes that S just in case, under certain *agent-centred* circumstances including *x's* desires and needs as well as *external circumstances*, x is disposed to act as if S, that actual or non-actual state of affairs, obtains" (p. 241). On this view, animals can be attributed beliefs. Whether this analysis does justice to our intuitions about belief is another matter. But it is clear that this sense of belief will not bear the sort of burden neo-Kantians require since it does away with any reference to concepts as linguistic, social or cultural constructs.

21. One could continue to maintain that perception has a conceptual component even in animals if one were willing to entertain the possibility that animals have their own language of thought (my thanks to Kim Sterelny for pointing this out to me). Two points mitigate against this move as far as McDowell is concerned. First, as noted above, it would entail abandoning the demanding sense of "concept" and "conceptual" to which he and other

neo-Kantians are committed. Second, there are doubts concerning the coherence of the language of thought hypothesis as depicted by Fodor and other cognitive scientists. Searle (1994) sets out many reasons for being suspicious of the various concepts employed by cognitive scientists. This is not the place to enter into this dispute, but Searle's charge (p. 229) that appeals to "rule following, information processing, unconscious inferences, mental models, primal sketches, 2½-D images, three dimensional descriptions, languages of thought and universal grammar" to account for the mind's activities are guilty of engaging in pre-Darwinian style anthropomorphising is particularly apropos. But whatever the merits of the language of thought hypothesis, they seem far more problematic to me than the adoption of Dretske's notion of non-epistemic seeing with its commitment to the non-conceptual content of some perceptions.

22. For some relevant passages in Aristotle see *De Anima*, Book III, Chapter 3, 427b 7–8, and *Nicomachean Ethics*, Book I, Chapter 7, 1098a. As for modern scientists, see Hubel (1988, p. 22).

23. Gibson makes the point as follows: "perception in the service of activity and orientation is the evolutionary primary kind of perception. Having reached some understanding of this kind of perception, [we can] then address the other varieties of awareness" (1979, p. 255f).

24. An important qualification is needed. I am currently concerned with perception in what can be loosely referred to as normal circumstances, that is, cases where perception is caused by the external world impinging on the sense organs of the perceiver. Visual perceptions can be caused by neuronal manipulations of the brain of the perceiver, but I am not currently interested in phenomena of this sort which, although producing a perception, bypass the eye (and are anything but normal). Nor do I deny that one can have visual *experiences* under unusual conditions, for example, the experience of "brain grey" or the visual experience produced by a ganzfeld. But neither of these sorts of experiences can be called visual perceptions in the sense outlined above, where something is visually differentiated from its immediate environment. Thanks to an anonymous referee for *Biology* and *Philosophy* for forcing me to be more precise on this matter.

25. This result was used by Koffka as a starting point of his *Principles of Gestalt Psychology*. The experiment has been repeated by numerous researchers (Avant, 1965; Cohen, 1957; Gibson and Waddell, 1952; Hochberg et al., 1951).

26. See Donald Mackay (1991), as well as Barlow (1953, 1958); Barlow and Levick (1965); Werblin and Dowling (1969).

27. Some have gone so far as to say that "The visual system ... does not respond to light at all, it responds rather to edges, changes, ratios, and relations" (T. G. R. Bower, 1974, p. 142).

28. Hubel writes, "In some animals we ... surgically sewed over one eye a thin, translucent, opalescent membrane, in effect, an extra eyelid called the nictitating membrane that cats possess and we don't. The plastic or the membrane reduced the light by about one-half but prevented the formation of any focused images. The results were the same: an abnormal cortical physiology; and abnormal geniculate histology. Evidently it was the *form* deprivation rather than light deprivation that was doing the damage" (pp. 197–198).

29. Of course, this has been the operating assumption of those working in cognitive psychology and neurophysiology. Bruce and Green write without any supporting argument that "the environment *structures* the light that reaches observers" (p. 2). The operating assumption has been that the presence or absence of structure in light is a function of the laws which govern the behaviour of the two types of light. Light radiating from energy sources can be thought of as an infinitely dense set of rays *diverging* in all directions, each ray being subject to the laws of photon tracks. Ambient light, on the other hand, is defined as light reflected from illuminated surfaces of the terrestrial world and *converging* upon a point of observations from all directions. Although ambient light is composed of rays, it is different in different directions because of the various natures and layout of the illuminated bodies which reflect light at different intensities. These differences in intensity structure the ambient light, producing a pattern or configuration in the light received by the eye, a structure altogether absent in radiant light which is not different in different directions.

30. This was brought to my attention by an anonymous referee for *Biology* and *Philosophy*.

31. I have said that a "rough" structural identity between the content of visual perceptions and the external world must be assumed rather than complete structural identity because (a) this is sufficient to explain oriented activity and (b) because the evolutionary argument does not permit more than this. There is no general argument from evolutionary theory that evolved perceptual systems accurately track the environment in all respects.

32. I borrow Dennett's apt phrase from *Darwin's Dangerous Idea*.

33. Following the work of Milner and Goodale (1998), some may wonder if the distinction between ventral and dorsal pathways in primate vision does not suggest that as the ventral pathway assumed greater prominence in mammalian vision it developed some independence from the more primitive visual system which served to guide oriented activities. (The dorsal pathway deals with directing action while the ventral pathway deals with identifying objects.) While this possibility cannot be discounted, it does not affect the primary point at issue. This semi-independent system is present in animals not in possession of linguistic concepts, nor does it affect the primary issue concerning the origin of structure.

6   Semantic anti-realism and the Dummettian reductio

1. I have taken this formulation of the key claim from Lievers (1998, p. 200) because he provides a recent and sympathetic formulation of the manifestation argument.

2. Of course, Tennant is right to insist that semantic anti-realism is not a crude form of verificationism (1995a, p. 17) inasmuch as it is not committed to sense datum reports or other protocol sentences as ultimate verifiers, not does it insist that meaningful sentences be either verifiable or falsifiable.

3. Ayer himself recognised this, and his solution was to distinguish between verification via logical analysis, which can be conclusive, and verification

via sensory experience, which almost never is. It is to Ayer's credit that he never tried to take mathematics as the guide to a general semantic theory.

4. Crispin Wright has offered another version of "recognition in principle" which relies on the notion of "superassertibility". More on this below.

5. The distinction between a capacity and its exercise is of no avail to the Dummettian anti-realist precisely because understanding must be currently manifestable in use.

6. Dummett tries to escape this dilemma in *The Logical Basis of Metaphysics* by suggesting that manifestation of the grasp of such sentences can be achieved if the speaker manifests a grasp of the component parts of the sentence in question by employing them correctly in other contexts. In particular, the capacity involved in understanding complex sentence p are manifested in general abilities with introduction and elimination rules governing the component logical operators and other expressions in p. I do not consider this argument here because its failings have already been exposed (Jim Edwards, 1995). But one might also ask why this strategy is not available to the semantic realist as well. When faced with the sentence "It rained on the Earth a million years ago" Appiah asked, "Why is it not evidence that someone assigns this sentence the correct truth conditions, that they use "rain" properly in sentences about present rain, that they can count to a million, know how long a year is, and display a grasp of the past tense in relation to the recent past?" (Appiah, 1986, p. 80) This response to the manifestation argument has usually been considered question begging. But it is not clear how Dummett could block this response given the strategy suggested in *The Logical Basis of Metaphysics*.

7. As Edwards points out, if superassertibility is identified with truth, then to have a warrant for *p* is to have a warrant for its superassertibility because it is a platitude about truth that to have a warrant for *p* is to have a warrant to claim that *p* is true (Edwards, 1996, p. 105).

8. Crispin Wright does offer another formulation of the notion of recognition, but it clearly belongs to another family of notions and will not serve Dummett's purposes. Wright states that a recognitional capacity is "an ability to recognise whether, and if so, what in a prevailing context renders a particular use of [a] sentence appropriate" (Lievers, 1998, p. 210) There is nothing in this formulation to suggest that this capacity always, or even in paradigmatically involves the recognition of a warrant to assert a statement.

9. Since semantic anti-realists are often accused of accepting the analytic-synthetic distinction too quickly, I expect I will be allowed this assumption.

10. In *Anti-Realism and Logic*, Tennant admits that extra-logical terms are understood in a holistic way. He writes: "it is quite plausible that non-logical concepts or expressions may be non-separable: and our theory of meaning for such expressions would accordingly be a holistic one. The existence of 'semantic fields', only within the whole of which can member-concepts properly be located, could turn a significant field of semantics into a preserve of the holist" (1987, p. 64). He is also sure that Dummett would have to allow for this limited use of holism, as these lines from "The Justification of Deduction" indicate: "Of course, even on a molecular view of this kind, no sentence can have a meaning which is independent of all the rest of the language. Its meaning depends on the meaning of the constituent words,

and these in turn depend upon the use of other sentences in which they may occur, and also expressions of a lower level to which they are logically related: a grasp of the meaning of any sentence must, even on a molecular view of language, depend upon a mastery of some fragments of the language, a fragment which may, in some cases, be quite extensive" (1992, p. 304).

7 Eliminating eliminative materialism

1. This is rather unnerving. But one of the good ways in which philosophy differs from real life is that instances of apparent philosophical lunacy which usually involve a degree of rationality.
2. It has been argued that the mind/body problem as described here was absent from ancient and medieval philosophy and arose only after the adoption of the corpuscular theory of matter (cf. Matson, (1966), King (2005)). But it is worth noting that the mind/body problem cannot be laid solely at the feet of the corpuscular theory of matter (although it certainly exacerbated the difficulties). The struggle to make sense of a minded material animal existed *before* the advent of the corpuscular theory of matter, although for different reasons. While Aristotle and the medievals did *not* have a problem explaining how material animals can enjoy sensation and perception, the same was not the case for abstract thought. Even Aristotle, a committed naturalist, was unable to reconcile the particularity of the bodily organs associated with cognition with the universality of abstract thought. See *De Anima*, Book III, Chapters 4–8, and my work (2006) for further discussion of this early version of the mind/body problem in ancient and medieval philosophy.
3. Sometimes this line of thought is taken to extremes. It is not uncommon to find a philosopher claiming that because he or she cannot conceive how a conglomeration of material entities and processes could give rise to consciousness and intentionality that it is not possible that such an occurrence should arise. This is an instance of the error the origins of which were exposed in Chapter 4. Failed attempts to conceive of x tell us nothing at all of the possibility or otherwise of x but only of the conceptual capacity of the conceiver – hence the need to be wary of certain kinds of thought experiments. I note that Patricia Churchland has also made precisely this point in this connection (1996, pp. 406–407). However, in making this point we must, in fairness, also note that a common criticism of Descartes – that Substance Dualism cannot be a true account of human nature because we cannot conceive how causal interaction between immaterial minds and material bodies can obtain – ought to be abandoned.
4. This is certainly a concern expressed by Bennett and Hacker (2003, p. 368). One would have to be a card-carrying radical empiricist for whom anything that is not a sense datum counts as a theoretical entity for the word "theory" to retain any meaning in this context. And I have already given reason to believe that the radical empiricist's framework is itself a product of theology's Trojan horse, and that the concern with the challenge of radical scepticism is misguided.
5. Ibid., p. 368.

6. This point has been made in this context by Bogdan (1993).
7. I might have mixed feelings about something, and so I might have to dwell on them for a while before arriving at a considered view of the matter. But this is not to say that my thoughts and feelings are "covert". In such cases, one is really just "weighing up" thoughts and emotions of which one is fully aware.
8. Ryle points out that those who take the problem of other minds seriously "come to suppose that there is a special mystery about how we publish our thoughts instead of realising that we employ a special artifice to keep them to ourselves" (1984, p. 27).
9. I owe this point to Searle (1999, pp. 71–77).
10. Not because to be real is to be causally efficacious, but because beliefs as the folk would have them are taken to be causally efficacious in the production of human behaviour.
11. This means that the defender of FP and common sense cannot argue, as Bennett and Hacker (2003) have done that FP is not a theory, and consequently that Churchland's argument for EM rests on a false premise. Nor can one argue, as Hannan (1993), Dennett (1987) and Clark (1989, 1993) have done, that the "theory–theory" argument of Churchland can be countered by adopting an *instrumentalist* approach to talk about beliefs and desires. Such an approach would deny beliefs and desires the required causal efficacy.
12. Churchland has a tendency to shift back and forth between the stronger versions of EM and EM3. As Austin would have it, there is the bit where they say it, and the bit where they take it back.

8 Freedom and responsibility

1. Chapter 9 of *De interpretatione*.
2. See *Physics* II, 8–9, and *On Generation and Corruption* II, 9.
3. See Chapter 6 of his *Ethics*. The crucial idea is that an agent acts freely if it is true to say that the agent could have performed another (unperformed) action if he or she had chosen to do so.
4. *Essays on the Active Powers*, IV, vi.
5. Of course there have been philosophers who have tried to develop such a theory, but it seems to me that all such theories face insuperable difficulties and are in fact unnecessary if one is keen principally to defend the notion of responsibility. For an interesting overview of such efforts see Chapters 4–6 of Kane's *A Contemporary Introduction to Free Will*. Oxford: Oxford University Press, 2005.
6. This account of the will seems to have fallen out of favour in the second half of the thirteenth century with the rise of radical voluntarism which sought to break the link between the will and the intellect for reasons explored in Chapter 4 of Part I. The Condemnations of 1277 undermined the Thomistic analysis of responsibility by condemning Aquinas's view that the will must follow the dictates of reason. See Korolec's "Free Will and Free Choice" in *The Cambridge History of Later Medieval Philosophy*. Kretzman, Kenny and Pinborg (eds) Cambridge University Press, 1990.

7. The following draws heavily upon Aristotle, but also Aquinas. For the latter's development of the Aristotelian analysis see his *Commentary on Aristotle's Nicomachean Ethics*, Book III, Lectures I–IV (Notre Dame: Dumb Ox Books, 1993); *On Evil*, q. 3, a. 6–8 (translation by Regan, Oxford: Oxford University Press, 2003); *Summa Theologicae*, I–II, q. 6, a 8 (*In Basic Writings of St. Thomas Aquinas*, Vol. 2. Indianapolis: Hackett, 1997). For more recent discussions see Meyer's *Aristotle and Moral Responsibility: Character and Cause*. Oxford: Blackwell, 1993, and her "Aristotle on the Voluntary" in *The Blackwell Guide to Aristotle's Nicomachean Ethics*. Kraut (ed.) Oxford: Blackwell, 2006. Irwin's "Reason and Responsibility in Aristotle" in *Essays on Aristotle's Ethics*. Rorty (ed.), University of California Press, 1980, is still very useful.
8. *Intention*, Section 6.
9. *Nicomachean Ethics*, 1111a3–1111a7.
10. See Bostock (2000, p. 118).
11. See her "Sanity and the Metaphysics of Responsibility" in *Free Will*, Kane (ed.) Oxford: Blackwell, 2002. This line of thought seems reasonable as long as not too much is built into our notion of sanity. Wolf's suggestion that being sane means something like being able to appreciate and conform one's behaviour to "the True and the Good" comes close to suggesting that moral competence, and not just cognitive competence, is an ingredient of sanity. See also Wolf (1990, p. 79).
12. See Chappell (1995, pp. 25–31).
13. See Siegler (1968).
14. It is very likely that Aristotle's account of responsibility grew out of his reflections on contemporary practices in the Athenian courts. But he does not distinguish between legal and non-legal responsibility, and would certainly have applied his account to unambiguously moral as opposes to legal cases. See Curren (1989) for a historical discussion.
15. This analysis fits very well with the evolutionary scenario sketched earlier in this chapter. If I am wondering whether to cooperate with another individual, what will weigh most heavily with me is what this individual has shown themselves to be willing to do, not the number of options that may or may not have been open to them.
16. This is an important point carried over from the preceding chapter.
17. See J. M. Camhi, (1984). *Neuroethology*. Sunderland: Sinauer, pp. 79–86.

9   On the existence of moral facts

1. For example, in his attempt to accurately characterise his version of moral realism, Railton (1997, p. 138) felt the need to provide answers to 13 different questions in order to locate his position in what has become a "multidimensional conceptual space". Realists can now expect to be asked for their views on cognitivism, the nature of truth, objectivity, reductionism, naturalism, empiricism, bivalence, relativism, pluralism, whether morality is determinable, whether moral imperatives are universal, whether existing moralities are acceptable as they stand or are in need of revision and so on.
2. For example, a biologically informed naturalistically inclined moral realist might be forgiven for thinking that Gibbard's attempt to understand the

acceptance of moral norms as a biological phenomenon includes precisely the sorts of material he or she needs to defend his or her own position.

3. Darwall, Gibbard and Railton (1997, p. 34) suggest that the proper distinction on which the debate now turns is the continuity or otherwise between ethics and the natural sciences (ibid., p. 9). But while it is no doubt true that this issue has occupied many meta-ethicists, it is also true that this question is usually pursued on the understanding that the correct answer to this question would provide the leverage needed to answer the old question. See Boyd (1997) for a good example.

4. Consider the different responses to the suggestion that moral properties are analogous to secondary qualities. McNaughton views this suggestion as part and parcel of a sophisticated version of non-cognitivism (1988, Chapter 4), while McDowell, usually classed as a non-naturalist moral realist, argues the suggestion is consistent with his version of realism (1998 (b), pp. 131–150).

5. See Railton (1996) for an interesting discussion of different kinds of independence.

6. Mackie, for instance, acknowledges that, "objectivism about values is not only a feature of the philosophical tradition. It has also a firm basis in ordinary thought, and even in the meanings of moral terms" (1977, p. 31).

7. Particularly, taxing has been the so-called "Frege-Geach problem". I am thinking in particular of Blackburn's attempt in *Spreading the Word* and "Attitudes and Contents" to develop a logic of attitudes and Gibbard's attempt to rework the general notion of validity in *Wise Choices, Apt Feelings*. For a good discussion of Blackburn's efforts, see Hale's "Can There Be a Logic of Attitudes?"

8. Aristotle's famous function argument in Chapter 7 of Book I of the *Nicomachean Ethics* is the locus classicus of his naturalistic moral realism, while his anti-Platonic views on the nature of the Forms are well known. As for Reid, Chapter 7 of his *Essays on the Active Powers of the Human Mind* is devoted to refuting Hume's suggestion that moral approbation does not include a real judgement, but is merely an "agreeable or uneasy feeling in the person who approves or disapproves". And in the fifth essay of the same work, we find the following: "From the constitution of every species of the inferior animals, and especially from the active principles which nature has given them, we easily perceive the manner of life for which nature intended them; and they uniformly act the part to which they are led by their constitution, without any reflection upon it, or intention of carrying out its dictates. Man only, of the inhabitants of this world, is made capable of observing his own constitution, *what kind of life it is made for*, and of acting according to that intention, or contrary to it. He only is capable of yielding an intentional obedience to the dictates of his nature, or of rebelling against them."

9. Frankena (1938) was a notable exception. He famously claimed that the argument begged the question because Moore assumed conceptual competence in the moral domain in order to draw a conclusion from the openness of any alleged analysis. It would be an interesting exercise to see if Moore could be defended from this charge along the lines suggested in Chapter 2, if the argument were not fatally flawed in other respects.

10. I take it that $[(x = y) \to \Box (x = y)]$ is a suppressed premise of Moore's argument.

11. This is not always the case, however. In his *The Biology and Psychology of Moral Agency* (Cambridge: Cambridge University Press, 1998) William Rottschaefer tries to make a case for moral realism on a mixture of biological and philosophical grounds.

12. For those interested in this debate, see Bekoff (2004) for a recent formulation of the reciprocity-based account and Sripada (2005) for a vigorous defence of the punishment-based account. What *is* interesting for our concerns, at least those of the last chapter, is that both accounts presuppose the ability to distinguish between actions done intentionally, deliberately and on purpose and those done by mistake or inadvertently.

13. See Jesse Prinz (2006) and J. Blair, A. A. March, E. Finger, K. S. Blair and J. Luo (2006) for examples of this kind of argument.

14. For examples, see Fine (2006), Kennett (2006) and Stone (2006).

15. It is important to notice, however, that the practicality claim does not entail that one will always act in accordance with one's moral judgements. Weakness of the will might prevent one from acting as one knows one should. But even those who suffer from weakness of the will remain motivated to act as they should; it is just that other motives overpower their better judgement.

16. For the non-cognitivist implications of this theory see Hume's *Enquiry*, Appendix I, pp. 285–294. For the tension between the objectivity and practicality claims, see also Chapter 1 of Mackie's *Ethics: Inventing Right and Wrong* and Blackburn's *Spreading the Word*, pp. 187–189. Hare's prescriptivism also leans heavily on the close connection between moral judgement and action. See also his *The Language of Morals* and *Freedom and Reason*.

17. See McNaughton's *Moral Vision*, p. 22; Blackburn's *Spreading the Word*, pp. 187–188; Smith's *The Moral Problem*, p. 61; Miller's *An Introduction to Contemporary Metaethics*, p. 7; and Chapter 1 of Dancy's *Moral Reasons*. The opposing view is called "externalism". Externalists contend that moral judgements are *not* conceptually connected to the corresponding motivation and require something in addition to itself to produce the corresponding motivation. See Brink's work (1986) for discussion of this point. "External moral realism", *Southern Journal of Philosophy*, 24, supplement, pp. 23–41.

18. For example, in his "Internalism's Wheel", Smith appears to retract the strong version of internalism which insists on the conceptual connection between moral judgement and motivation, and to replace it with a much weaker version which requires only that there be a "normative" connection (p. 74). While I consider this weaker version to be the more plausible, for reasons which will become clear, it is not sufficient in conjunction with (3) to generate the tension required to threaten (1). I shall ignore it for present purposes.

19. This appears to have been Mackie's understanding of moral realism. He took the moral realist to be committed to the objectivity of moral judgements *and* to their being "prescriptive", "directive" or "action-guiding" (1977, p. 23). Taking Plato as a paradigm case of the moral realist, he wrote, "The philosopher-kings in the *Republic* can, Plato thinks, be trusted with unchecked power because their education will have given them knowledge of the Forms. Being acquainted with the Forms of the Good and Justice and Beauty and the rest they will, *by this knowledge alone*, without any further motivation, be impelled to pursue and promote these ideals" (ibid., pp. 23–24, emphasis added).

20. There is need for care here. Some Humeans insist that the appropriate beliefs and desires *produce* the corresponding motivation in some sort of causal sense, while others insist merely that the appropriate beliefs and desires be *present*. For an extended discussion, see Smith's (1987) "The Humean Theory of Motivation", *Mind*, 96, pp. 36–61. For Hume's statement of his belief/desire theory, see *A Treatise of Human Nature*, Book II, Part III, section iii (Oxford: Clarendon Press, 1989).

21. He writes, "reason alone can never be a motive to any action of the will" (1987, p. 413). In the same vein, we read that "Abstract or demonstrative reasoning, therefore never influences any of our actions concerning causes and effects" (ibid., p. 414).

22. Hume writes, "Reason being cool and disengaged is no motive to action, and directs only the impulse received from appetite or inclination, by showing us the means of attaining happiness or avoiding misery: taste, as it gives pleasure or pain, and thereby constitutes happiness or misery, becomes a motive to action and is the first spring or impulse to desire or volition (*Enquiry*, p. 294).

23. Hume writes, "As it's [sic] proper province is the world of ideas, an as the will always places us in that of realities, demonstration and volition seem, on that account, to be totally remov'd, from each other" (ibid., p. 413).

24. See Nagel (1970), McDowell (1979) and McNaughton (1988) for examples.

25. This is true even of ascription theories of motivation. Such theories, while admitting that a desire accompanies a belief in the production of a motivation, nonetheless deny that the desire plays a Humean role in that production. On this view, the desire is an additional but unnecessary extra. According to such theories, the moral judgement must have both the mind-to-world direction of fit characteristic of beliefs, but also a world-to-mind direction of fit associated with desires.

26. Aristotle writes, "Anger may be defined as an impulse, accompanied by pain, to a conspicuous revenge for a conspicuous slight directed without justification towards oneself or towards what concerns one's friends...it must always be felt towards some particular individual, e.g. Cleon, and 'man' in general. It must be felt because the other has done or intended to do something to him or one of his friends." *Rhetoric*, Book 2, Chapter 2.

27. For example, if I am too distracted to pay attention to the relevant beliefs, or if I have other concerns that take priority, I might fail to engage with the relevant beliefs in the fashion required for the emotion to arise. But more importantly, the relevant beliefs may not be sufficient to produce the emotion if I am not psychologically well-ordered. For example, if I am suffering from depression, I might not have the same affective responses to events I would otherwise have. Moreover, if my moral education has been defective, or if I happen to be amoral or wicked, or if I am psychologically tormented or oppressed, then it is far from certain that the appropriate emotion will emerge in the presence of the relevant belief.

28. See all of Book 2 of Aristotle's *Rhetoric*. One might also consider Part III of Spinoza's *Ethics*, particularly the section entitled "Definitions of the Emotions". It is interesting to note in this respect that recent work on the psychology of the emotions has reached similar conclusions. In his *Emotion*

and Adaptation, Lazarus argues that psychology is just now beginning to claw its way back to conclusions Aristotle took for granted in his *Rhetoric* (New York: Oxford University Press, 1991).

29. See note 27.
30. Not "minor qualifications" as Smith pretends (*Companion to Ethics*, p. 401).
31. As McNaughton points out, one of the consequences of Hume's belief/desire theory of motivation is that one's beliefs place no constraints on one's desires at all (1988, pp. 110–111). And Hume implies that all of these logically possible desires are equally immune to rational criticism because "[a] passion can never, in any sense, be called unreasonable" (1987, p. 416).

Afterword

1. See Sterelny (2003, Chapter 6) for a very useful discussion of these epistemological challenges. One might also include in this list of strictly epistemological challenges the difficulties involved in the tracking of modal facts (an issue touched upon briefly in Chapter 4).

Bibliography

Alexander, R. D. (1979). *Darwinism and Human Affairs*. Seattle, Washington University Press.

Alexander, R. D. (1985). "A Biological Interpretation of Moral Systems." *Zygon* 20: 3–20.

Alexander, R. D. (1987). *The Biology of Moral Systems*. New York, Aldine DeGruyter.

Anderson, J. (1991). "Is Human Cognition Adaptive?" *Behavioural and Brain Science* 14: 471–517.

Anscombe, E. (1981). *Collected Papers*. Oxford, Blackwell.

Anscombe, E. and P. T. Geach, Ed. (1976). *Descartes: Philosophical Writings*. Hong Kong, Nelson's University Paperbacks.

Appiah, A. (1986). *For Truth in Semantics*. Oxford, Blackwell.

Aquinas, S. T. (1963). *Summa Theologiae*. London, Blackfriars.

Aquinas, S. T. (1993). *Commentary on Aristotle's Nicomachean Ethics*. Notre Dame, Dumb Ox Books.

Aquinas, S. T. (2003). *On Evil*. Oxford, Oxford University Press.

Ariew, R., J. Cottingham and T. Sorell, Ed. (1998). *Descartes' Meditations: Background Source Materials*. Cambridge Philosophical Texts in Context. Cambridge, Cambridge University Press.

Aristotle, Ed. (1941). *The Basic Works of Aristotle*. New York, Random House.

Armstrong, D. M. (1961). *Perception and the Physical World*. New York, Routledge and Kegan Paul.

Atran, S. (2002). *In Gods We Trust: The Evolutionary Landscape of Religion*. Oxford, Oxford University Press.

Austin, J. L. (1964). *Sense and Sensibilia*. Oxford, Oxford University Press.

Austin, J. L. (1979). *Philosophical Paper*. Oxford, Clarendon Press.

Avant, L. L. (1965). "Vision in the Ganzfeld." *Psychological Bulletin* 64: 246–258.

Axelrod, R. (1984). *The Evolution of Cooperation*. New York, Basic Books.

Ayer, A. J. (1960). *Language, Truth and Logic*. London, The Camalot Press Ltd.

Baker, L. R. (1987) unpublished. "The cognitive status of common sense."

Barlow, H. B. (1953). "Summation and Inhibition in the Frog's Retina." *Journal of Physiology* 119: 69.

Barlow, H. B. (1958). "Temporal and Spatial Summation in Human Vision at Different Background Intensities." *Journal of Physiology* 141: 337.

Barlow, H. B. and W. R. Levick (1965). "The Mechanism of Directionally Sensitive Units in the Rabbit's Retina." *Journal of Physiology* 178: 477.

Bekoff, M. (2004). "Wild Justice and Fair Play: Cooperation, Forgiveness and Morality in Animals." *Biology and Philosophy* 19: 489–520.

Bennett, M. R. and P. M. S. Hacker (2003). *Philosophical Foundations of Neuroscience*. Oxford, Blackwell.

Berkeley, G. (1960). *A New Theory of Vision*. London, Dent and Sons.

Berkeley, G. (1975). *Berkeley: Philosophical Works*. London, Dent.

Blackburn, S. (1984). *Spreading the Word*. Oxford, Oxford University Press.

Blakemore, C. (1974). "Reversal of the Physiological Effects of Monocular Deprivation in Kittens." *Journal of Physiology* 237: 195.

223

Blakemore, C. (1978). "The Physiological Effects of Monocular Deprivation and Their Reversal in the Monkey's Visual Cortex." *Journal of Physiology* **282**: 223.

Blair, J., A. A. Marsh, E. Finger, K. S. Blair and J. Luo (2006). "Neuro-Cognitive Systems Involved in Morality." *Philosophical Explorations* **9**: 13–28.

Bogdan, R. J. (1993). "The Architectural Nonchalance of Commonsense Psychology." *Mind and Language* **8**(2): 189–205.

Boghossian, P. (1990) 'The status of content.' *Philosophical Review* **99**: 157–184.

Boghossian, P. and J. D. Vellemar (1991). "Physicalist Theories of Colour." *Philosophical Review* **100**: 67–106.

BonJour, L. (1986). "A Reconsideration of the Problem of Induction." *Philosophical Topics* **14**: 93–124.

Bonjour, L. (1994) Problems of Induction. *A Companion to Epistemology*, Dancy, J. and Sosa, E. (Eds). Oxford: Blackwell.

Bosley, R. N. and M. Tweedale, Ed. (1999). *Basic Issues in Medieval Philosophy*. Toronto, Broadview Press.

Bostock, D. (2000). *Aristotle's Ethics*. Oxford, Oxford University Press.

Boulter, S. J. (1997). "Putnam's 'Home Coming'." *Philosophy* **282**(7): 595–601.

Boulter, S. J. (2002). "Hume on Induction: Genuine Problem or Theology's Trojan horse?" *Philosophy* **77**: 67–86.

Boulter, S. J. (2006) Aquinas and Searle on Singular Thoughts, *Analytical Thomism: Traditions in Dialogue*. Paterson, C. and Pugh, M. S. (Eds). Aldershot: Ashgate. pp. 59–78.

Bower, T. G. R. (1974). The Evolution of Sensory Systems. *Perception: Essays in Honour of J. J. Gibson*. R. B. MacLeod and El. C. Picks. Ithaca, Cornell University Press.

Boyer, P. (1994) *The Naturalness of religious ideas*. Berkeley: University of California Press.

Boyd, R. (1997). How to Be a Moral Realist. *Moral Discourse and Practice*. G. R. Darwall. Oxford, Oxford University Press. pp. 105–136.

Brickhouse, T. (1991). "Roberts on Responsibility for Action and Character in the Nicomachean Ethics." *Ancient Philosophy* **11**: 137–148.

Brink, D. (1986). "External Moral Realism." *Southern Journal of Philosophy* **24**: 23–41.

Bruce, V. and P. R. Green (1990). *Perception, Physiology and Ecology*. New Jersey, Lawrence Erlbaum.

Camhi, J. M. (1984). *Neuroethology*. Sunderland, Sinauer.

Chappell, T. (1995). *Aristotle and Augustine on Freedom: Two Theories of Freedom, Voluntary Action and Akrasia*. Houndsmill, Macmillan.

Churchland, P. (1981). "Eliminative Materialism and the Propositional Attitudes." *Journal of Philosophy* **78**(2): 67–90.

Churchland, P. (1983). "Stalking the Wild Epistemic Engine." *Nous*: 5–18.

Churchland, P. (1995). Folk Psychology. *A Companion to the Philosophy of Mind*. S. Guttenplan. Oxford, Blackwell. pp. 308–316.

Churchland, P. (1996). "The Hornswoggle Problem." *Journal of Consciousness Studies* **3**(5–6): 402–408.

Clark, A. J. (1987). The Philosophical Significance of an Evolutionary Epistemology. *Evolutionary Epistemology: A Multiparadigm Program*. W. Callebaut and R. Pinxten. Dordrecht, Reidel. pp. 223–244.

Clark, A. (1989) *Microcognition: Philosophy, Cognitive Science and Parallel Distributed Processing*. Cambridge, MA: MIT Press.

Clark, A. (1993) "The Varieties of Eliminativism." *Mind and Language* 8(2): 223–233.

Cohen, W. (1957). "Spatial and Textural Characteristics of the Ganzfeld." *American Journal of Psychology* 70: 403–410.

Curren, R. (1989). "The Contribution of Nicomachean Ethics iii 5 to Aristotle's Theory of Responsibility." *History of Philosophy Quarterly* 6(3): 261–277.

Dennett, D. (1987). *The Intentional Stance.* Cambridge, MA, MIT Press.

Dancy, J. (1993). *Moral Reasons.* Oxford, Blackwell.

Darwall, G. R. (1997). Towards Fin de siecle Ethics: Some Trends. *Moral Discourse and Practice.* G. R. Darwall. Oxford, Oxford University Press. pp. 3–50.

Darwin, C. (1987). *Charles Darwin's Notebooks 1836–1844: Geology, Trasmutation of Species, Metaphysical Enquiries.* Ithica, NY, Cornell University Press.

Dawkins, R. (1999) *The Extended Phenotype: The Long Reach of the Gene.* Oxford: OUP.

Deacon, T. and P. Feyerabend (1999). Language Evolution and Mechanics. *A Companion to Cognitive Science.* W. Bechtel and G. Graham. Oxford, Blackwell.

Dedrick, D. (2005). *Objectivism and the Evolutionary Value of Colour Vision.* Retrieved 20 June 2005, www.cogprints.org/366/00/dialogue.html.

Descartes, R. (1975). *Discourse on Method.* London, Everyman's Library.

Descartes, R. (1986). *Meditations on First Philosophy.* New York, Macmillan.

Descartes, R. (1990) *The Philosophical Writings of Descartes*, Vol. 1. Cottingham, Stoothoff and Murdoch (Eds). Cambridge: CUP.

Devitt, M. (1997). *Realism and Truth.* Princeton, Princeton University Press.

Dretske, F. (1969). *Seeing and Knowing.* London, Routledge and Kegan Paul.

Dretske, F. (1999). *Knowledge and the Flow of Information.* United States, CSLI Publications.

Dretske, F. (2002). Conscious Experience. *Vision and Mind.* N. Thompson. Cambridge, MA, MIT Press.

Dummett, M. (1991). *The Logical Basis of Metaphysics.* London, Duckworth.

Dummett, M. (1992). *Truth and Other Enigmas.* London, Duckworth.

Edwards, J. (1995). "The Universal Quantifier and Dummett's Verificationist Theory of Sense." *Analysis* 55(2): 90–97.

Edwards, J. (1996). "Anti-Realist Truth and Concepts of Superassertibility." *Synthese* 109: 103–120.

Evans, J. (1989). *Bias in Human Reasoning: Causes and Consequences*, Erlbaum.

Everson, S. (1990). "Aristotle's Compatibilism in the Nicomachean ethics." *Ancient Philosophy* 10: 81–103.

Feyerabend, P. (1991). *Against Method.* London, Verso.

Fine, C. (2006). "Is the Emotional Dog Wagging Its Rational Tail, or Chasing It?" *Philosophical Explorations* 9: 83–98.

Fodor, J. (1975). *The Language of Thought.* New York, Crowell.

Fodor, J. (1981). Three Cheers for Propositional Attitudes. *Representations.* Cambridge, Cambridge University Press.

Forbes, G. (1999). Essentialism. *A Companion to the Philosophy of Language.* C. Wright and B. Hale. Oxford, Blackwell.

Frankena, W. (1938). "The Naturalistic Fallacy." *Mind* 48: 464–477.

Frankfurt, H. (2003). Freedom of the Will and a Concept of a Person. *Free Will.* G. Watson. Oxford, Oxford University Press. pp. 322–336.

Frankfurt, H. C. (1969). "Alternative Possibilities and Moral Responsibility." *The Journal of Philosophy* 66: 829–839.

Fratantaro, S. (1998). *The Methodology of G.E. Moore*. Aldershot, Ashgate.

Frede, M. (1988). "A Medieval Source of Modern Scepticism." *Gedankenzeichen*: pp. 65–70.

Gibbard, A. (1990). *Wise Choices, Apt Feelings*. Oxford, Clarendon Press.

Gibson, J. J. (1967). "New Reasons for Realism." *Synthese* 17: 162–172.

Gibson, J. J. (1979). *The Ecological Approach to Visual Perception*. Boston, Houghton Mifflin.

Gibson, J. J. (1982). A History of the Ideas Behind Ecological Optrics. *Reasons for Realism*. R. Jones. New Jersey, Lawrence Erlbaum.

Gibson, J. J. and E. Gibson (1982). Perceptual Learning: Differentiation or Enrichment? *Reasons for Realism*. E. S. Reed and R. K. Jones. New Jersey, Lawrence Erlbaum.

Gibson, J. J. and D. Waddell (1952). "Homogenous Retinal Stimulation and Visual Perception." *American Journal of Psychology* 65: 263–370.

Godfrey-Smith, P. (1991). "Signal, Decision, Action." *Journal of Philosophy* 88: 709–722.

Goldman, A. (1986). *Epistemology and Cognition*. Cambridge, MA, MIT Press.

Gould, S. J. and R. Lewontin (1979). The Spandrels of San Marco and the Panglossian Paradigm: A Critique of the Adaptionist Programme. *The Evolution of Adaptation by Natural Selection*. J. M. Smith and R. Holliday. London, Royal Society. pp. 147–164.

Grice, P. (1989). *Studies in the Way of Words*. Cambridge, MA, Harvard University Press.

Griffiths, P. J. (1999) *Religious Reading*. New York: OUP.

Guttenplan, S. (1975). *Mind and Language*. Oxford, Oxford University Press.

Haldane, J. (1993). Mind-World Identity Theory and the Anti-Realist Challenge. *Reality, Representation and Projection*. J. Haldane and C. Wright. Oxford, Oxford University Press.

Hale, B. (1999). Modality. *A Companion to the Philosophy of Language*. B. Hale and C. Wright. Oxford, Blackwell.

Hamilton, W. D. and R. Axelrod (1981). "The Evolution of Cooperation." *Science* 211: 1390–1396.

Hannan, B. (1993). "Don't Stop Believing: The Case Against Eliminative Materialism." *Mind and Language* 8(2): 165–179.

Hare, R. M. (1952). *The Language of Morals*. Oxford, Oxford University Press.

Hare, R. M. (1963). *Freedom and Reason*. Oxford, Oxford University Press.

Hatfield, G. and W. Epstein (1979). "The Sensory Core and the Medieval Foundations of Early Modern Perceptual Theory." *Isis* 70(253): 363–384.

Hilbert, D. R. (1987). *Color and Color Perception: A Study in Anthropocentric Realism*. Stanford, CSLI.

Hochberg, J., W. Triebel and G. Seaman (1951). "Color Adaptation Under Conditions of Homogenous Visual Stimulation (Ganzfeld)." *Journal of Experimental Psychology* 41: 153–159.

Hubel, D. H. (1988). *Eye, Brain and Vision*. New York, Scientific American Library.

Hudson, W. D. (1977) "What Makes Religious Beliefs Religious?" *Religious Studies* 13: 221–242.

Hume, D. (1985). *Enquiries Concerning Human Understanding and Concerning the Principles of Morals*. Oxford, Clarendon Press.

Hume, D. (1989). *A Treatise of Human Nature*. Oxford, Clarendon.

Inwagen, P. v. (1983). *An Essay on Free Will*. Oxford, Clarendon.

Irwin, T. H. (1980). Reason and Responsibility in Aristotle. *Essays on Aristotle's Ethics*. Rorty, University of California Press.

Ittelson, W. H. (1960). *Visual Space Perception*. New York, Springer.

James, W. (1977). The Will to Believe. *The Writings of William James: A Comprehensive Edition*. W. James and J. J. McDermott. Chicago, University of Chicago Press.

Jackson, F. (2000) *From Metaphysics to Ethics: A Defence of Conceptual Analysis*. Oxford: OUP.

Johnson, M. (1992). "How to Speak of the Colors." *Philosophical Studies* **68**: 221–263.

Kahneman, D. and A. Tversky (1984). "Choices, Values and Frames." *American Psychologist* **39**: 341–350.

Kane, R. (2005). *A Contemporary Introduction to Free Will*. Oxford, Oxford University Press.

Kant, I. (1902). *Prolegomena*. La Salle, Open Court.

Kant, I. (1965). *Critique of Pure Reason*. New York, St Martin's Press.

Kauppinen, A. (Forthcoming). "The Rise and Fall of Experimental Philosophy." *Philosophical Explorations*.

Kennett, J. (2006). "Do Psychopaths Really Threaten Moral Rationalism?" *Philosophical Explorations* **9**: 69–82.

King, P. (2005). Why Isn't the Mind/Body Problem Medieval? *Forming the Mind: Conceptions of Body and Soul in Late Medieval and Early Modern Philosophy*. H. Lagerlund and O. Pluta. Berlin, Springer.

Kirk, G. S., J. E. Raven and M. Schofield (1991). *The Presocratic Philosophers*. Cambridge, Cambridge University Press.

Klemke, E. D. (1969). *The Epistemology of G.E. Moore*. Evanston, Northwestern University Press.

Korolec, J. B. (1990). Free Will and Free Choice. *The Cambridge History of Later Medieval Philosophy*. N. Kretzmann, A. Kenny and J. Pinborg. Cambridge, Cambridge University Press.

Kraut, R. (2001). Aristotle on Method and Moral Education. *Method in Ancient Philosophy*. J. Gentzler. Oxford, Clarendon Press. pp. 271–290.

Kuffler, S. (1953). "Discharge Patterns and Functional Organisation of Mammalian Retina." *Journal of Neurophysiology* **16**: 37.

Kuhn, T. (1970). *The Structure of Scientific Revolutions*. Chicago, University of Chicago Press.

Langford (1942). The Notion of Analysis in Moore's Philosophy. *The Philosophy of G. E. Moore*. Schilpp, Open Court Publishing Company.

Lazarus, R. (1991). *Emotion and Adaptation*. New York, Oxford University Press.

Lievers, M. (1998). "Two Versions of the Manifestation Argument." *Synthese* **115**: 199–227.

Lipton, P. (1991). *Inference to the Best Explanation*. London, Routledge.

Lowe, E. J. (2002). *A Survey of Metaphysics*. Oxford, Oxford University Press.

Lycan, W. (1988). *Judgement and Justfication*. Cambridge, Cambridge University Press.

Mackay, D. (1991). *Behind the Eye*. Oxford, Blackwell.

Mackie, J. L. (1977). *Ethics: Inventing Right and Wrong*. Harmoundsworth, Penguin.

Marcus, R. B. (1993). *Modalities: Philosophical Essays*. Oxford, Oxford University Press.

Marr, D. (1996). *Vision: A Computational Investigation into the Human Representation and Processing of Visual Information*. New York, Freeman.

Matson, W. (1966). Why Isn't the Mind/Body Problem Ancient? *Mind, Matter and Method*. P. Feyerabend and G. Maxwell. Minneapolis, University of Minnesota Press. pp. 92–102.

Maturana, H. R. and F. J. Varela (1980) Autopoiesis and Cognition: The Realization of the Living. D. Reidel.

Maturana, H. R and F. J. Varela (1987) The Tree of Knowledge: The Biological Roots of Human Understanding. Shambhala.

Mayr, E. (2000). *The Growth of Biological Thought: Diversity, Evolution and Inheritance*. Cambridge, MA, Harvard University Press.

McDowell, J. (1979) "Virtue and Reason." *The Monigt* 62: 331–350.

McDowell, J. (1994a). "The Content of Perceptual Experience." *The Philosophical Quarterly* **44**: 175.

McDowell, J. (1994b). *Mind and World*. Cambridge, MA, Harvard University Press.

McDowell, J. (1998a). Are Moral Requirements Hypothetical Imperatives? *Mind, Value and Reality*. Cambridge, MA, Harvard University Press.

McDowell, J. (1998b). Values and Secondary Qualities. *Mind, Value and Reality*. Cambridge, MA, Harvard University Press. pp. 131–150.

McNaughton, D. (1988). *Moral Vision: An Introduction to Ethics*. Oxford, Blackwell.

Metzger, W. (1953). *Gesetze des Sehens*. Frankfurt, W. Kramer.

Metzger, W. (1974). Can the Subject Create His World? *Perception: Essays in Honour of James J. Gibson*. R. B. MacLeod and H. L. Picks. Ithaca, Cornell University Press. pp. 62–65.

Meyer, S. S. (1993). *Aristotle and Moral Responsibility: Character and Cause*. Oxford, Blackwell.

Meyer, S. S. (2006). Aristotle on the Voluntary. *The Blackwell Guide to Aristotle's Nicomachean Ethics*. R. Kraut. Oxford, Blackwell.

Miller, A. (2003). *An Introduction to Contemporary Metaethics*. Cambridge, Polity Press.

Millican, P. (2004) "The One Fatal Flaw in Anselm's Argument." *Mind* **113**: 437–476.

Millikan, R. (1984). "Naturalistic Reflections on Knowledge." *Pacific Philosophical Quarterly* **65**: 315–334.

Millikan, R. (1987). *Language, Thought and Other Biological Categories*. Cambridge, MA, MIT Press.

Milner, A. and M. Goodale (1998). *The Visual Brain in Action*. Oxford, Oxford University Press.

Misak, C. J. (1995). *Verificationism*. London, Routledge.

Mitchell, D. E. (1988). "The Extent of Visual Recovery from Early Monocular or Binocular Deprivation in Kittens." *Journal of Physiology* 395: 639.

Moore, G. E. (1951). The Refutation of Idealism. *Philosophical Studies*. London, Routledge and Kegan Paul.

Moore, G. E. (1963) *Philosophical Papers*. New York: Macmillan.

Moore, G. E. (1965). *Some Main Problems of Philosophy*. New York, Macmillan.

Moore, G. E. (1991). *The Elements of Ethics*. Philadelphia, Temple University Press.

Moore, G. E. (1993). *Principia Ethica*. Cambridge, Cambridge University Press.

Nagel, T. (1970) *The Possibility of Altruism*. Oxford: Clarendon Press.

Natsoulas, T. (1991). "Why Do Things Look as They Do? Some Gibsonian Answers to Koffka's Question." *Philosophical Psychology* 4: 2.

Nietzsche, F. (1966) *Beyond Good and Evil*. New York: Vintage Books.

Nozick, R. (1993). *The Nature of Rationality*. Princeton, Princeton University Press.

O'Connor, D. (1982). *The Metaphysics of G. E. Moore*. Dordrecht, Reidel Publishing.

O'Hear, A. (1997). *Beyond Evolution: Human Nature and the Limits of Evolutionary Explanation*. Oxford, Clarendon Press.

Ockham, W. (1990). *Philosophical Writings*. Indianapolis, Hackett.

Ockham, W. (1991). *Quodlibetal Questions: Quodlibets 1–7*. New Haven and London, Yale University Press.

Papineau, D. (1993). *Philosophical Naturalism*. Oxford, Blackwell.

Papineau, D. (2000). The Evolution of Knowledge. *Evolution and the Human Mind: Modularity, Language and Meta-cognition*. P. C. A. Chamberlain. Cambridge, Cambridge University Press.

Phillips, D. Z. (1976) *Religion without Explanation*. Oxford: Blackwell.

Plato (1961). *Collected Dialogues*. New Jersey, University of Princeton Press.

Plato, Ed. (1987). *The Collected Dialogues of Plato*. Bollingen Series. Princeton, Princeton University Press.

Popper, K. (1959). *The Logic of Scientific Discovery*. London, Hutchison.

Popper, K. (1972). *Objective Knowledge*. Oxford, Clarendon.

Priest, G. (2003). "Where Is Philosophy at the Start of the 21st Century?" *Proceedings of the Aristotelian Society* CII(I).

Prinz, J. (2006). "The Emotional Basis of Moral Judgments." *Philosophical Explorations* 9: 29–44.

Putnam, H. (1981). *Reason, Truth and History*. Cambridge, Cambridge University Press.

Putnam, H. (1994). *Words and Life*. Cambridge, MA, Harvard University Press.

Quine, W. V. (1953). Reference and modality. *From a Logical Point of View*. Cambridge, MA, Harvard University Press.

Quine, W. V. (1968). Ontological Relativity. *Ontological Relativity and Other Essays*. New York, Columbia University Press.

Quine, W. V. (1975). The Nature of Natural Knowledge. *Mind and Language: Wolfson College Lectures*. S. Guttenplan. Oxford, Clarendon Press.

Quine, W. V. (1980). Two Dogmas of Empiricism. *From a Logical Point of View*. Cambridge, MA, Harvard University Press.

Railton, P. (1996). Subjective and Objective. *Truth in Ethics*. B. Hooker. Oxford, Blackwell.

Railton, P. (1997). Moral Realism. *Moral Discourse and Practice*. G. R. Darwall. Oxford, Oxford University Press. pp. 137–166.

Rand, B., Ed. (1908). *Modern Classical Philosophers: Selections Illustrating Modern Philosophy from Bruno to Bergson*, Boston: Houghton Mifflin.

Rauschecker, J. and W. Singer (1981). "Visual Deprivation, Stripe Rearing and Hebb Synapses." *Journal of Physiology* 310: 215.

Ravizza, M. and J. M. Fischer (1998). *Responsibility and Control*. Cambridge, Cambridge University Press.

Reichenbach, H. (1938). *Experience and Prediction*. Chicago, University of Chicago Press.

Reichenbach, H. (1949). *Theory of Probability*. Berkeley, University of California Press.

Reid, T. (1994). *The Works of Thomas Reid*. Bristol, Thoemmes Press.

Reid, T. (2005). *The Works of Thomas Reid*. Boston: Adamant Media Corporation.

Roberts, J. (1989). "Aristotle on Responsibility for Action and Character." *Ancient Philosophy* 9: 23–36.

Roitblat, H. L. (1999). Animal Cognition. *A Companion to Cognitive Science.* W. Bechtel and G. Graham. Oxford, Blackwell.

Rorty, R. (1979). *Philosophy and the Mirror of Nature.* Princeton: Princeton University Press.

Rottschaefer, W. (1998). *The Biology and Psychology of Moral Agency.* Cambridge, Cambridge University Press.

Ruse, M. (1986). *Taking Darwin Seriously.* Oxford, Blackwell.

Russell, B. (1912). *The Problems of Philosophy.* Oxford, Oxford University Press.

Russell, B. (1995). *History of Western Philosophy.* London, Routledge.

Ryle, G. (1931). "Systematically Misleading Expressions." *Proceedings of the Aristotelian Society* 32: 139–170.

Ryle, G. (1984). *The Concept of Mind.* Chicago, University of Chicago Press.

Ryle, G. (2002). *Dilemmas.* Cambridge, Cambridge University Press.

Sage, J. (2003). "Truth–Reliability and the Evolution of Human Cognitive Capacities." *Philosophical Studies* 117(1–2): 95–106.

Scotus, D. (1987). *Philosophical Writings.* Indianapolis, Hackett.

Searle, J. (1987). "Indeterminacy, Empiricism and the First Person." *Journal of Philosophy* 84: 123–146.

Searle, J. (1992). *The Rediscovery of the Mind.* Cambridge, MA, MIT Press.

Searle, J. (1999). *Mind, Language and Society: Philosophy in the Real World.* London, Phoenix.

Sellars, W. (1956). Empiricism and the Philosophy of Mind. *Minnesota Studies in the Philosophy of Science.* H. Feigl and M. Scriven. Minnesota, University of Minnesota Press. Vol. 1. pp. 251–328.

Sellars, W. (1962). Philosophy and the Scientific Image of Man. *Frontiers of Science and Philosophy.* R. G. Colodny. Pittsburgh, University of Pittsburgh Press.

Siegler, F. A. (1968). "Voluntary and Involuntary." *Monist* 52: 268–287.

Skyrm, B. (1975). *Choice and Chance: An Introduction to Inductive Logic.* Encino, Dickenson.

Smart, J. J. C. (1975). On Some Criticisms of a Physicalist Theory of Colors. *Philosophical Aspects of the Mind–Body Problem.* C-Y. Cheng. Honolulu, University of Hawaii Press. pp. 54–63.

Smith, J. M. (1998). Science and Myth. *The Philosophy of Biology.* D. L. Hull and M. Ruse. Oxford, Oxford University Press.

Smith, M. (1987). "The Humean Theory of Motivation." *Mind* 96: 36–61.

Smith, M. (1994). *The Moral Problem.* Oxford, Blackwell.

Smith, M. (1996). Internalism's Wheel. *Truth in Ethics.* B. Hooker. Oxford, Blackwell. pp. 69–94.

Sober, E. (1981). "Evolution and Rationality." *Synthese* 46: 95–120.

Solnick, J. V. (1980). "An Experimental Analysis of Impulsivity and Impulse Control in Humans." *Learn Motiv* 11: 61–77.

Sorenson, R. (1992). *Thought Experiments.* New York, Oxford University Press.

Sosa, E. (2007). "Experimental Philosophy and Philosophical Intuitions." *Philosophical Studies* 132: 99–107.

Spinoza, B. (1955). *The Ethics.* New York, Dover Publications.

Sripada, C. S. (2005). "Punishment and the Strategic Structure of Moral Systems." *Biology and Philosophy* 20: 767–789.

Stalnaker, R. (1999). Reference and Necessity. *A Companion to the Philosophy of Language*. B. Hale and C. Wright. Oxford, Blackwell.

Stanley, J. (1999). Names and Rigid Designation. *A Companion to the Philosophy of Language*. B. Hale and C. Wright. Oxford, Blackwell.

Sterelny, K. (1993). "Refuting Eliminative Materialism on the Cheap?" *Mind and Language* 8(2): 306–315.

Sterelny, K. (2003). *Thought in a Hostile World: The Evolution of Human Cognition*. Oxford, Blackwell.

Steven, C. (2001). "When Is It Selectively Advantageous to Have True Beliefs? Sandwiching the Better Safe than Sorry Argument." *Philosophical Studies* 105: 161–189.

Stewart-Williams, S. (2005). "Innate Ideas as a Naturalistic Source of Metaphysical Knowledge." *Biology and Philosophy* 20(4): 791–814.

Stich, S. (1990). *The Fragmentation of Reason*. London, MIT Press.

Stone, V. (2006). "The Moral Dimension of Human Social Intelligence." *Philosophical Explorations* 9: 55–68.

Strawson, G. (1986). *Freedom and Belief*. Oxford, Oxford University Press.

Strawson, P. (1952). *Introduction to Logical Theory*. London, Methuen.

Strawson, P. (2006). *Individuals: An Essay in Descriptive Metaphysics*. London, Routledge.

Tennant, N. (1987). *Anti-Realism and Logic*. Oxford, Clarendon Press.

Tennant, N. (1995a). Antirealism. *A Companion to Metaphysics*. J. Kim and E. Sosa. Oxford, Blackwell.

Tennant, N. (1995b). "On Negation, Truth and Warranted Assertibility." *Analysis* 55(2): 98–104.

Thomas, N. (1970). *The Possibility of Altruism*. Princeton, Princeton University Press.

Thompson, E., A. Palacios, and F. J. Varela (1992) Ways of Colouring: Comparative Colour Vision as a Case Study for Cognitive Science. *Vision and Mind*, Noë and Thompson (Eds). Cambridge, Mass: MIT Press, pp. 351–418.

Turvey, M. T., R. E. Shaw, E. Reed and W. Mace. (1981). "Ecological Laws of Perceiving and Action: In Reply to Fodor and Pylyshyn." *Cognition* 9: 241–244.

Tversky, A. and D. Kahneman (1982). Evidential Impact of Bases Rates. *Judgement under Uncertainty: Heuristics and Biases*. D. Kahneman, P. Slovic, and A. Tversky. New York, Cambridge University Press.

Vision, G. (1998). "Perceptual Content." *Philosophy* 73(285): 395–427.

Wachtershauser, G. (1987). Light and Life: The Nutritional Origins of Sensory Perception. *Evolutionary Epistemology, Rationality, and the Sociology of Knowledge*. G. Radnitzky and W. W. Bartley. La Salle, Open Court. pp. 121–137.

Warrington, E. K. and A. M. Taylor (1973). "The Contribution of the Right Parietal Lobe to Object Recognition." *Cortex* 9: 152–164.

Watson, G. (2003). Free Agency. *Free Will*. G. Watson. Oxford, Oxford University Press.

Werblin, F. S. and J. E. Dowling (1969). "Organisation of the Retina of the Mudpuppy: Intracellular Recording." *Journal of Neurophysiology* 32: 339.

White, A. R. (1958). *G.E. Moore: A Critical Exposition*. Oxford, Blackwell.

Whitehead, A. N. (1932). *Science in the Modern World*. Cambridge, Cambridge University Press.

Whorf, B. (1956). *Language, Thought and Reality*. Boston, MIT Press.

Williams, G. C. (1988). "Huxley's Evolution and Ethics in Sociobiological Perspective." *Zygon* **23**: 383–407.

Williams, G. C. (1989). A Sociobiological Expansion of Evolution and Ethics. *T.H. Huxley's Evolution and Ethics with New Essays on its Victorian and sociobiological context.* J. Paradis and G. C. Williams. Princeton, Princeton University Press. pp. 179–214.

Wilson, E. O. (1978). *On Human Nature.* Cambridge, MA, Harvard University Press.

Wittgenstein, L. (1974). *Tractatus Logico-Philosophicus.* London, Routledge.

Wittgenstein, L. (1953). *Philosophical Investigations.* New York, Macmillan.

Wittgenstein, L. (1998). *On Certainty.* Oxford, Blackwell.

Wolf, S. (1990). *Freedom Within Reason.* Oxford, Oxford University Press.

Wolf, S. (2002). Sanity and the Metaphysics of Responsibility. *Free Will.* R. Kane. Oxford, Blackwell.

Wright, C. (1992). *Truth and Objectivity.* London, Harvard University Press.

Wright, C. (1993). "Eliminative Materialism: Going Concern or Passing Fancy?" *Mind and Language* **8**(2): 316–325.

Wright, C. (2002). "(Anti)-sceptics Simple and Subtle: G.E. Moore and John McDowell." *Philosophy and Phenomenological Research* **LXV**(2): 330–348.

Index

action explanation, 173–4, 189, 191
action, *see* beliefs; free agency; responsibility; determinism
altruism
  origins of, 160–1
  tit-for-tat, 160–1
Anscombe, Elizabeth, 94, 166
anti-realism
  with respect to the external world, *see* perception; metaphysical realism
  with respect to intentional states, *see* eliminative materialism (EM); folk psychology
  with respect to moral facts, 177–97; *see also* moral realism and cognitivism
  with respect to the past, *see* Dummett, Michael, Dummettian reductio
  semantic anti-realism, 118–36
Appiah, Anthony, 121, 123, 127
Aquinas, Thomas, 16, 165–6, 175–6
Arcesilaus, 91
argument from differential certainty, 34–5
Aristotle
  action explanation, 191
  on the cognitive basis of the emotions, 193
  and the common sense tradition, xiv, xv, 1, 26, 200; on the nature of philosophy, 8–12, 15, 18; on the preservation of *endoxa*, 22–4
  criterion of existence, 119
  on the difficulty of philosophy, 65
  and metaphysical realism, 99–103
  moral realism, 182
  on natural kinds and essential properties, 95, 97
  the rejection of the principle of separability, 88–91

on responsibility, 159, 163, 165–76
on when proofs are required, 66
Armstrong, David, 3
Atran, Scott, 48–9
Austin, John, 24, 26, 37–8, 60
Averroes, xii, 89, 141
Avicenna, 89
Axelrod, R., 160–1
Ayer, A. J., xiii, 67, 77, 127–8, 179

Bacon, Francis, 5
Baker, 152–3
Barcan Marcus, Ruth, 80, 85, 95, 106
beliefs, 22
  allegedly false but adaptive beliefs, 46–9
  and emotions, 192–5
  and free agency and responsibility, 173–6
  and moral judgements, 187
  and perception, 105–7
  as decoupled representations, 41–2, 174–5, 191–2
  co-evolved with oriented activity, 40, 113
  primary function is action guidance, 40, 144, 176
  see also action explanation, and Hume, David, theory of motivation
Bergson, Henri, 5
Berkeley, George, xii, 11, 54, 81, 86, 92–3, 99, 104
Blackburn, Simon, 132, 187
Boethius of Dacia, 89
Boghossian, Paul, 152–3
Bosley, R. N., 89–93
Boyer, Pascal, 48
Boyle, 90
Bradley, 5
Brentano, Franz, 6
Brink, D., 190
Bruno, 5